Free to Be Mohawk

New Directions in Native American Studies
Colin G. Calloway and K. Tsianina Lomawaima, General Editors

Free to Be Mohawk

Indigenous Education at the Akwesasne Freedom School

Louellyn White

University of Oklahoma Press : Norman

Published through the Recovering Languages and Literacies of the Americas initiative, supported by the Andrew W. Mellon Foundation

RECOVERING LANGUAGES & LITERACIES OF THE AMERICAS

Free to Be Mohawk: Indigenous Education at the Akwesasne Freedom School is published as part of the Recovering Languages and Literacies of the Americas initiative. Recovering Languages and Literacies is generously supported by the Andrew W. Mellon Foundation.

Library of Congress Cataloging-in-Publication Data
White, Louellyn, 1968–
Free to be Mohawk : indigenous education at the Akwesasne Freedom School / Louellyn White.
pages cm. — (New directions in Native American studies series ; volume 12)
Includes bibliographical references and index.
ISBN 978-0-8061-4865-6 (hardcover : alk. paper) —
ISBN 978-0-8061-5154-0 (pbk. : alk. paper)
1. Mohawk Indians—Education—Akwesasne Indian Reserve (Québec and Ont.)
2. Akwesasne Freedom School. 3. Mohawk Indians—Education—New York—Saint Regis Mohawk Indian Reservation. 4. Mohawk Indians—Ethnic identity. 5. Mohawk language—Study and teaching—Case studies. 6. Indians of North America—Education.
I. Title. II. Title: Indigenous education at the Akwesasne Freedom School.
E99.M8W48 2015
971.3004′975542—dc23 2015021059

Free to Be Mohawk: Indigenous Education at the Akwesasne Freedom School is Volume 12 in the New Directions in Native American Studies series.

The paper in this book meets the guidelines for permanence and durability of the Committee on Production Guidelines for Book Longevity of the Council on Library Resources, Inc. ∞

1 2 3 4 5 6 7 8 9 10

To all those who came before,

to my mother, Eleanor R. Currie (1933–2007),

and my father, Louis J. White (1922–2008),

to my beloved son Skye Louis White,

and to the seven generations ahead

Contents

Illustrations

Figures

Maps

Table

Preface

A Journey Home

The process of writing this book has been an intensely personal journey full of rewards, continual internal reflection, and ultimately healing. As I reflected upon the past several years of my work with the Akwesasne Freedom School, forging deeper connections with family, and ultimately trying to understand what it means to be Kanien'kehaka (Mohawk or People of the Flint), I realized that I have emerged as a different person than I was when I started. In the early years of the new millennium I was a doctoral student in American Indian Studies at the University of Arizona. In July 2004, the day I was to begin fieldwork at Akwesasne (the Mohawk community straddling the border of Canada and the United States on the St. Lawrence River), my father, Louis John White, suffered a severe stroke. As I was his only child, it was my responsibility to care for him. I gladly accepted that charge, and for several years I traveled back and forth between Arizona and where my father was living in central New York and Akwesasne. Three years later my mother, Eleanor Ruth Currie, died of an unexpected heart attack, and my father passed on that same year after a lengthy illness.

After my father's death, I was faced with an existential crisis. I had to know what happens when we die. Was there more? Is this it? As I began to question the meaning of existence and the purpose of life, I turned to the Creation Story and traditional cultural knowledge of my father's people—the Mohawks of the Haudenosaunee (Iroquois) confederacy. The Creation Story, it has been written, "Opens doors to ways of thinking about the nature of the universe and about life and death" (Mohawk 2005, p. xvii). In a quest to understand my place in the universe I spent months searching for the answer to John Mohawk's question about our identities as Haudenosaunee people: "Who are we?" Mohawk's response: "We [Haudenosaunee] are the people who carry on the tradition of ceremonials of thanksgiving" (p. v).

As an insider in some ways but an outsider in others, searching for answers at the same time I experienced intense mourning, I tried to compartmentalize my life into the personal and the academic. However, I came to realize that this separation was not possible or necessary. Neither could I separate myself into a Mohawk half and an academic half. I was writing about identity, about becoming "fully Mohawk" (and fully human), and about Mohawk values, but I had been somewhat removed from the context of my work. As a researcher I had stepped back and tried to be objective. I had not denied my insider perspective, but this had been limited to my involvement in the Mohawk world through family connections, familiarity with the physical space of Akwesasne, and an attempt to learn the Mohawk language. But what did it mean to "*feel* Mohawk?" I stopped writing for a few months after my father's death and reflected on my own identity and what it meant to be Mohawk.

As I experienced the pain of grief, explored our Creation Story, and tried to understand the meaning of life and death, the borders fell away and I became fully immersed in my work. No longer just a researcher, I was now living the process of what it means to be Mohawk. I began to question my own values, my identity, and this book unfolded as a series of related questions. How do I form the concept of self? The idea of *Mohawkness*? What does it mean to be "fully Mohawk"? Chapter 6, "Becoming Fully Mohawk," is a direct result of that period of reflection.

I was close to both of my parents, and their deaths devastated me. Grieving their loss, I eventually reflected on the values they had instilled in me, considered my obstacles and struggles, and came to appreciate life more than ever and feel gratitude. But who was I? Was I really Mohawk? I had a tribally issued ID card. Did that make me Mohawk? I didn't have a clan, because my mother was non-Native, so traditionally speaking I am not Mohawk at all. My mother descended from a long line of European ancestors including Scottish and English. My father was a proud Mohawk. While my father aged and his health declined, I had pondered how I would feel when he was gone. I had looked to him as my sole connection to my identity as a Mohawk woman. I wondered if I would be able to maintain the strong kinship ties to our family in Akwesasne and whether I would lose my sense of what it meant to be Mohawk. While writing this book and taking care of my father during his long illness, I spent a lot of time with family in Akwesasne. This was a gift, and I began to realize that my Mohawk family grounded me in who I am. My father made sure I knew our relatives in Akwesasne, and he taught me the value of family. For me, then, family encompasses a large part of being Mohawk. Since his death, I now have a son, Skye Louis White, who I bring to Akwesasne often. My cousin Connie Thompson has taken on the role of his *tota* or grandmother and teaches him Mohawk words and songs. I want my son to know where he comes from and who he is. So, rather than losing Mohawk identity with my father's passing, his death strengthened me as one of the Onkwehonwe (Original People) and as a human being. While I still have not found the answers to all of life's big questions, this book is an attempt to understand what it means to be Kahnien'kehaka in today's world. Several months later, my great aunt Mildred Bero passed at ninety. Then in 2013 another great aunt, Beatrice Jacobs, died at the age of one hundred. An era is ending. Elders are leaving us, taking with them vast knowledge and lifetimes of stories, but one great solace to me is knowledge of places like the Akwesasne Freedom School. There young people are taught to respect elders, and the stories live on, helping to ensure that the Mohawk way of life continues for future generations.

Acknowledgments

I would like to thank all of my family and friends for their love and encouragement. Thank you to my brothers and sisters and nieces and nephews, who have helped me with the confidence needed to go out into the world with my feet on the ground. I thank my relatives at Akwesasne, especially Connie Thompson and family, Darlene and Pete Sunday, and my late aunt Mildred Bero, for their support and for taking care of me while working on this book. To the mothers, fathers, students, alumni, staff, and volunteers of the Akwesasne Freedom School, I owe a big *niawenko:wa* (thank you) for sharing and for trusting me with your stories. *Niawen* (thank you) to Kaweienón:ni (Margaret) Cook-Peters for her unwavering passion and perseverance in keeping our language alive. Niawen to Konwanahtotani (Elvera) Sargent for her patience and kindness throughout the last several years. And to Barry Montour for providing me with feedback on early drafts of this manuscript and to John Kahionhes Fadden for reading drafts and allowing me to use his wonderful artwork. Niawenko:wa to Sue Ellen Herne for her constructive commentary and assistance with the final manuscript. Niawen to Orenda Boucher, who spent many hours conducting library searches and editing drafts of the manuscript and to Darren Bonaparte and Brian Rice who provided insight into a greater understanding of the Haudenosaunee Creation Story. I would also like to thank K. Tsianina Lomawaima, my former dissertation advisor, for her mentorship, patience, kind understanding, and invaluable feedback during the process of completing the manuscript. Also instrumental in the early stages of my writing were Teresa McCarty, Joseph "Jay" Stauss, and Mary Jo Tippeconnic-Fox who served on my dissertation committee; I thank you. To Matt Sakiestewa Gilbert, thank you for your kind encouragement and support during manuscript revisions. Thank you to Robert Warrior and the faculty and staff in the American Indian Studies Program at the University of Illinois at Urbana-Champaign, where I was fortunate enough to have spent a year as a chancellor's postdoctoral fellow. I am grateful to Concordia University in Montreal for providing financial support by way of an Aid to Research-Related Events (ARRE) grant. And thank you to my colleagues at Concordia University for supporting me throughout my early years as a new faculty member. I have to express my gratitude to the Creator for blessing me with my son Skye, who has taught me to laugh again, and who has given my life new meaning. Finally, I want to thank my parents: my mother for her unconditional love and for always telling me I could do anything I set my mind to, and my father for being a proud Mohawk who pounded his fists on the table and said, "The goddamn white man took everything, but he'll never take away your education!" I hope I make them proud. Niawenko:wa.

Kanienke:ha Blues

Theresa "Bear" Fox

I would wish on birthday candles
I would wish on falling stars
I would wish on four leaf clovers
Throw my money in wishing wells

How I wish it could be that easy
But I know it cannot be
To wake up in the morning
And speak my language fluently

I have the Kanienke:ha blues
Oh my *tota*
All I want is to speak my language with you

I know you get frustrated
'Cause I don't know what you say
But you know that television didn't help me in any way

I would close my eyes and pray
With all my heart
Put my pinky around a wishbone
And pull real hard

"Kanienke:ha" is a Mohawk term referring to the Mohawk language.

And even though I'd win the finger wish
I'd still wake up in the morning speaking English

I have the Kanienke:ha blues
Oh my *tota*
It's not easy to speak with you

I enrolled in classes
Each day from nine to four
In Tsi Snaihne at I:iohahio
Our Mohawk language course

I am trying to learn my language
That is so beautiful
Returning to school as an adult
Is not an easy thing to do

My wishing days are over
I have to try real hard
No more relying on birthday candles
Or relying on the stars

I have the Kanienke:ha blues
Oh my *tota*
All I want is to speak my language with you

I have the Kanienke:ha blues
Oh my *tota*
All I want is to speak my language with you

 Bear has become a nationally recognized, award-winning singer and songwriter. She writes songs about Mohawk culture, growing up poor, and life with her "iron-working hubby."

Free to Be Mohawk

Introduction

> "The prophecies say that the time will come when the grandchildren will speak to the whole world. The reason for the Akwesasne Freedom School is so the grandchildren will have something significant to say."
>
> —*Sakokwenionkwas [Tom Porter], qtd. in "Curriculum," Akwesasne Freedom School, www.freedom-school.org/index.php/curriculum*

The song "Kanienke:ha Blues" was written and performed by Theresa "Bear" Fox, an alumnus of the Akwesasne Freedom School (AFS), a small grassroots Mohawk language and cultural immersion school located in the Akwesasne Mohawk community. Bear, who began singing at a young age, sings passionately about her deep desire to learn her language, her struggles and frustrations, and her deep commitment to family.[1] When I asked about "Kanienke:ha Blues" she said, "This song came to me when I was in my Mohawk language class in Tsi Snaihne.[2] I was thinking about my father and how angry he would get when I couldn't understand what he was saying in Kanienke:ha to me" (Interviewee AP: October 11, 2004).[3] When she was growing up, Bear couldn't effectively communicate with her father, who primarily spoke to her in Kanienke:ha, while her mother spoke to her in English. She says she was ridiculed by a Catholic priest from the church her mother belonged to because she couldn't speak Kanienke:ha to her father. From a young age she felt ashamed because she didn't know her language, and she began to "put up a wall," she says. "I was kind of scared of it [Kanienke:ha]" (Interviewee AP: October 11, 2004). Like many others, Bear wishes she could communicate with her parents and her *tota* (grandmother) in Kanienke:ha, but the influx of English through television and other mass media complicates her efforts. She remains determined to learn her ancestral language and has sent all five of her children to the AFS in hopes that they can carry on this important element of their culture. Her story echoes that of many Indigenous people who are likewise faced with the challenges of loss of culture (including language) and Indigenous identity.

This book covers the struggles and complexities of language revitalization and retention in the community of Akwesasne, while telling the story of the AFS, a Kanienke:ha language and cultural immersion school started by Mohawk parents. The school arose out of extreme political conflict in the late 1970s and continues to provide an opportunity for negotiating language and identity in a space designed to transcend a long history of colonization. The AFS is an example of a self-determined, self-sufficient, independent, and culturally appropriate educational initiative. Because "Indigenous language revitalization is never only about language, but also about the identities and experiences of speakers and communities" (Hornberger 2008, p. 2), this book explores the complex relationship between language and identity and addresses questions like "How can you be Mohawk if you don't know your language?" Using community-based research within a Mohawk community while addressing issues relevant to working from home (that is, doing research as an insider), it outlines an Indigenous model of holistic education that employs traditional approaches to education while instilling specific Mohawk cultural values. Through first-person narratives it examines how the school affected the lives of students, parents, and teachers. Overall, the book focuses on the AFS as an example of how one community asserted its sovereign right to self-education and made schooling an agent of positive change. Ultimately it addresses what it means to be "fully Mohawk."

Background of the Akwesasne Freedom School

In 1979 an unprecedented effort to revitalize the Mohawk culture and language began with the establishment of the community-based Akwesasne Freedom School, which would in time become a Mohawk language immersion school. Uniquely situated in two countries, two provinces, and one state, the Mohawk territory of Akwesasne (also known as St. Regis) lies across the US-Canadian border intersecting New York State, Ontario, and Quebec (see map 1).

Located on the US side of the territory, the AFS arose out of conflict within the community and in response to public education systems in both countries, where Mohawk culture, including language, was desperately lacking.

The AFS employs a traditional Mohawk approach to education:

> Through our language the Akwesasne Freedom School will support and encourage a process for each child to learn . . . roles and responsibilities as Rotinosonni [Haudenosaunee] through an understanding of the *Ohenton Kariwahtekwen* [Thanksgiving Address] as the core of their learning experience. The guiding principles of *Skennen* (Peace), *Kasatstensera* (Strength), and *Kanikonriio* (Good Mind) will thrive and be heard in the voices of our children for the next 7 generations. (Akwesasne Freedom School, n.d.)

The AFS is essentially a space for cultural and linguistic survival. When the school was named, the word "freedom" was chosen because, according to founder Ron LaFrance, "it is precisely what our traditions teach us, to be a free people, conscious of our rights and obligations to ourselves, to other nations, and to our Mother Earth" (LaFrance 1982). While the school's name reflects these values, some who opposed the idea referred to it as the "Free to Be Dumb School." Over the years students were teased for going to a school that wasn't considered academically challenging, was small in comparison to public schools, and was conducted entirely using the Mohawk language. One former student remembers:

> It wasn't considered a very cool place to go to school. . . . Other kids thought we didn't have to do the things they did, like the curriculum wasn't the same, but actually it was. We learned math and science—we learned all our subjects, and we learned in the language. That in itself was twice as hard. We had to deal with name-calling and teasing. (Interviewee A8: July 15, 2005)

The school also drew criticism because it lacked many of the amenities of modern schools: it had no gymnasium, no cafeteria, and no sports program. Today the modest buildings are often in need of repair, with leaky roofs and occasional flooding. Financial constraints prevent the school from having top-notch facilities or even keeping up with repairs and having enough classroom materials. Long-standing divisions within the community also contribute to ongoing

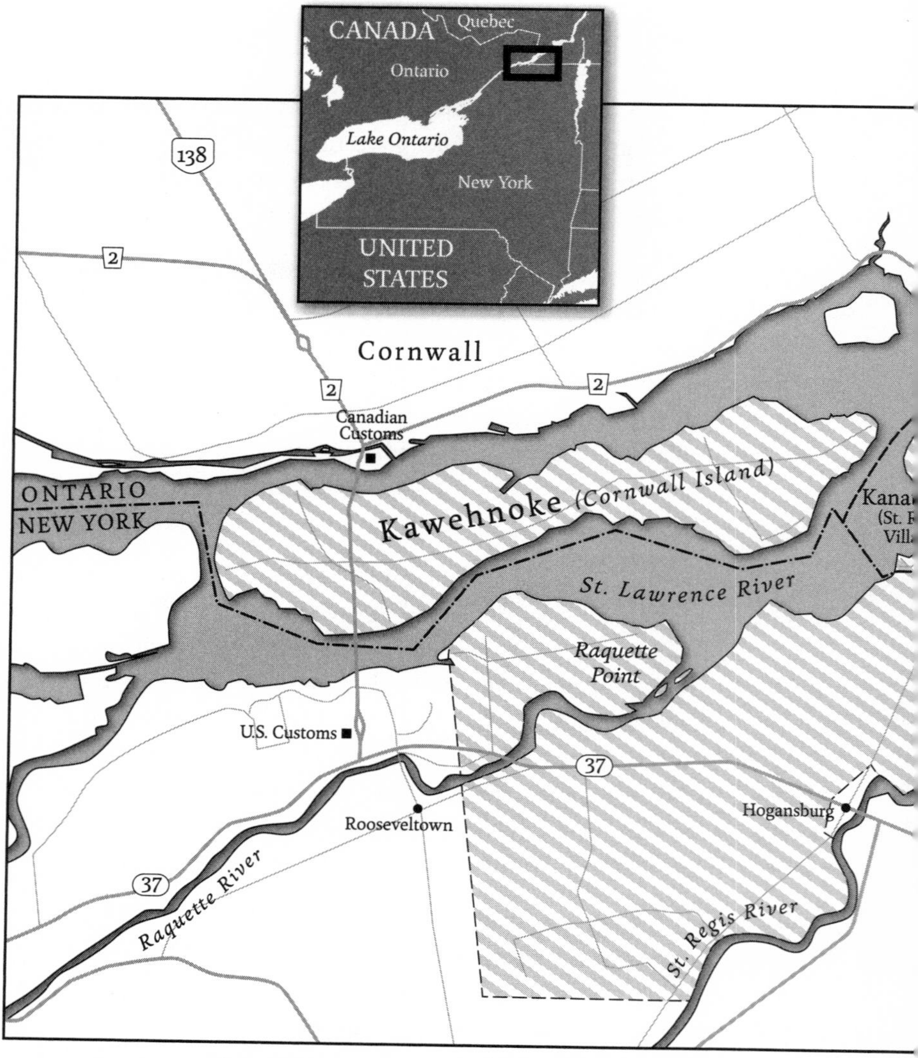

MAP 1. Akwesasne (St. Regis). Based on a map by John Kahionhes Fadden; reproduced with permission. Copyright © 2015, University of Oklahoma Press.

criticisms of the school. Over the years parents have occasionally withdrawn their children from the school, under the impression that teachers were negatively influencing children against other members of the community. Other parents have thought that the school was becoming more like a public school and thought its mission and goals were changing: "People forgot the true meaning of the school. I think we seem to forget here who is who and whose blood

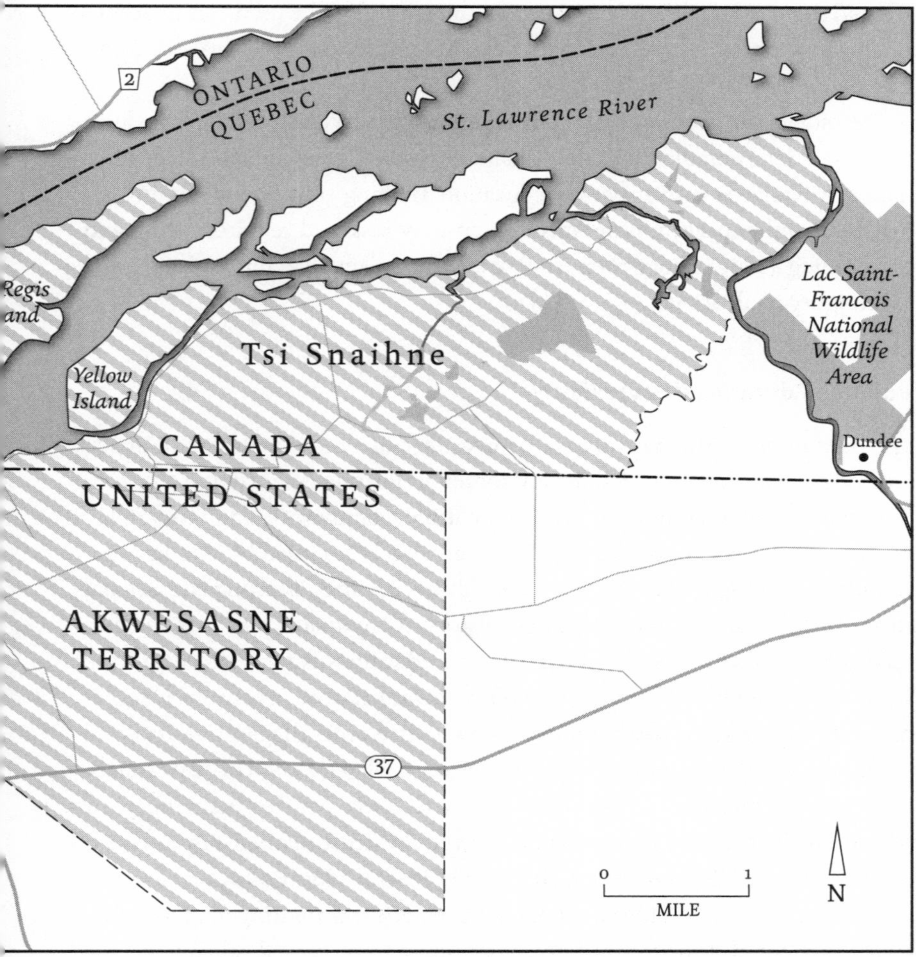

it is in these woods" (Interviewee A9: July 15, 2005). Others didn't like how the language was being taught. The school was also criticized for taking indirect funding from the Canadian government that was filtered through local organizations (Interviewee P10b: May 19, 2005). However, parents continue to send their children to the school because "they want their people to survive" (Interviewee A12: July 14, 2005). One mother sent her children to AFS because she wanted them to learn their language and culture and "to be proud and not confused about who they are," saying that was her responsibility as a parent (Interviewee P1: October 18, 2004).

Despite its shortcomings, the AFS continues to serve as a model for educational self-determination and as a reminder to the Canadian and US governments of Native sovereignty over education. Gaining control and administering successful education programs isn't an easy task and requires facing and overcoming a long history of oppressive legislation aimed at diminishing tribal sovereignty in all arenas.

Building Educational Sovereignty

The educational challenges Native peoples face in United States and Canada are widespread, complex, and deeply rooted in historic colonizing discourses. Traditional Native education, in which culture, community, and family play major roles in the lives of children, has been largely replaced by colonial education that long ago led to language and cultural decline. Asserting educational sovereignty requires addressing a long history of oppressive practices and attitudes of settler societies. Tribal control over education is fairly recent. In the United States a federal trust responsibility toward Native Americans is recognized through various treaty provisions, executive orders, legislative acts, and court decisions.[4] This unique trust relationship obligates the US government to protect the interests of federally recognized Native peoples, including their education (Deloria and Lytle 1983). However, this trust relationship has been tarnished by the US government. Historically, federal education systems served as tools for assimilation into the dominant society, contributing to Native language loss, the destruction of family systems, and increased reliance on the state to provide appropriate education (Adams 1995; Lomawaima 1995; Lomawaima and McCarty 2006).

Numerous problems in US federal schools for Indians were reflected in the Meriam Report of 1928.[5] In response to the report and as a consequence of federal legislation and New Deal programs, the Johnson-O'Malley Act (1934) allowed for contracts with the states to provide services for federally recognized tribes, including education. A House of Representatives resolution in 1953, announcing a policy of "termination," attempted to end the federal-tribal relationship and federal trust responsibility to provide education for many Indian students. This responsibility was partially shifted to the states (Reyhner 2006; Reyhner and Eder 1988, 2004). Throughout the history of the imposition of colonial forms of education and governmental oversight that have marginalized Native peoples, education has remained fraught with inadequate funding, culturally inappropriate curriculum, and poorly trained teachers (Reyhner 1994, 2006; Swisher and Hoisch 1992).

In the modern era, scholars have advocated for Native nations to control their own schools while asserting their sovereign rights (Cajete 1994; McCarty and Watahomigie 1998; Swisher and Tippeconnic 1999; Tippeconnic 2000). Tippeconnic (2000) states that Indian control "means that Indian people have the power to decide what their youth and adults are to be taught, how they will be taught and what human and fiscal resources will be used to support teaching and learning—without outside forces influencing or dictating the educational program" (p. 44). He further clarifies that there is an important distinction between "tribal control" and "local community control." The former means that the tribal government has control over education as opposed to community members through school boards. Furthermore, Indian parental involvement is sometimes confused with Native control over education—but it does not necessarily mean the same thing. How we define "Indian control" of education is important because "we often use these terms interchangeably without making distinctions and assume we have Indian control of education—but do we?" (p. 44).[6] The AFS is not specifically tribally controlled, as the tribal council and band council do not directly oversee the school. Additionally, a school board does not govern the school. Parents do have a high level of involvement with the school, which in the unique case of the AFS means actual control over all aspects of education. I hope this will become more clear in later chapters that describe how the school functions.

Many Native communities are increasingly creating tribally controlled and community-controlled schools in an effort to address the failure of mainstream educational methods (Swisher and Tippeconnic 1999). Blackwater, a Gila River Indian community in Arizona, began operating a US Bureau of Indian Affairs (BIA) school in the 1960s under a local school board (Lomawaima and McCarty 2006). A leader in tribal community-controlled schools in the United States is the Rough Rock Demonstration School of the Navajo nation. Rough Rock began in 1966 as a demonstration project of the BIA, the Office of Economic Opportunity, and local tribal school boards (McCarty 2002). Rough Rock's success helped initiate other Navajo community-controlled schools like Rock Point, which started in 1972 (Holm and Holm 1995; McCarty and Lomawaima 2006). The number of community-controlled Native schools expanded during this era. According to Lomawaima and McCarty, "By the late 1970s, there were 34 American Indian community-controlled schools" (2006, p. 118).

The Indian Education Act of 1972 and the Indian Educational Assistance and Self-Determination Act of 1975 (PL 093-638) and amendments to the latter enabled tribal councils and Native communities to contract for the operation of schools and other social services formerly operated by the BIA or that were funded by the BIA and privately operated. Tribal governments or councils could receive direct funding, and tribal education departments could work with contract and grant schools to coordinate tribal education standards, implement tribal education policies, and promote educational goals (Castile 1998).

Contracting in schools under PL 93-638 was an important advancement as it opened up opportunities for tribal control that did not previously exist. However, control was still limited by bureaucratic systems. Schools had to meet BIA accreditation and other requirements and fell under the BIA's budget. Fishman (1991) explained that because some tribally controlled schools depended on federal funding, they were not "entirely masters of their own fate" (p. 298). Senese (1986) called 93-638 contracting merely an "illusion of control" (p. 154) and identified how it reinforced BIA control while weakening tribal communities. Local or tribal control of schools is inherent to the sovereign status of Native American tribes, a status that gives tribal governments the legal right to make decisions about how to educate their members (Swisher and Tippeconnic 1999). Tribal nations operate and design their own school boards, but funding still comes from outside the community, and, with external funding sources, real autonomy is limited. Without local control, outside regulations on curricula, school administration, teacher credentialing, and school boards must be adhered to, undermining the decision-making authority of the tribal community. In this era of standards-based reform, schools are required to be accountable for student performance in order to receive funding. Content standards drive school curricula, which in some cases can be beneficial for Indian education—if states allow the development of local standards to include more culturally relevant curricula. Unfortunately, this is not the norm because standards-based testing is often culturally biased against the Indian student (Fox 2001). Reyhner and Eder (2004) warn about modern educational reforms: "Perhaps the greatest danger facing Indian education at the beginning of the twenty-first century is the push for outcomes assessment, state and national standards, and the associated increased use of high stakes testing in all facets of education but especially for promotion to the next grade" (p. 11).

McCarty (2002) details struggles the Rough Rock School experienced because of unpredictable BIA funding and program instability. Inconsistent and uncertain BIA funding sent Rough Rock on a "perilous financial path" (p. 124). Debt accrued over the years, and there was high teacher turnover. During the mid-1970s, budget and contracting issues were "making a mockery of self-determination and jeopardizing the very future of community contract schools" (p. 125). McCarty asserts that the volatility and inadequate funding that Rough Rock experienced stemmed from the "manifestations of power relationships" (p. 178) between the tribe and congressional appropriations. But Indian control of Indian education is crucial in combating problems within colonial forms of schooling, including reversing language loss. In the United States, bilingual education was important in the 1960s movement for control of Indian education. Approved in 1968 as Title VII of the Elementary and Secondary Education Act, the Bilingual Education Act "provided an opportunity and some financial means to build on Indian students' lived experiences by bringing their language and local knowledge directly into the school curriculum" (McCarty 1993, p. 18). Taking advantage of newly available funds after passage of the act, Rough Rock was the first school to teach in a Native language and to have a Native school board. Due to the "essential role of indigenous educators in bilingual programs" (McCarty 1993, p. 27) bilingual and bicultural education became "the lightning rod for Indigenous self-determination in the latter part of the 20th century" (Lomawaima and McCarty 2006, p. 119) and provided increased opportunities for Native education. Rough Rock has now lasted for over forty years, however, proving that the difficulties encountered with tribally controlled schooling are not insurmountable.

Challenges with government authority, colonial forms of education, and the forced assimilation of Indigenous people through schooling are not restricted to the United States. Since it straddles the United States and Canada, Akwesasne and its people have been affected by both governments' policies of assimilation. The Canadian government's treatment of Native people closely parallels the situation in the United States, as it too has failed to fulfill trust responsibilities in Native education and adopted similar policies designed to eradicate Native cultural identity (Brady 1995; Milloy 1999). The Indian Act of 1876 assigned federal jurisdiction over Native education in Canada, and in their attempts at assimilation the government entered agreements with Christian churches to provide "civilized education." The Jesuits assumed this task in Mohawk territory and attempted to assimilate Native students into French culture (Montour 2000). A subsequent Indian Act amendment in 1951 allowed the federal government to make agreements with provinces to provide education to Native students. In 1972 the National Indian Brotherhood wrote the document "Indian Control of Indian Education," which called for Native control over education (1972).[7] In response to this, the Canadian government issued "Indian Education Paper, Phase One," recognizing the need to improve Indian education and for Indian control (Brady 1995). Brady perceived that "neither the proactive approach of the United States nor the passive approach of the Canadian government [had] led to significant change, or at least reform substantive enough to alter the locus of control over Native education from the federal to Native governments" (p. 361).

However, some Native communities in Canada have successfully administered their own education programs. Community "survival" schools, focused on maintaining Native culture (including language), sprang up across Canada in the late 1970s through the 1980s (McCaskill 1987). The Mohawks of Kahnawà:ke started the first Aboriginal community-controlled school on the reserve in 1972, the Indian Way School. By 1978 Kahnawà:ke community members had started another school, the Kahnawake Survival School (KSS). This initiative was in response to Bill 101 enacted in 1978 by the Quebec government, making French the official language of the province (Arbuthnot 1984; Hoover 1992). The community began withdrawing their children from local public schools in protest and started their own high school, KSS, focusing on Mohawk culture, while continuing to follow a Quebec-mandated curriculum. Currently administered by the Kahnawake Education Center, the KSS teaches the Mohawk language as a subject along with French.

The Mohawks of Kahnawà:ke did not stop with the KSS. In 1988, a group of parents started a small school called Karihwanon:ron Tsi ionterihwaienstahkhwa, in hopes of their children achieving increased proficiency in Kanienke:ha. Here Mohawk children learn their own language in a homelike setting, learn traditional songs, talk with elders, and take nature walks (see www.karihwanoron.com). Children at Karihwanon:ron are in pre-K through sixth grade.

The school also faces the same kinds of financial challenges as other community schools where funding often falls short and cutbacks are a constant threat. Karihwanon:ron receives donations, relies on fund-raisers, and receives tuition money from Aboriginal Affairs and Northern Development Canada (AADNC) (Horn 2011).

On Canada's northeastern coast, the Innu of Labrador asserted their sovereignty and began managing their own educational programs in 2009. A study conducted in collaboration with the government of Canada showed Innu schools desperately lacking Innu culture and language. It is still too early to tell if this shift can improve the lives of Innu youth, but it looks promising (Philpott 2010).

Language Loss through Residential Schooling[8]

Native communities have opportunities through local control over education to provide culture and language programming to combat years of forced governmental assimilation policies. Such policies aimed to eradicate Indian languages in order, it was said, to "civilize the Indian" (Adams 1988, 1995; Dick and McCarty 1996; Hoxie 1984; Lomawaima 1993, 1994, 1995; McCarty 2002; Skutnabb-Kangas 2000). In many Native families, residential school experiences negatively affected the ability to transmit traditional cultures, including languages, to subsequent generations (Johnston 1988; McBeth 1983; Reyhner and Eder, 2004). Numerous autobiographical accounts (Eastman 1971; Johnston 1989; LaFlesche 1978) attest to the many and varied experiences of Indian residential school survivors, and internal feelings of shame, embarrassment, and inferiority continue to prevent older generations from teaching young people their culture, including traditional languages (Archuleta, Child, and Lomawaima 2000; Child 1998). Thousands of Native children were subjected to these colonial institutions throughout the United States and Canada.

From the late 1880s through 1973, over 150,000 Native children attended Canadian residential and industrial schools, where thousands suffered emotional, physical, and sexual abuse, while many lost their lives from disease and other undocumented reasons (J. R. Miller 1996; Milloy 1999). Beginning in the early 1990s, residential school survivors in Canada began bringing forward individual lawsuits regarding abuses. As numerous stories and cases became public, the Assembly of First Nations (AFN) formed and began negotiating with the federal government and church groups for an out-of-court settlement. Finally, in 1998 the Canadian government admitted wrongdoing and offered apologies in a "Statement of Reconciliation." Six years later, after further class-action suits filed by individual survivors and ongoing negotiations between the AFN and the Canadian government, the AFN called for a plan that included payments to survivors, the establishment of a truth and reconciliation commission (TRC), and a commemoration fund. In 2006, the government approved a settlement that offered $1.9 billion in survivor payments (Niezen 2013; Stanton 2011). In 2008 the prime minister of Canada, Stephen Harper, offered a full apology for the residential school policies and acknowledged that the Canadian government had "contributed to social problems that continue to exist in many communities today" (Harper 2008). While there have been numerous criticisms of Harper's apology, Canada's TRC, and the compensation process, the United States still lags far behind in officially and publicly acknowledging the government treatment of Native peoples. There was a symbolic, semi-public apology in 2009 by Obama; however, it included no mention of financial reparations.[9]

Although government policies that forced the English language upon Mohawk people are no longer in full force today, the damage to the Mohawk language has been done, and the effects still linger. The guiding principles of the Mohawk people have been carried out for generations through their language, which is used in ceremonies, prayers, and everyday life. However, since European contact, drastic changes have taken place in the lives of Mohawk people as a result of warfare, disease, trade, and governmental policies designed to eradicate Indigenous cultures and languages (Bates 2001; Beauchamp 1905; Grant 1984; Hanzeli 1969). Evolving forces such as mass media and popular culture have become increasingly powerful temptations for young people to reject Mohawk culture, especially in more urban areas. Today's Native youth feel constant pressure to assimilate into mainstream society and often leave their traditional culture and language behind.

The rapid rate of Indigenous language decline and the possibilities of language extinction are alarming. According to Krauss (1998), of approximately 210 Indigenous languages that exist in the United States and Canada today, only 34 are still spoken by all generations. Although language revitalization and maintenance efforts have been underway for years, the danger of the Mohawk language disappearing remains a serious concern. The status of Kanienke:ha is further discussed in chapter 4.

Through language and cultural immersion strategies, the AFS attempts to reverse the assimilative forces that have caused significant declines in Mohawk language use. Language immersion has proven to be an effective strategy for Native language renewal (Arviso and Holm 2001; Cummins 1998; Genesee 1994; Harrison 1998; Holm and Holm 1995; Kipp 2000; Slaughter 1997; Warner 2001; Wilson and Kamanā 2001).

Language Immersion Programs

Early language immersion research began in Canada with French-language instruction for middle-class Anglophone students (Cummins 1998; Genessee 1994; Lambert and Tucker 1972; Swain and Lapkin 1986). Although the sociocultural and sociopolitical context of Native communities is strikingly different from French-language immersion movements, Native people have adapted immersion techniques to teach Native languages. The Māori of New Zealand (Harrison 1998) and Native Hawaiians (Warner 2001; Wilson and Kamanā 2001) have successful immersion programs that extend through twelfth grade. One of the first programs was the ʻAha Pūnana Leo (Language Nest) program, a privately funded, Hawaiian-language-immersion preschool program that was modeled after the successful Māori language immersion program, Te Kōhanga Reo (Slaughter 1997). A Navajo school in Fort Defiance, Arizona, also uses language immersion strategies (Arviso and Holm 2001; Holm and Holm 1995). The Blackfeet Nation of Montana immerses students from kindergarten through eighth grade in the Blackfeet language and is producing the first fluent speakers in a generation (Kipp 2000).

Immersion, however, still lacks a clear standard definition. In the case of the French programs, immersion refers to "at least 50% instruction through the target language (French) in the early stages. . . . Early immersion usually involves 100% French in kindergarten and grade 1 with one period of English language arts introduced in grades 2, 3, or sometimes as late as grade 4" (Cummins 2000). According to Holm and Holm (1995), Navajo immersion at the Fort Defiance Elementary School is conducted "almost entirely in Navajo" (p. 150) and entails "developmental Navajo, reading and writing (first in Navajo and then in English), and mathematics (in both languages)" (p. 149). Hawaiian immersion programs delay any English instruction until fifth grade, when students begin receiving one hour of English per day (Warner 1990, 1999).

In 1985 the AFS began language immersion for pre-kindergarten children through fourth grade. In 1992 its program extended through fifth grade, while English was the instructional language for sixth and seventh grade students. In 1993 immersion extended through sixth grade, and English was the instructional language for seventh and eighth grade (Jennings and Montour 1992, p. 13). For many years the parents and teachers hoped to someday have complete immersion through all grades. That dream has become a reality: seventh graders at AFS were included in Mohawk immersion beginning in 2011, and since then immersion has grown to include eighth and ninth grades with plans to add advanced levels each year to complete a high school program. Then in 2014 a language nest was created at the AFS with approximately nine children, ages eighteen months to three years, who are completely immersed in the language and culture (Kanerahtens Tara Skidders, personal communication, January 21, 2015).

While immersion schools can make tremendous strides in Native language revitalization efforts, we must question whether schools alone should be responsible for teaching Native languages to children. Can they do this successfully? Or should it be the sole responsibility of the parents and other elders at home to pass their language on to subsequent generations? I argue in this book that we need concerted efforts in the school and at home to revitalize Native languages in our communities. Schools can be effective places for language reclamation, especially when the community controls them, as is the case with the AFS. But schools cannot bear this burden alone. Even a successful immersion school like the AFS requires considerable dedication on the part of the parents, other family members, and the community. The ubiquitous presence of English is powerful—young people are bombarded with pop culture and mass media. It becomes too easy to slip into English, even for fluent Mohawk speakers. Deeper and more ingrained reasons also explain why parents do not pass on their languages to their children, reasons stemming from beliefs and ideologies connected to their own experiences with Western schooling.

A commonly held belief by some parents is that language immersion will be detrimental to their children's academic success. However, as this book claims, language immersion does not impede academic performance. In fact, learning a language through immersion, which is the most effective way to learn a language, leads to increased academic skills and academic success (Cummins 2000; Genessee 1994; Harrison 1998; Holm and Holm, 1995; Kana'iaupuni and Ishibashi 2005; McCarty 2003; Slaughter 1997; Stiles 1997). Students at the AFS have shown high academic performance, but perhaps more importantly they are grounded in their individual and cultural identities, have high self-esteem and self-confidence, and are given the necessary tools to be successful in their future endeavors.

Language and Identity

As AFS students are learning to be Kanienkeha:ka (Mohawk) and discovering their unique identities, we must wonder what role language plays in the construction of identity. The politics of identity are simplified in this description by Ojibwe scholar Scott Lyons: "Identity orients you in space and time, connects you to the past, helps you develop a vision for the future, and provides you with a story" (2010, p. 39). For Native people in the twenty-first century, individual and cultural identity stems from connection to our ancestors, from stories and traditions passed down through the generations that inform us of our lineage, from ties to the land that holds memories of our people, from our relationships with our tribal communities and families, and from our various roles and responsibilities as Native people. Indigenous identity in North America has become complicated given colonial impositions of "blood quantum" and documentation attesting to one's membership. Membership in a federally recognized tribe has become an important part of belonging for many, while excluding others.[10] But traditional ideas about Native identity have included "culture, ethnicity, language and allegiance—not blood or biology—as determinants" (Lyons 2010; p. 56). Indigenous identities are constructed and molded, fluid and dynamic, often complex. They cannot simply be reduced to "either you are or you're not." Identities are "not so much a thing at all, but are rather a social process. Indian identity is something people do, not what they are, so the real question is, what should we do?" (Lyons 2010; p. 40). This idea of doing, acting out, or behaving is a social process that young children are exposed to at the AFS, and they increasingly live their lives acting out the norms, customs, and behaviors of Mohawk citizens.

How does language fit into the complex nature of what it means to be Indigenous? I have often heard Native people say that you can't be Native if you don't know your language. Language is a central aspect to identity, but in this book, as I illustrate the complex nature of Indigenous identities, I argue that

Mohawk language alone does not constitute the basis of Mohawk identity. Language can serve as a marker of Mohawk identity, the components of which also include knowing traditional songs, stories, and dances, and living by the community's cultural values.

But if language alone were the sole aspect of Indigenous identity, then it would follow that fluent speakers all have strong cultural identities. However, I found this was not the case with adult Mohawk speakers. Some fluent speakers felt that some cultural identity was lacking because they didn't know the deep cultural meanings embedded in the Mohawk language. Many fluent speakers grew up with teachings from the Catholic Church and other Christian religious denominations and without cultural knowledge of the Haudenosaunee Creation Story or the founding of the Haudenosaunee Confederacy. In addition to language, cultural values are strongly connected to identity. In her study of Hopi contemporary youth and their cultural and linguistic practices, Nicholas (2008, 2009, 2010) found that while they lacked proficiency in speaking or understanding Hopi, they actively participated in a Hopi way of life through thinking, acting, and feeling Hopi, thereby developing a strong foundation in their cultural identities as Hopi. In contrast to adult speakers of the Mohawk language who felt that they were missing other aspects of Mohawk culture and didn't feel "fully Mohawk," the Hopi language was the "missing piece" (2009, p. 322) for the Hopi youth in Nicholas's study.

Becoming "Fully Mohawk"

Generally, cultural values or principles provide stability and cohesion in a community, guide us through life by helping us distinguish between right and wrong, and provide a role in cultural identification (Wan et al. 2007). Cultural values that comprise Mohawk identity include respect, kinship, responsibility, cooperation, leadership, and stewardship. These values, as identified through interviews with AFS students, alumni, parents, and teachers, are fully articulated in this book and lead to an understanding of what it means to be Mohawk today.

The cosmological process of becoming fully Mohawk as one follows traditional teachings and original instructions is also discussed in the book. Similar to becoming "fully Hopi," in which a moral and spiritual path leads to spiritual fulfillment (Nicholas 2009), becoming fully Mohawk means having a sense of completeness and being spiritually fulfilled. Both Hopi and Mohawk identity are assured through cultural "markers of identity" such as traditional naming, clan affiliation, and being part of a community (Nicholas 2008, p. 157). Identify formation is an ongoing process of becoming, not a state of being that is fixated in time and space. For Mohawk people, this process of becoming leads to our ultimate purpose, which is to live our lives adhering to our cultural values and traditions, in preparation for returning to the Skyworld, the place of our creation. The AFS is one place that nurtures and encourages children toward becoming fully Mohawk.

Insider/Outsider Research

My familial ties to Akwesasne and my own family history of linguistic and cultural loss prompted me to write this book. During the process of learning the Mohawk language I realized it was in danger of disappearing altogether, and I wanted to focus my work on language revitalization programs in the community. As a language immersion school, the AFS seemed the perfect place to begin my research. However, telling the full story of the AFS requires that I first share my story as a Mohawk woman.

My paternal grandfather, Mitchell Aronhiawakon White, attended the Carlisle Indian Industrial School in Pennsylvania from approximately 1900 to 1911, beginning when he was around eight years old. At Carlisle and many other residential schools for Native children, students were forbidden to speak their Native languages or practice their traditional ways of life. Carlisle's founder and school superintendent Richard H. Pratt, associated with the phrase "kill the Indian, save the man," was in charge of the first government-run, all-Indian-student, off-reservation residential school where complete assimilation into mainstream white America was the goal (Bell 1998; Fear-Segal 2006; Landis 2006). Thousands of Native students in these schools were subjected to harsh punishment, exploitation, malnourishment, and physical and sexual abuse. The trauma of residential school experiences has had detrimental effects on subsequent generations of Native people. Motivated by a feeling of personal responsibility to recover what has been lost and reclaim a piece of my familial and cultural heritage, writing this book has been part of a healing process for me.

My connection with the AFS started during the summer of 2001, when I started learning the Mohawk language through an adult language immersion program at Kanatsiohareke, a community established by Mohawk elder Tom Porter, in the Mohawk Valley of central New York. It was then that I met the AFS office manager, Konwanahtotani (Elvera) Sargent, and a former AFS teacher, Kaweienón:ni (Margaret) Cook-Peters. My relationship with these women evolved over the years as we talked about the Mohawk language and community efforts at language revitalization. After visiting the AFS during the summer of 2003, I asked Sargent, "What do you need?" Asking this question is critically important for researchers, particularly those working in Native communities. Historically, Native people did not control or share in the design or outcomes of research, and community needs often went unmet. These unmet needs have created a call for more Native researchers and a call for an increased understanding of Native peoples by non-Native researchers (Smith 1999; Swisher and Tippeconic 1999). This book evolved from the expressed interest and needs of the people at the AFS into a formal study to address how the school has affected the lives of students and to document the history of the school. When I initially inquired about the possibility of conducting research at the AFS, a former teacher and parent remarked: "The Akwesasne Freedom School has been researched by many people but we've never actually seen any results" (Cook-Peters, personal communication, November 15, 2001). It was important that I involve the AFS community as much as possible in the process of writing this book and that I saw it through to completion.

As with many Native communities, a long history of academic research that has at times exploited Native people has created a general distrust of researchers. Gaining the trust of participants was always at the forefront of my work. Since I had never lived in this community full-time, some residents of Akwesasne saw me as an outsider. In my previous experiences, kinship ties have helped to break through some of the initial distrust felt by community members. "Who's your family?" is the first thing I am asked when meeting other Mohawk people. In response, I would name my father, Louis John White, and his family, naming names until finding someone they knew, at which point they would nod, and a sense of community kinship was established. This was important, not only to link me to the community but also to foster trust. I grew up away from Akwesasne in the Mohawk Valley with only a few words of the Mohawk language. Most of my family members at Akwesasne are Catholic and do not follow the traditional longhouse ceremonies. I did, however, grow up understanding the importance of kinship ties within my community.

Ojibwe historian Thomas Peacock has this to say about his research: "I refuse to distance myself from my research. My representation of the history of the Ojibwe will always contain some of my own story because I am Ojibwe. I am part of the story" (Peacock and Wisuri, 2002, p. 12). In this way I too cannot separate myself from my work. It is not possible, and it is not necessary. I am Mohawk and I am a part of this story.

As an enrolled member of the Akwesasne community who grew up and lived away from the community, my role in this book is as an insider/outsider researcher. Stemming from the field of linguistics, there are several scholarly conversations and debates surrounding use of the terms "insider/outsider" and "emic/etic." Simply put, "emic" operations rely on insiders, while "etic" operations are based on categories formed by outside observers (Harris 1990; Pike 1990).

The insider/outsider researcher paradigm is complex and has multiple layers.[11] Smith (2012) states: "Indigenous research approaches problematize the insider model in different ways because there are multiple ways of being an insider or an outsider in Indigenous contexts" (138). For example, I am a member of the Haudenosaunee Confederacy, the Mohawk Nation, and more specifically, a member of the Akwesasne Mohawk community. As an insider, or even a partial insider, my view is quite different from that of an outside researcher who is not familiar with the Akwesasne community. As an insider I have an understanding of the history, a familiarity with the region, and strong familial ties and other relationships with the people and the land. There may be some immediate elements of trust because I am Mohawk, because I know some of the social mores and the best places to get corn soup, because I eat at the Bear's Den, and because I have fished in the St. Lawrence River. Although I am not much of an insider to the AFS, I know what it is like to be a part of the Akwesasne community to some extent.

Insider/outsider status is not black-and-white but is on a continuum where I had to balance and negotiate my multi-positionality (Loftlin 2002). I situated myself on this research continuum through constant self-reflection and critical inquiry regarding my personal relationships in the community and in serving the needs of the AFS. In writing this book I gained a greater awareness of myself as a researcher and as a Mohawk woman.

My insider status helped me understand and gave insight into what people were experiencing as I both witnessed and shared in some of those experiences.

Working in my home community has brought a greater sense of personal, professional, and moral responsibility than if I were to research an area unrelated to my personal background. Unlike researchers who have no familial ties to the communities they are studying, my family lives at Akwesasne. It is a place to which I will always return and be connected. I cannot disconnect myself from this reality, as Akwesasne is a place I will always return to. Some may assume that researching one's own community is easy, but the responsibility is greater when one must answer to their family. I have a family counting on me and a community that has trusted me to be a voice for them. As Maori scholar Linda Tuhiwai Smith writes, I "have to live with the consequences of [my] processes on a day-to-day basis for ever more" (Smith 2012, p. 138). So do my family and community. Community members are hoping to receive something meaningful in return.

I am burdened and blessed to bear responsibility to mothers who became teary as they told me how proud they were that their children were learning the language of their ancestors, to teachers who shared their stories of being paid with sacks of potatoes, and to fathers who helped build the AFS. I carry the voices of those I interviewed with me. It is my responsibility to share their stories with dignity. I must be of service to them and provide a medium for sharing.

Conducting the Research

Influenced by my sense of personal responsibility and a history of community research conducted by outsiders, I felt it important to involve the AFS in the research process as much as I could. When I initially asked Konwanahtotani (Elvera) Sargent about the possibility of researching the AFS, she thought it was a perfect time: several parents and teachers had indicated that they wanted to document the history of the school and wanted to know how the school had affected its students. Sargent then helped frame the following research questions: How did Akwesasne establish and maintain its own grassroots community school to reverse cultural and linguistic loss? How has the AFS affected the lives of its students? How have students' experiences at the AFS affected their perceptions of who they are as Mohawk people? What does it mean to be Mohawk?

With these questions in mind, I set out to document the circumstances surrounding the founding of the school in 1979 and its subsequent history. I aimed to understand the impact the school has had on its students and how it shaped their identities as Mohawk people.

It was imperative that peoples' experiences, thoughts, and opinions be voiced in this book. Because I wanted to know how the AFS has affected the lives of its students and how the school has been maintained over the years, I chose the case study approach. This work is descriptive, reflecting the process, meaning, and understanding inherent in qualitative research. It is ethnographic, in that it is an analysis of a particular cultural group, and historic, as it provides a description and analysis of how the AFS has evolved over time (Merriam 1998).

In attempting to gather participants' many and varied stories regarding their cultural and linguistic histories, I relied on in-depth interviewing techniques that would allow participants to "actively reconstruct their experience within the context of their lives" (Seidman 1998, p. 8). The Mohawk culture retains an important focus on oral tradition recounting stories of creation and the rich and vibrant Mohawk history. The people maintain this tradition throughout the community, in ceremony, and at the AFS. It is fitting then, because "stories are a way of knowing" (Seidman 1998, p. 1), that the participants could express themselves in this way. Therefore, I asked questions such as "What was happening in the community twenty-five years ago?"; "What were the goals of the AFS when it began?" ; "How has the school been able to achieve financial independence?"; "What does it mean to be Mohawk?"; and "How did your experience at the AFS influence your life?" By insuring confidentiality, participants were allowed to speak openly about their stories, reflect upon their experiences, and make sense of them (Seidman 1998).

I conducted forty interviews with students, alumni, teachers, parents, and staff. To maintain confidentiality I have only used interviewees' names when given explicit permission to do so.[12] No one declined an invitation to be interviewed, and most of the participants were found by word of mouth. Many responded with enthusiasm and appeared eager to tell their stories. Most of the interviews took place in participants' homes, on their porches, in their offices, and most frequently at a kitchen table.

As a participatory observer, I attended fund-raising events, parent meetings, and social gatherings, and I spent many hours in the homes of the participants. During classroom observations, I spent time with pre-kindergarten children, first graders, and children in grades 6–8. I also observed teachers and students while on the playground and before and after school. I spent considerable time searching through school files and archival materials at the Akwesasne Library, and I kept copious field notes.

Framework for the Book

Mohawk people have a long history of fighting for their sovereign rights to self-governance and self-education. It is important to understand Native education in the context of power relations, given the history of cultural and linguistic attacks by outside authoritative forces in control of Native education (Lomawaima and McCarty 2002). By first thoroughly examining relations of power, inequity, and domination within Native communities, and then better understanding social injustices, one can work toward positive social change in education and other areas.

This book is situated within an overarching framework of critical pedagogy, which attempts to understand and transform the power relations between the dominant society and those who are marginalized and oppressed. The goal of critical pedagogy is to empower and transform oppressed peoples (Freire 1970; Giroux, 2001). It is within critical pedagogy that Freire (1970) says, "The pedagogy of the oppressed is the pedagogy of people engaged in the fight for their own liberation" (p. 53). Critical pedagogy is significant for Indigenous peoples because "social change, action, and justice can be equated with a restoration of Indigenous values, knowledge, and ways of life. [It restores] Indigenous educational philosophy by calling attention to the effects of colonization and by empowering students to become critically conscious and aware of their own worth" (Lee 2006, p. 7).

However, Quechua scholar Sandy Grande (2004) warns that because Indigenous peoples are not like other marginalized groups that are fighting for inclusion in the mainstream but struggling to remain distinct and sovereign, a new pedagogy is needed that "cultivates a sense of collective agency to curb the excesses of dominant power and to revitalize Indigenous communities" (Grande 2004, p. 26). She calls this "red pedagogy." Informed by critical educational theory, she says that red pedagogy is "historically grounded in local and tribal narratives, intellectually informed by ancestral ways of knowing, politically centered in issues of sovereignty, and morally inspired by the deep connections among the Earth, its beings, and the spirit world" (p. 35).

The AFS is an example of Indigenizing education as it engages in red pedagogy by instilling Mohawk values and traditional knowledge, which serves to empower students as they engage in restoring Indigenous epistemologies and are liberated from oppressive colonial forms of education. This book examines how the community of Akwesasne regained its power and brought education back into the hands of the people. They fought for their sovereign rights and overcame powerful obstacles in providing a truly parent-controlled, culturally based education for their youth. Tipping the balance of power in favor of Native communities creates opportunities for renewed strength and vision for the future because. "Power means sovereignty, and sovereignty means self-government, self-determination, and self-education" (Lomawaima 2000, p. 9).

Outline of the Book

This book is for educators, researchers, and those interested in language revitalization, language immersion in education, and Indigenous identity issues. It is intended for both Indigenous and non-Indigenous readers and those interested in multiculturalism and diversity in education. Iroquois studies scholars and Native studies scholars in particular may find it useful. I hope this book will serve as a guide to others who are trying to find ways to develop culturally relevant curricula, establish and maintain language revitalization and retention programs, conduct community-based research.

I begin with background on the Haudenosaunee and the Mohawks of Akwesasne. In Chapter 1, I provide a cultural and historical background of the Haudenosaunee Confederacy in order to contextualize how the AFS is situated within its framework. I describe Haudenosaunee cosmology and follow the history of the founding of the confederacy with the coming of the Peacemaker and subsequent historical events that were instrumental in shaping contemporary Haudenosaunee life. In chapter 2, I give a detailed account of events leading up to the establishment of the AFS as well as its precursors. Here I rely on archival as well as personal accounts from Akwesasne community members who were a part of a divisive conflict within the community. In chapter 3, I make a case for a model of education based on the AFS holistic pedagogical model. This model is my interpretation of how the overall structure of the school allows its students the freedom to be Mohawk. Chapter 4 presents the current condition of the Mohawk language and provides accounts of language use by the AFS community. I briefly discuss language ideologies at Akwesasne, the roles of home and school in language revitalization efforts, and language immersion strategies and benefits, and I conclude with other language initiatives at Akwesasane. Chapter 5 tackles the questions of cultural identity and addresses Mohawk identity in particular. Here I argue that home and school are both necessary for language preservation. I also discuss the notion of "feeling Mohawk" and "thinking Mohawk" through use of the Mohawk language. Mohawk names are important markers of identity, and a brief discussion of them is included here. I argue that language alone does not equal identity and offer examples of how AFS students and adults value the language although they may not speak it fluently. Chapter 5 concludes with a section titled "I Knew I Was Indian but Didn't Know What It Meant," which relays how many adults rediscovered what it meant to be Mohawk through their participation in the AFS community. Chapter 6 covers what it means to be a "good Mohawk." Here I identify what it means to be Mohawk according to the AFS community and describe the values of respect, kinship, responsibility, stewardship, cooperation, and leadership. I also discuss the cosmological process of what it means to be Mohawk. Finally, a conclusion summarizes my thoughts on educational self-determination.

ONE

The Haudenosaunee

> Humans exist in a context of nature and not vice versa. Everything we ever had, everything we have, everything we will ever have—our health, our good looks, our intelligence, everything—is a product not of our own merit but of all that which created our world. That which created our world is not society but the power of the universe.
>
> —*(Mohawk 2005, p. xviii)*

Among Indigenous peoples around the world, storytelling is a method for teaching history, values, beliefs, and life skills. "Stories hold the key to the traditions, the rituals, and the social ways of Indigenous peoples. They passed on messages about loyalty, respect, responsibility, honesty, humility, trust, and sharing" (Maclean and Wason-Ellam 2006, p. 9). Indigenous stories also hold tremendous power: "They create people, they author tribes. . . . Creation stories, as numerous as Indian tribes, gave birth to our people" (Howe 1999, p. 118).

The guiding principles for the Haudenosaunee, or Iroquois (the confederacy of Mohawk, Oneida, Onondaga, Cayuga, Seneca, and Tuscarora people), are found within the stories of creation and the Great Law of Peace.[1] Other stories that comprise the foundation for a Haudenosaunee worldview include the Ohenton Kariwahtekwen (the Thanksgiving Address) and the Karihwi:io (the Code of Handsome Lake). These narratives express stories and cultural history with the "power to transform." Choctaw scholar LeAnne Howe (2002, 1999) calls the rhetorical space that holds such narratives "tribalography." Tribalographies relate origins, legends, and tribal history, and they connect to our contemporary lives. Haudenosaunee tribalography provides the cultural foundation for the Haudenosaunee way of life as well as the curriculum at the Akwesasne Freedom School (AFS). When such Indigenous stories are incorporated into the curriculum, they provide students with meaningful and transformative learning opportunities that are culturally based (Maclean and Wason-Ellam 2006).

In a sense this book is a tribalography of Mohawk people in the community of Akwesasne, as it weaves traditional stories and sociopolitical histories together and gives voice to community members who tell their own stories and share their own memories. The telling of Indigenous stories gives voice, honor, respect, and acknowledgment to our ancestors and serves as an act of empowerment and critical pedagogy. The AFS engages students in the telling of tribal traditional stories from the perspective of Haudenosaunee peoples, empowers students to reconnect with these stories and traditions, and therefore challenges Western education in which Indigenous epistemologies have been largely ignored.

The narratives of Indigenous peoples have been threatened by colonialism, Western religious indoctrination, and Western ideas of education. The history of the Haudenosaunee has been wrought with war, disease, land theft, and displacement. The community of Akwesasne has evolved from that history into one of complex political and geographical systems, and against long odds it has managed to perpetuate the tribalography of the Haudenosaunee. This tribalography begins with a great epic narrative: the Creation Story.

Creation Story

> In the distant past, all the earth was covered by deep water, and the only living things there were water animals. There was no sun, moon, or stars, and the watery earth was in darkness. Sky Beings lived above the great sky dome. A tree of life grew there in the cloud world, where it shaded the councils of the supernatural beings. One day the Great Chief became ill, and he dreamed that if the tree were uprooted he would be cured. He further commanded that his pregnant wife, Sky Woman, look down at the watery darkness. He told her to follow the roots of the tree, and to bring light and land to the world below.

> The animals of the sea saw Sky Woman as she fell from the sky world. Waterfowl rose to cushion Sky Woman's descent with their wings. Beaver dove to find earth to make dry land for Sky Woman. But Beaver drowned and floated lifelessly to the surface. Loon, Duck, and others all tried and failed as well. Finally Muskrat tried, and came back with a paw-full of dirt that would spread and grow. He placed the dirt on Turtle's back where Sky Woman landed. The dirt on Turtle's back grew and became the earth.
>
> Time passed and Sky Woman gave birth to a daughter. The daughter grew rapidly, and when she reached maturity a man visited her. He placed two arrows on her stomach, one tipped with chert and the other not. The daughter in turn bore twin brothers. The left-handed twin was Sawiskera (Mischievous One) and the right-handed one was known as Teharonhiawako (Holder of the Heavens). The left-handed twin forced himself out through his mother's armpit, killing her in the process. Corn, beans, squash, and tobacco grew from her body, and she became one with the earth. Teharonhiakwako created animals, medicine, and flowers, while Sawiskera created the thorns on the rose bush and the mountain lion to kill the deer his brother created. After much fighting the brothers decided to divide the world in half. The nighttime would belong to Sawiskera, and Teharionhiawako would get the daytime. The Onkwehonwe (Original People) were created by Teharionhiawako out of red earth and were to watch over his creations on Earth. Black soil, tree bark, and saltwater were used to create other beings. Teharionhiawako told the beings that he was to be called "Sonkwaiatison" (The Creator) and that they were to be respectful of one another and all living creatures. He instructed the people to appreciate each other's differences and to share the world.[2]

The Creation Story illustrates the worldview of the Haudenosaunee as one of duality, in which balance must be adhered to between opposing forces. Teharonhiawako represents generosity, peace, and harmony, while Sawiskera tempts us with greed and tests us with fear and darkness. Balancing this duality of opposing forces of human nature rests on an individual's choices to live with a "good mind."[3]

For the Haudenosaunee, the original instructions from the Creator are to live in balance, peace, and harmony while expressing gratitude for all living beings. By living one's life according to these instructions, one accumulates *orenda*—the spiritual force or power that flows in all things and connects us to all life and to the earth itself, the moon, sun, stars, wind, and spirits.[4] Orenda is a balance of light and dark, good and "evil."[5] By following the original instructions and accumulating orenda, one moves toward becoming fully Mohawk, fully Onkwehonwe, fully human. The idea of orenda and how it manifests through the Akwesasne Freedom School is discussed more fully in chapter 6.

Central to the Creation Story is the power of women as life givers and sustainers, as illustrated by Sky Woman. This story has cultivated an attitude of respect and gratitude to all women throughout Haudenosaunee history. Female elements are also found in the story of the "three sisters" that sprung forth from Sky Woman's body: corn, beans, and squash, which are sources of nutrients and vitality. Tobacco, which also grew from her body, is still used by the Haudenosaunee as a means for prayers to be carried skyward to the Creator.

The Creation Story is not a mere "myth" but illustrates the Haudenosaunee vision of the relationships and interconnectedness among all living things. "From the time we first hear this story as children through the voices of our own mother and grandmother we are given direction and understanding of our place in the world and our relationship to the other elements of creation" (HETF 1998, p. 2). This cultural foundation is an essential element in developing a strong identity as Haudenosaunee. The Creator gave responsibilities to the Onkwehonwe that have been passed down for many generations and are essential for survival; these responsibilities "help to set the framework for our cultural thinking" (HETF 1998, p. 2). With an understanding of where we come from we can better plan for where we are going and take comfort in who we are. We can look skyward and see the place where our ancestors have returned.

The Ohenton Kariwahtekwen

During the time of Creation, when Skyholder (Creator) returned to the earth, he instructed the original people to conduct ceremonies and to be thankful for having life. He told them to be grateful for the earth, the sun, grandmother moon, the thunder beings, and all other life forms. He instructed them that giving thanks in this way brings all of our minds together as one (Mohawk 2005; Rice 2013). As with many elements of Haudenosaunee tradition, there are several versions of the Ohenton Kariwahtekwen. The central theme of giving thanks runs through all, while the ordering and specific details may vary slightly. An excerpt taken from a school brochure (Akwesasne Freedom School, n.d.) reads:

> *Onkwehshon:a (The People)*
> May we now gather our minds as one and give one another greetings and thanks that we are gathered here in good health and in peace (all agree).
>
> *Iethinistenha Onhwéntsia (Mother Earth)*
> May we now gather our minds together as one and greet and give our thanks to our mother the earth for all that she gives us so we may live.
>
> *Ohnekashon:a (The Water)*
> May we now gather our minds together as one and turn to the spirit of the waters of the world. With oneness of mind, we now send our thanks to the waters of the world for quenching our thirst and purifying our lives.
>
> *Kariota'shon:a (Animal Life)*
> May we now gather our minds together as one and give our words of greetings and thanks to the animals.
>
> *Okwire'shon:a (Trees of the Forest)*
> May we now gather our minds together as one and give greetings and thanks to the trees of the forest for the fruits we eat, for the shade in summer, and for the shelter of our homes.
>
> *Ohontehshon:a (Green Plants)*
> May we now gather our minds together as one and give greetings and thanks to the plant life for giving us food and medicine.
>
> *Otsi'ten'okon:a (Bird Life)*
> The creator instructed the birds to sing upon the arrival of each new day, and to sing so that all life will not know boredom. With one mind we now greet and thank the bird life.
>
> *Ratiwe:ras (Grandfather Thunders)*
> The creator instructed the grandfather thunders to put fresh water into the rivers, lakes, and springs to quench the thirst of life. So with one mind we give our greetings and thanks to our grandfathers.
>
> *Ehtsitewahsti:a Kiehkehnekha Karahwkwa (Our Eldest Brother the Sun)*
> We are the younger siblings and our brother sun shines the light so we

may see and radiates warmth that all life may grow. We now with one mind give greetings and thanks to our eldest brother the sun.

Iethihsotha Ahsonthenehka Karahkwa (Our Grandmother the Moon)
Our Creator placed her in charge of the birth of all things and made her leader of all female life. All babies of all nations are born by her orchestration. May we now gather our minds into one and send our greetings and our thanksgiving to our grandmother the moon.

Shonkwaia'tison (Our Creator)
Our creator made all of life with nothing lacking. All we humans are required to do is waste no life and be grateful daily to all life. And so now we gather all our minds into one and send our greetings and our thanksgiving to our maker, our creator.

The Ohenton Kariwahtekwen is a central and foundational Haudenosaunee teaching. It conveys appreciation for all living things, recognition of the human relationship with the natural world, and concomitant responsibility to live on the land respectfully. The Ohenton Kariwahtekwen helps people achieve "one-mindedness" and is a "preamble to our [Haudenosaunee] way of life, our society" (Thomas 1992, p. 10). It calls for a gathering of minds and a unification of thought and belief in our interrelatedness. What one does affects all others, and we must live our lives according to what is best for all. For the Haudenosaunee there is no separation of this philosophy from daily life. An expression of Haudenosaunee culture that has guided its people since time immemorial, the Ohenton Kariwahtekwen reminds us of how to live our lives in a good way.

The Peacemaker and the Great Law of Peace

Haudenosaunee "tribalography" continues with the coming of the Peacemaker, the formation of the Great Law of Peace, and the founding of the Haudenosaunee Confederacy.[6] As the founding constitution and guiding principle of the Haudenosaunee Confederacy, the Kaianerekowa's (Great Law of Peace) message of peace and how to live as a responsible Haudenosaunee have been passed down and carried out for many generations. Although the date of the original founding of the confederacy varies among scholars, it is thought to be long before the coming of Europeans. Although no one knows for certain, the dates for the founding of the confederacy are thought to fall somewhere between 1142 and 1451 or later (Mann and Fields 1997; Snow 1994; Tooker 1978).[7]

It was the Peacemaker who provided the original Five Nations of the confederacy—the Mohawks, Oneidas, Onondagas, Cayugas, and Senecas—with the Kaianerekowa. The Creator sent the Peacemaker to end warfare and bloodshed among these peoples. The Peacemaker came into being when a Huron mother, who had never been touched by man, became pregnant. As a child he demonstrated superior abilities and was tested by some in his village who didn't believe he had been bestowed with supernatural powers. His grandmother tried to burn him when he was an infant because she thought he was evil. After he went unscathed, she next tried to drown him. Again he reappeared intact. Years later, when he was a young man, villagers threw him over a waterfall only to see him surface in perfect condition. Finally he was accepted for his abilities and his message of peace. Once he reached adulthood he left his home on the Bay of Quinte, now part of the Tyendinega Mohawk Reserve located on the north shore of Kaniatari:io (Beautiful Lake), now Lake Ontario. The Peacemaker created a stone canoe for the trip that was able to carry him to the other side of Lake Ontario where the Mohawk people accepted his message of peace. Traveling over the course of many years, the Peacemaker eventually reached a village called Ganondagon (White Town). Once a capitol of the Senecas, it is located about twenty miles southeast of present-day Rochester, New York. While in Ganondagon, the Peacemaker met a woman, Jikonsasay, who accepted his message of peace. In turn she became the head clan mother whose duty was to confer with the council of clan mothers on matters to be brought before the Grand Council (Mann 2010). Jikonsasay is still known as the Mother of Nations for her role in promoting peace and unity. Her body is buried near Ganondagan (George-Kanentiio 1993, 2003; Ryle 2002, p. 11).

With the help of Hiawatha, a great orator, the Peacemaker spread the message of the Great Law of Peace throughout all of Haudenosaunee territory—to the Mohawks, Oneidas, Onondagas, Senecas, and Cayugas—and thus the confederacy was formed (George-Kanentiio 1993). The Peacemaker used a quiver of arrows to demonstrate the importance of peace between nations. He demonstrated how one arrow could break easily but five held together in a bundle could not break. Therefore, he said, in unity you will find strength. He then

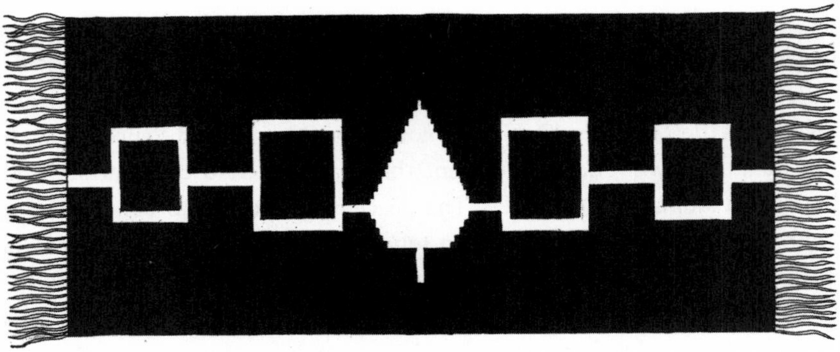

FIGURE 1. Hiawatha Belt. Drawing courtesy of John Kahionhes Fadden.

had each of the five nations bury their weapons of war under a white pine tree, which became known as the Tree of Peace (Ryle 2002). The original Tree of Peace was planted in Onondaga territory, where the council fire of the Haudenosaunee Confederacy has burned ever since. The Onondagas came to be known as the Keepers of the Central Fire.

In the Great Law of Peace, as instructed by the Creator, the Haudenosaunee found a way to live in peace and unity. This message was woven into a belt made of wampum and the story has been passed down over the centuries through oral tradition (see fig. 1).[8] In the Hiawatha Belt pictured in figure 1 there are thirty-eight rows of wampum. White wampum beads signifying the unity of the confederacy connect the symbols. The white tree in the middle symbolizes the Onondaga Nation and is reminder of Haudenosaunee loyalty to the Great Law. The belt, read right to left, symbolizes the journey of the Peacemaker through Haudenosaunee territory. The squares represent, in order, the Mohawks, the Oneidas, the Cayugas, and the Senecas. The colors of wampum hold particular significance for the Haudenosaunee: "The color white symbolizes purity and keeping of evil thought from the minds of the Sachems while in Council. Peace, charity, love and equality shall surround and guard the Confederacy" (Barnes 1984, p. 52).

The original instructions of unity and peace structure the social, political, and spiritual aspects of Haudenosaunee life. Passed down through oral tradition and committed to memory, instructions on choosing chieftain positions, duties and responsibilities of the people, the matrilineal clan system, use of wampum, procedures for ceremonies and adoptions, songs and prayers, and what to do in case of warfare—all are provided in the Great Law:

> These words constitute a new mind, which is the will of Tharonhiawako, the Holder of the Heavens. There shall be Righteousness when men desire justice, Health when men obey reason, Power when men accept the Great Law. These things shall be given form in the Longhouse, *Kanonsionni,* where five nations shall live as one family. In Unity there is power, these are the people of the Hotinonshonni. Their voice shall be the voice of the Great Law. All men shall hear this and find peace. (Barnes 1984, p. 62)

The concepts of peace, power, and righteousness" are embedded in the original teachings of the Great Law. Peace does not mean merely the absence of war or passivity but is achieved through a strong sense of cooperation and community. Power is not domination or military power but is achieved by the people having one mind, one heart, and one body, embodying the strength of working together. This type of power allowed the confederacy to remain united despite facing numerous obstacles. To be righteous, one lives according to the original teachings and the values embedded within those teachings. "Righteousness means justice practiced between men and between nations. It means a desire to see justice prevail. It also means religion, for justice enforced is the will of the Creator and has his sanction" (Barnes 1984).

The Grand Council of the Haudenosaunee

The Great Law of Peace is manifested in contemporary Haudenosaunee life through the Grand Council, which has continued to be active in many areas of Haudenosaunee political, social, and spiritual life. When all Five Nations accepted the Great Law of Peace, a protocol was established to confer a chief's title upon a descendant in a matrilineal line: "Each nation must select a certain number of their wisest, and kindest men to be the Chiefs, *Roiane*. These men will be the advisers of the people. They will sit in Council and make the decisions for their respected nations. The women (clan mothers) holding the hereditary titles will make the selections and confirmations (Barnes 1984, p. 30)." Nine chiefs were selected for the Mohawks, nine for the Oneidas, fourteen for the Onondagas, eight for the Senecas, and ten for the Cayugas. The total, fifty male representatives of the Five Nations, came to comprise the Grand Council of the Haudenosaunee (Barnes 1984).

Thus, the Peacemaker established the principles of representation in the confederacy. Each leader's title, duties, and authority are derived from the people, and the people have the right to impeach him, a right bestowed upon the clan mothers. The Peacemaker had established a "government of absolute democracy, the constitution of the Great Law with the spiritual law" (Lyons and Mohawk 1992, p. 32). It was written, "Five bound arrows symbolize our complete union. Our power is now one within the Hotinonshonni. We have tied ourselves together in one head, one body, one spirit and one soul to settle all matters as one. We shall work, counsel and confirm together for the future of coming generations. We shall each eat one bowl of cooked beaver tails being careful not to use a sharp object for if we do we might cut one another and bloodshed will result" (Barnes 1984, p. 31).

Haudenosaunee chiefs' titles are still passed along the matrilineal line through a system of clan names, thus carrying on a long lineage that goes back to the original council. Although today some political bodies do not recognize the traditional council, the central fire still burns in Onondaga territory. The Grand Council still carries on the oral tradition of the Great Law of Peace by calling meetings, opening with the Ohenton Kariwahtekwen, and continuing to affirm the identities of the Haudenosaunee. The Grand Council continues to ensure the survival of the Great Law of Peace.

Sociopolitical History of the Haudenosaunee

According to some Haudenosaunee oral tradition, the people originally came from the Southwest, near the land of the Hopis. Eventually the Haudenosaunee moved eastward to the Midwest, and after many generations of following the Ohio River, bands split off in all directions and became the Huron, Erie, Cherokee, Wenro, Nottoway, Meherrin, Susquehannock, Neutral, and Petun Nations. The rest continued to the Great Lakes and the St. Lawrence River. The Kanienkeha:ka (Mohawks) settled in the lower valleys near the Mohawk River.[9] Others settled further west: the Oneniota:a:ka (Oneidas), Onontowa:ka (Onondagas), Kaiokwenha:a (Cayugas), and Onontowa:ko (Senecas) (George-Kanentiio 2000). Around 1722 the Tuscaroras joined the confederacy, thereby forming the Six Nations Confederacy as it is known today.

Prior to European contact, the Haudenosaunee populated much of what are now New York State, southern Ontario, and Quebec. Morgan (1962) claimed that the Haudenosaunee occupied these areas during the Dutch explorations around 1609. Guided by rich traditions of agriculture, hunting, and fishing, the Haudenosaunee prospered along the vast rivers and fertile valleys of this region (Fenton 1968; Fenton and Tooker 1978; George-Kanentiio 2000; Morgan 1962). The Mohawk territory extended from the Delaware River north to the St. Lawrence, encompassing most of the Adirondack Mountains. Their eastern boundaries were Lake Champlain, Lake George, and the Hudson River (George-Kanentiio 2000; Schneider 1997). Mohawks once occupied all of what is now Adirondack Park, the largest publicly protected area in the United States at over six million acres (apa.ny.gov). They hunted in the lower regions of the park and made their homes in nearby valleys.

Akwesasne[10]

Akwesasne (Where the Partridge Drums) land is home to a rich hunting and fishing environment. Akwesasne Mohawk territory, also known as St. Regis, is located in northern New York and straddles the international border, extending into Quebec and Ontario (see map 1 in introduction). Akwesasne is located along the scenic St. Lawrence River and also encompasses islands in the St. Lawrence River. In 1700 two-thirds of the Mohawks in the Northeast were living in Canada. Beginning in the seventeenth century, Mohawk converts to Christianity often left the Mohawk Valley (in what is now central New York State) and headed to missions in Canada to avoid invasions and warfare (Fenton and Tooker 1978; Snow 1994). Some Mohawks left the mission at Kahnawà:ke, near present-day Montreal, and settled down the St. Lawrence River in traditional hunting and fishing territory (Akwesasne) sometime between 1755 and 1759. A new mission site known as St. Regis, named after French priest Jean François Régis (Saint Francis Regis), was established under French Jesuit authority (Fenton and Tooker 1978; Frisch 1970; Snow 1994).[11] The reservation boundaries for the St. Regis Mohawks were officially delineated in 1796 when New York State illegally entered into treaties with unauthorized individuals said to represent the St. Regis Mohawks (George-Kanentiio 2006; Frisch 1970). New York State established the St. Regis reservation, while recognition by the federal government did not occur until 1972 (George-Kanentiio 2006). Although the commu-

MAP 2. Haudenosaunee communities in the United States and Canada. Based on a map by John Kahionhes Fadden; reproduced with permission. Copyright © 2015, University of Oklahoma Press.

nity predates the founding of the United States and Canada, the boundaries of both countries have been laid across it.

Akwesasne territory is relatively small: approximately forty-one square miles of land and water. It has approximately thirteen thousand residents and is composed of four residential districts. Two districts, Kanatakon (St. Regis Village) and Tsi Snaihne (Snye) are located within Quebec's boundaries. A third district, Kawehno:ke (Cornwall Island), is located within Ontario, while the fourth southernmost district lies within New York State's boundaries. The AFS is located in this southern part of the territory, just west of Hogansburg, New York.

Jurisdiction and Governance at Akwesasne

Akwesasne's system of governance is complicated by the fact that the community overlaps two countries, two Canadian provinces, and one state. In 1783, the Treaty of Paris drew the international boundary between Canada and the United States; it went right down the middle of Akwesasne territory. Although all parties ignored the international boundary for a few years, the War of 1812 changed the sociopolitical situation at St. Regis drastically. After the war the Canadian and US governments refused to acknowledge Mohawks on their opposing sides of the international border (Fenton and Tooker 1978; Frisch 1970).

Akwesasne has a complicated system of three interlocking jurisdictions. The US federal government and New York State government only recognize the St. Regis Mohawk Tribe (SRMT). An 1802 New York State statute allowed for the election of three trustees to manage affairs and negotiate with the state on behalf of the St. Regis Mohawks (Herne, October 25, 2009, personal communication; Snow 1994).[12]

In 1888 the Canadian government instituted the second jurisdiction, the Mohawk Council of Akwesasne (MCA), to replace the traditional twelve-member council with an elected body (Snow 1994). Due to the relocation of Mohawks in the Mohawk Valley following the American Revolution, there had been a void in the Haudenosaunee Confederacy for a century with the absence of the Mohawks. But in 1885, Akwesasne was brought into the confederacy as a seat of the official Mohawk Nation and its traditional council. The community had adopted an Indigenous form of leadership, which incorporated Haudenosaunee principles but also showed evidence of new circumstances: widespread conversion to Christianity and distancing from the Haudenosaunee Confederacy. The third Mohawk government then is the Mohawk Nation Council of Chiefs (MNCC), a traditional system that has been in existence for generations and is composed of hereditary chiefs, clan mothers, and "faithkeepers" (those responsible for ensuring that the traditional ceremonies are carried out). Canadian and US officials do not formally recognize the MNCC, despite the fact that early Canadian and US treaties were made with the traditional council. However, the MNCC has considerable influence and is recognized by the larger Haudenosaunee Confederacy as the official government of Akwesasne. The MNCC adheres to the Great Law of Peace and belongs to the Grand Council of the Haudenosaunee.

It is important to understand that the MNCC considers itself a sovereign entity designated as a distinct "nation," rather than a "tribe" within the nation-states of the United States and Canada. Sue Ellen Herne, AFS parent and Akwesasne Museum curator, provides the following explanation of the MNCC's sovereign status:

> When Europeans came to this land, there were hundreds of distinct nations of people—with their own recognized territories and distinct ways of governing themselves. Today, each still chooses its own form of governance but that is generally within the confines of the larger nation (U.S. or Canada) around them. The United States defines native nations as "domestic sovereign nations," seeing them as part of the United States, but with a limited sovereignty. "Tribe" is often used as the designation, rather than "nation." Each of these tribes or nations has its own unique way of governing its people and addresses their needs as [each sees] fit but most are intimately tied to the federal government through funding and regulations. . . . The Haudenosaunee are unique in that the central council in Onondaga has remained strict in its definition of sovereignty and has kept the traditional form of government throughout history, into the present, without an administrative government that is tied to the United States or Canada and not accepting the designation of U.S. citizenship. Akwesasne's traditional government is recognized by Onondaga as the Mohawk Nation. (personal communication, October 25, 2009)

The distinction of MNCC's sovereign status as a nation becomes important when addressing educational policies including those surrounding the development of the AFS. The status of the AFS as an independent entity supported by the MNCC and separate from the education regulations and policies of the United States and Canada is discussed in detail in later chapters.

The Mohawk Nation Council of Chiefs is also responsible for making decisions based on Haudenosaunee laws and traditional teachings, the foundation of Mohawk existence and sovereignty. The MNCC offers governmental and spiritual services such as membership registration and documentation, birth and marriage certificates, marriage ceremonies, border crossing credentials, and funeral rites, as well as fostering language promotion. The degree of cooperation and the intersection of jurisdiction among these three independent and distinct councils is not always clear to tribal members, let alone to outsiders. As each council has its own membership codes and requirements, it is a complicated, dizzying task to decide which council to address for which purposes. The "divide and conquer" tactics of federal and state authorities have created a complex political situation. Regardless, as Darren Bonaparte writes, "These elected councils, conceived by Canadian and American authorities and imposed by force in the 19th century, have evolved over time to reflect the wishes and aspirations of the community. All three councils, to varying degrees, share the responsibility of keeping the fire of Mohawk nationhood burning at Akwesasne" (Bonaparte n.d.).

The Code of Handsome Lake

We now come to one of the most recent narratives in Haudenosaunee tribalography: the life of controversial prophet Handsome Lake. The controversy surrounding Handsome Lake has created geographical, political, and spiritual divisions among the Haudenosaunee. Many generations after the coming of the Peacemaker, during the height of social upheaval caused by early European influences and American Revolution, a Seneca named Handsome Lake (1735–1815) purportedly received a series of visions, which came to be known as "The Good Message" or the Karihwi:io (Parker 1913). As a result, Handsome Lake renewed Haudenosaunee midwinter ceremonies that had gone dormant: the Feather Dance, Thanksgiving Dance, the Rite of Personal Chant, and the Peach Stone Game. He spent fifteen years traveling and speaking throughout Haudenosaunee territories in the United States and Canada, spreading the Karihwi:io (Tooker 1970).

Spanning four days of recitations, with over 130 sections, the basic tenets of the Karihwi:io include everything from repenting for "evil things," abstaining from alcohol, and forbidding wife abuse to instructions for child-rearing.[13] Regarding education, the Karihwi:io states:

> We feel that the white race will take away the culture, traditions, and language of the red race.
>
> When your people's children become educated in the way of the white people, they will no longer speak their own language and will not understand their own culture. Your people will suffer great misery and not be able to understand their elders anymore.
>
> Your relations will appoint twelve children to be educated by the white race. They will select two children from each of the Six Nations. We feel that when they become educated, not a single child will come back and stand at your side because they will no longer speak your language or have any knowledge of their culture. (Thomas and Boyle, 1994, p. 41)

Handsome Lake's teachings also included prophecies of a dark future with a weakened Haudenosaunee government, lack of faith in the Karihwi:io, unknown diseases, and loss of language: "In the future you will see a day coming when we will no longer be able to carry on our ceremonies, for our children will not be able to speak their own language. It will be at this time that all the great changes of the earth will take place in the not too distant future" (Barnes 1984, p. 81).

The Karihwi:io views alcohol as a drink given for "white brothers" for their labors but that was then abused by whites, causing their minds to "split." Part of the controversy of the Karihwi:io stems from the fact that Handsome Lake himself was a severe alcoholic and had been near death when he began receiving his visions. Yet his teachings about abstaining from alcohol remain a powerful message for many: "For the *Onkwehonwe* it will bring great misery and hardship. When you have touched the firewater called '*Oneka*' you will like it. You must remember what will result from drinking it. Anyone who has [drunk] the firewater will know it as the 'mind changer.' They must reaffirm their faith and renewal to *Sonkwaiatison* and pledge never to touch it again" (Barnes 1984, p. 73).

Perhaps the most controversial tenets in the Karihwio:io are elements of Christianity, including acts confession and repentance of sins. Handsome Lake

FIGURE 2. Model of traditional Haudenosaunee longhouse, Ganondagan, New York. Photo by L. White.

also believed that traditional medicine societies should be disbanded, because of their association with witchcraft. Sometimes those who refused to confess and give up such practices were killed by members of their own community (Snow 1994). Handsome Lake's "New Religion," as it is sometimes referred to, divided the already fragile confederacy into factions of those who followed the old order and those who followed the new teachings of Handsome Lake (Lemelin 1997). Some say he became "dictatorial and even grandiose," declaring himself divine (Wallace and Steen 1972, p. 253). But in an already factionalized confederacy plagued by alcoholism and torn by Christianity, Handsome Lake's message became more widely accepted and by the 1840s was formalized into a religion. Many Haudenosaunee believe that without Handsome Lake's message, the original midwinter ceremonies that he helped reinvigorate might have been weakened beyond repair (Herne, personal communication, October 25, 2009).

The Longhouse

The traditional dwelling of the Haudenosaunee was the longhouse, a wooden structure forty to two hundred feet long and twenty feet wide (see fig. 2) that housed extended families organized by clan (ganondagan.org). By the mid to late eighteenth century, people had moved into small log cabins holding single

FIGURE 3. Contemporary longhouse, Akwesasne. Photo by L. White.

families. Upon formalization of Handsome Lake's message, his followers began rituals in a building similar to the old longhouse, thus the birth of the "Longhouse religion" (Wallace and Steen 1972, p. 335).

It was not until the 1930s that Longhouse ceremonies and the Karihwi:io were openly practiced in Akwesasne. Prior to that time, many Mohawks of Akwesasne belonged to the Catholic Church, while those keeping traditional ceremonies alive practiced in secret, often in family homes. An elder describes the cultural revitalization brought to a primarily Christian community: "Back in 1935, that was the big year for the establishment of the longhouse. It was built then. . . . They had to relearn most of what was forgotten. A small movement began. It started to increase. Eventually, it kept going, and people kept getting more knowledgeable about their own ceremonies, beliefs, and history" (Interviewee T2, July 19, 2005).

Many Mohawks sought to return to the traditional ways of the Longhouse religion and tried to distance themselves from Christianity or anything resembling Christianity. The Karihwi:io has continued to be subject to controversy and rejection by some community members (Lemelin 1997).

Today there are two longhouses at Akwesasne. One belongs to the traditional Handsome Lake followers who also abide by the Great Law of Peace. Supporters of the Warrior Society attend the other. This militant faction split off from the Handsome Lake longhouse after violent conflicts erupted in the

1990s and built their own longhouse (Thomas and Boyle 1994, p. 143). Dissension and factionalism among spiritual Mohawks at Akwesasne is still prevalent, as relayed by this community member:

> One of the things that we have a hard time with is religion. That in itself is another reason why there was a split in the longhouse. Handsome Lake's religion . . . we say we don't need it. We were given our original instructions [before Handsome Lake]. . . . Handsome Lake comes around in the 1930s and he says he's got another message. . . . Every generation adds a little to his message and it changes over time. . . .We respect them if they want to follow it, but they don't respect us for not wanting to follow it. So they downgrade us and discredit us in the community. They say you have to follow it. . . . Religion has destroyed our people. . . . Religion is not a God thing, it's a government. And its president sits in Rome. (Interviewee P10: May 19, 2005)

Although it has come with the high price of internal hostility, the continually changing social structure of Akwesasne and the Longhouse religion has meant a continual resurgence and renewal of traditional practices. Guided by original teachings held in the Great Law of Peace and the Karihwi:io, Mohawks have continued to fight as tenacious activists for their unique place in the world.

The Haudenosaunee have been guided by stories of creation, the Great Law of Peace, the Ohenton Kariwahtekwen, and the Karihwi:io for generations. As part of the Haudenosaunee Confederacy, the Akwesasne Mohawk Nation still adheres to the tribalography that has been passed down for centuries. The complex sociopolitical history and current jurisdiction at Akwesasne has certainly created numerous challenges. Despite these, Mohawks have "continued to adhere to a collective identity defined by family, the bonds of a common ancestry, and the desire, however vague or muted, to preserve a distinct aboriginal heritage" (George-Kanentiio 2006, p. 134). The Mohawks of Akwesasne have experienced pressures of acculturation for more than two hundred years yet have preserved their distinct cultural identity as members of a once powerful confederacy.

TWO

Drums along the St. Regis

> We were standing up for our own freedom to be who we were, also to be free to raise our children the way we felt they should be raised, for them to be able to think freely, think for themselves, to judge for themselves, not to be told by someone else what to think, how to feel, how to be.
>
> —*Interviewee P8: October 8, 2004*

Indigenous peoples have long and rich cultural histories predating European contact. After contact, governmental authorities, religious organizations, and Western educators began an ongoing war to destroy and assimilate these cultures. However, Indigenous peoples have continued to resist attacks on their culture and sovereignty.

In the 1960s Native people around the country were coming together and taking a stand against the US government. Native nations vocalized their treaty rights, fought racism, reclaimed land bases, and sparked cultural revitalization movements. Policies began to shift in favor of Indigenous rights with the passage of the Indian Education Act of 1972 and the Indian Self-Determination and Education Assistance Act of 1975, which are often viewed as the most "significant pieces of legislation aimed at establishing indigenous control" (Grande 2004, p. 45). Sandy Grande states that Indigenous control over education must be accompanied by a vision of "social transformation and emancipation" (p. 165). A brief overview helps set the stage for the activist movement that led to the Akwesasne Freedom School (AFS) and educational self-determination for the people of Akwesasne.

The Haudenosaunee, "especially the Tuscaroras and Mohawks, were instrumental in the emergence of Red Power in the late 1960s" (Hauptman 1986, p. 235). Haudenosaunee activism, however, had a history dating back to at least the 1920s with the Indian Defense League of America (IDLA), which organized to advocate for treaty rights (Hauptman 1986). These movements set the stage for Ray Fadden (Tehanetorens), a visionary Mohawk teacher who would take some brave steps to radically transform Mohawk education.

Mohawk Education and Social Movements

Nestled in the Adirondack Mountains in upstate New York, is the Six Nations Museum, a small establishment full of Haudenosaunee artifacts, drawings, and paintings. Ray Fadden built the museum in 1954 as a place to preserve Haudenosaunee history with dignity and honor, and it is still run by his family. Fadden was an accomplished artist who re-created many traditional wampum belts. His legacy of revitalizing Mohawk culture, however, began in the classroom.

Fadden began his teaching career in Tuscarora territory in the 1930s before coming to Akwesasne to teach at the St. Regis Mohawk School. He did what no other teacher dared at the time, which was to teach Mohawk students their own history and culture in a public school setting. Using knowledge of the elders, traditional music, and especially nature, Fadden instilled a sense of cultural pride in his students.

Around 1940, Fadden took his teaching outside of the classroom, founding the Akwesasne Counselor Organization to train young Mohawk boys and girls in the history, traditions, and crafts of their people. He modeled the organization after the Boy Scouts of America but sought to counter the racism and anti-Native negative stereotypes of the predominantly white group. Members—largely Fadden's students from the St. Regis Mohawk School—learned skills that had been dying out in Mohawk communities, like deer tanning and flint knapping. The group traveled throughout New York State and beyond, visiting museums and historical sites, even going to Washington, D.C., and to the 1967 World's Fair in Montreal. Members studied Mohawk history and sought elders from whom to learn culturally relevant information. The Akwesasne Counselor Organization had an enormous impact on the Akwesasne community and Mohawk cultural revitalization (R. Fadden n.d.; George-Kanentiio 2006; Jennings 1998).

Ray Fadden passed into the spirit world on November 14, 2008. He left behind a lasting legacy that will be revered by future generations. When I asked Ray's son, John Kahionhes Fadden, when the Akwesasne Counselor Organization had ended, he replied, "It simply faded. To some degree it never ended. I still have my membership card" (John Kahionhes Fadden, personal communication, 2006).

Another early effort for Native education at Akwesasne began around 1971, when a Mohawk clan mother, Kariohiwanoron Ann Jock of the Bear Clan, started the Indian Way School. The school taught Native values, natural life cycles, crafts, Native history, and academics. The teachers worked in return for room and board. The humble school building located on Ann Jock's land had wooden benches, approximately twenty students, and little money. The school raised funds through bingo games and craft sales. Ray Fadden was also involved in this effort. He obtained a small grant for supplies and showed students how to make replica wampum belts while studying their cultural meanings. Students made several belts and wampum strings that can still be seen in the publication *Wampum Belts of the Iroquois* (Tehanetorens 1999). Students also learned to trap animals and even made muskrat stew. One student claimed, "It's not so much an education, it's a way of life we're getting" ("Indian Way School" 1972).

Like many programs that have come and gone in Indian country, the Indian Way School could not operate long without adequate funding and closed its doors after a few years. Even though Ann Jock's dream of teaching the traditional ways was short lived, she spurred renewed interest in revitalizing a rich culture that was on the brink of being forgotten.

A major event in the history of Akwesasne was the publication *Akwesasne Notes,* which was distributed internationally and covered events worldwide. Started in 1969 by Ernest M. Kaientarionkwen Benedict and Jerry Rarihokwats Gambill, *Akwesasne Notes* was the official publication of the Mohawk Nation at Akwesasne but its publishers called it "the voice of Indigenous peoples" (Akwesasne Notes 1972; Hauptman 1986). The publication began modestly as a few pieces of paper stapled together, with copies of newspaper clippings describing the International Bridge Blockade of 1968. That year several hundred Mohawks blocked traffic on the international bridge crossing the St. Lawrence River between the United States and Canada, demanding their rights to free passage as guaranteed in the Jay Treaty (Frisch 1971).[1]

The Jay Treaty of 1794 stated: "It is agreed that it shall at all Times be free to His Majesty's Subjects, and to the Citizens of the United States, and also to the Indians dwelling on either side of the said Boundary Line freely to pass and repass by Land, or Inland Navigation, into the respective Territories, and Countries of the Two Parties on the Continent of America (the Country within the limits of the Hudson's Bay Company only excepted) and to navigate all the Lakes, Rivers, and waters thereof, and freely to carry on trade and commerce with each other" (Miller 1931). The Mohawk Council of Akwesasne states: "The Jay Treaty is not a Treaty with Aboriginal Peoples and it is not a Treaty which *gives* [emphasis added] border crossing rights to the First Nations People. It is however, a Treaty which *confirms* [emphasis added] those rights and which adds to the constitutional protection of those rights. It also does not create the range of Aboriginal Rights that have been exercised by Aboriginal People since time immemorial" (http://www.akwesasne.ca/node/119).

Since the imposition of the international border between the United States and Canada in 1783, Mohawks have had to fight for border crossing rights, despite the provisions of the Jay Treaty. In 1956 a customs office and toll collection booths for the international bridge were constructed on Cornwall Island. Mohawks on the island were required to pay tolls and customs duties on all goods purchased in the United States. After much protest, including the bridge blockade in 1968, Mohawks finally won the dispute in 1969, and the Canadian government agreed to the duty-free status of Akwesasne residents and exempted them from the toll (Hauptman 1986).

Around the same time, a small group of Mohawks took their message directly to the people. Headed by Gambill, they formed the White Roots of Peace, a mobile activist troupe designed to provide instruction on Native culture and contemporary issues. Composed mostly of Mohawk performers and instructors and other artists from North America, their mission was to promote Native sovereignty and treaty rights and to deepen the teaching of Native history to include a Native perspective. Inspired by the civil rights movement, the group printed posters and other educational materials and traveled around the world inspiring others to organize at the grassroots level (George-Kanentiio 2006). Benedict and Gambill were also responsible for starting the North American Indian Travelling College in 1969, considered to be a "major educational force" (Hauptman 1986, p. 222).[2]

Members of White Roots of Peace distributed *Akwesasne Notes* throughout their travels and the publication grew to be the largest Native-owned newspaper in North America. The Indian Studies Department at Wesleyan University in Connecticut took on printing of the newspaper, while the editorial headquarters were at Akwesasne. Later, teachers at the newly formed AFS would use the newspaper to teach history, social studies, and Indigenous culture. The award-winning journal remained in publication until 1995.

All this Haudenosaunee activism set the stage for a shift in educational self-determination. That shift began with a major community conflict among the people of Akwesasne who were once again fighting for sovereignty and self-determination.

Drums along the St. Regis

> Native American community life today is framed by two value systems that are fundamentally opposed. One, still rooted in traditional teachings, structures social and cultural relations; the other, imposed by the colonial state, structures politics. This disunity is the fundamental cause of factionalism in Native communities.—*Alfred 1999, p. 1*

Mohawk scholar Taiaiake Alfred (1999) speaks to the divided nature of contemporary Native communities. At Akwesasne these divisions were linked to generations of internal and external struggle, which finally culminated in an outright civil war. From 1979 to 1982 regional newspapers around Akwesasne featured headlines reading, "Traditionalists under Siege," "Unrest at Indian Reservation," and "Drums Along the St. Regis: Indians Fighting for Their Heritage" (Friedman 1980; Thompson 1979a; "Traditionalists under Siege" 1980). On one side of this conflict were Mohawks who supported the tribal police and the elected St. Regis Tribal Council. On the other side were "traditionalists," who opposed any imperialistic form of governance and were proponents of the Longhouse religion and the Great Law of Peace. The Awkwesasne Freedom School was born out of this turmoil.

Describing details of this conflict is beyond the scope of this book, but description of the events leading up to it and the evolution of the AFS may provide insight and perspective on how the community was able to develop and sustain a school in the context of so much unrest.[3] Interviews with those who

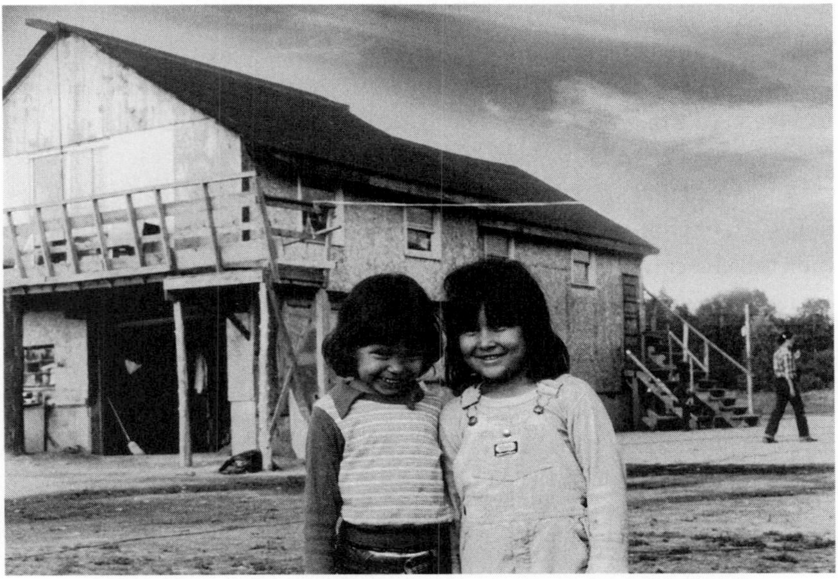

FIGURE 4. AFS students Karonienhawi Cook Thomas (on left) with Wahiahawi Barreiro Fitch, around 1979–80. Photo courtesy of Mary Rojas.

were present during that time and archival records present an account of a fractured community struggling for cultural survival. Many of the stories from those who spoke about the events of that time are filled with painful memories but also glimpses of hope for healing. As a scholar, it is my intention to remain as unbiased as possible concerning the issues that led to the 1979 conflict at Akwesasne. I will present differing opinions and various points of view in order to shed light on how the AFS came about and how it has persevered over the years.

On May 29, 1979, the *Watertown Times*, daily newspaper of nearby Watertown, New York, reported that Loran Thompson, a chief of the Mohawk Nation Council of Chiefs and Longhouse member or "traditionalist," had been arrested on charges of grand larceny after confiscating chainsaws owned by the Young Adult Conservation Corps (Elder 1979), which was a federally sponsored conservation-related employment and education program. The YACC had been using the chainsaws to build a fence on Thompson's property on the western edge of Akwesasne's boundary. The fence-building had been initiated by the St. Regis Tribal Council to "delineate Akwesasne's boundaries with the help of physical markers, thereby exposing the geo-national (American, Canadian) differences in the community" (Lemelin 1997, p. 103). Traditional Mohawk members were opposed to any fencing that might weaken the claim to traditional territory outside of Akwesasne's boundaries.

Alleged victims of police brutality while resisting arrest by the Mohawk police, Thompson and other traditionalists demanded a disbanding of what they called a corrupt Mohawk police force. The St. Regis Tribal Council had created its own tribal police force in the early 1970s with federal funding in order to enforce New York State laws, creating an immediate clash between traditional and elected councils (George-Kanentiio 2006).

The arrest of Thompson was described by the local newspapers as "an armed invasion of Mohawk lands," and traditionalists accused the Akwesasne police of being "an occupation army serving the purposes of New York State" who were being "used by New York State to force illegal laws" onto Mohawk lands (Elder 1979). The traditionalists claimed that the presence of state police and the New York State–sponsored Young Adult Conservation Corps on their territory violated their jurisdiction as a sovereign nation because they had never accepted New York State's treaty laws. These Longhouse members supported the Mohawk Nations Council of Chiefs, the governing body instituted by the Peacemaker to carry the Great Law of Peace. New York State claimed that treaties signed two hundred years earlier obligated the Mohawks to the state rather than to the federal government.[4]

A Franklin County grand jury indicted Thompson for third-degree grand larceny and for resisting arrest, on the grounds of violating state law. After attempts at a peaceful resolution, several traditional Mohawks seized the elected chief's council house in protest of the arrest. Fifty state police officers then entered the community and arrested three Mohawks involved in the takeover of the council house (Boyer 1979). Adding fuel to the fire, while traditional Mohawks were in the council house, they discovered secret negotiations between the St. Regis Tribal Council and New York State to relinquish land claims in exchange for $12 million dollars without consulting with the Mohawk Council of Akwesasne or the Mohawk Nation Council of Chiefs (George-Kanentiio 2006).

After the remaining criminal indictments regarding the council house takeover were issued, 100–150 Mohawks gathered near Thompson's residence to

FIGURE 5. Encampment at Raquette Point, 1980. Drawing courtesy of John Kahionhes Fadden.

prevent law enforcement officers from serving the warrants. In doing so, they also constructed a roadblock located on Raquette Point. The Mohawks prepared for "an Attica-style attack" (George-Kanentiio 2006, p. 37).[5] Behind the barricades, people stayed in tents, slept on living room floors, and stood their ground. The traditionalists insisted they comprised a sovereign nation, governed by their own laws of the Mohawk Nation Council of Chiefs, which opposed the state police and the Mohawk police. The Mohawk police reported to the elected St. Regis Tribal Council, which traditionalists claimed had no jurisdiction on Akwesasne land because the council was an imposed form of government that had never been accepted by tribal members. They demanded that the police force disband and the tribal council be replaced.[6] The latter responded to the crisis by stating, "The majority of Indians on this reservation do not support this small group of 'traditional' people who persist in ignoring the laws of New York State and the United States of America" (Thompson 1979a).

Over the next two years, the standoff continued, the encampment grew, and no one would budge on either side. Snipers fired shots into the camp, helicopters hovered, guns were waved, and fists were thrown. People shot at cars, set fire to a building, made death threats, and set off pipe bombs, and police beat up a traditional Mohawk. Sharpshooters were stationed around the encampment and a state police checkpoint was set up near the barricaded road (Brothers and Emery 1980; Thompson 1980). With the road blocked, the only access to the camp was by boat along the St. Lawrence River. A local newspaper photographed Mohawk men bearing rifles while a young boy and his dog looked on from nearby. An alumna of the AFS recalls the frightening conditions she endured: "They [the traditional Mohawks] took all of us across the water because they said they were coming in to shoot us. It was horrifying. I wanted to go home but I couldn't. It was like a nightmare" (Interviewee A9: July 16, 2005).

The division at Akwesasne was not a simple split between traditional Mohawks and those who were on the side of the elected St. Regis Tribal Council (Garte 1981). It was complex and crossed family, political, and religious lines. One Longhouse member who took the side of the tribal council described his experience: "I have relatives who haven't talked to me in two or three months since this incident started. It's splitting people and families" (Thompson 1979b). The sentiments toward authorities were mistrust and disdain: "Any kind of uniform represents evil or bad. They're not there to help you" (Interviewee P12: July 16, 2005). And the Akwesasne police chief, whose brother sided with the traditionalists, could not get to his home behind the barricades.

The Birth of the Akwesasne Freedom School

> You got people with guns coming in. [We saw] it, when we were young. You remember these things. There were moats [ditches] for the men to run [in] and not get shot at. We really didn't think about them coming to shoot us because we were so young. That was right here at the Freedom School. We used to play in the bunkers and stuff.—*Interviewee A9: July 16, 2005*

FIGURE 6. Traditional Mohawks negotiate with New York State Police. Photo courtesy of *Watertown (N.Y.) Times.*

In the first year of the encampment problems ensued when Mohawk students in the encampment were harassed while they attended public school and when buses could not run because of the roadblocks. Parents did not want to send their children back out into the public schools where they were forced to dress up like George Washington and taught that Columbus was a hero. One parent explained, "I was never going to send my child to public school. I would home school or something else" (Interviewee P8: October 8, 2004). The traditionalists felt they were losing the language and culture, and they were tired of the laws and regulations imposed on them.

Most of the public schools on and near Akwesasne at that time did not teach Mohawk culture, with the exception of the Salmon River High School, located away from Akwesasne, in New York State. Salmon River had a Title VII bilingual program in fourth and fifth grades, where Mohawk culture (including language) was taught in an effort to increase awareness of Haudenosaunee history and identity (Emery 1979).[7] Approximately one thousand Mohawk students attended the school, which received appropriations for Indian education and large per-student grants. Parents were no doubt distrustful about their children's education after audits of the school in 1972 found inadequate and incomplete financial records and misuse of funds (Akwesasne Notes 1972).

Mohawk parents and others behind the barricade were determined to take education into their own hands, and started the Akwesasne Freedom School. The parents stood their ground despite threats from the New York State school system: "The state sent letters threatening . . . that if we didn't send our kids back to school we could be jailed" (Interviewee P12: July 16, 2005). New York State considered the AFS students to be truant and criticized the school for not being certified or accredited. It seems the local public school district was mostly concerned with losing funding because of its contract with New York State to provide education to Mohawk students (Kennedy 1981). The Mohawk Nation Council of Chiefs asserted its status as a sovereign nation with its own traditional form of government and oversight, including support of the AFS. New York State eventually backed down, deferring the education of Mohawk children to the Akwesasne Mohawk Nation.

While state police sharpshooters stood nearby and gunfire was occasionally exchanged between opposing groups, young Mohawk children were learning to speak their people's language. They walked in the woods looking for medicine and learned the Haudenosaunee Creation Story and Haudenosaunee history. Parents and community members, as well as Native and non-Native volunteers from outside the community taught the young people behind the barricades. Classrooms were put together in barns, living rooms, and trailers until a small building could be constructed. Some classes were held above a garage on Loran Thompson's property. At any given time throughout the two-year standoff, approximately twenty to twenty-five students attended, from pre-kindergarten through high school. Desks, chairs, and school supplies were donated, the local churches supplied food, and volunteers came from as far away as France and Germany to support the school and the Mohawk people's fight for sovereignty. The encampment was home to hundreds of people over two years, people living communally, sharing space, cooking and eating together, having a ceremony each morning, and protecting one another. Most importantly, they were united by a determination to keep Mohawk culture alive. An alumna reminisced about the kinship she felt: "We were a big family. We knew everybody. Even now when we see them, it can still feel like a bond in a sense because of all the animosity that went on and it just brought us closer. Although it was a school, it was like a family" (Interviewee A9: July 16, 2005).

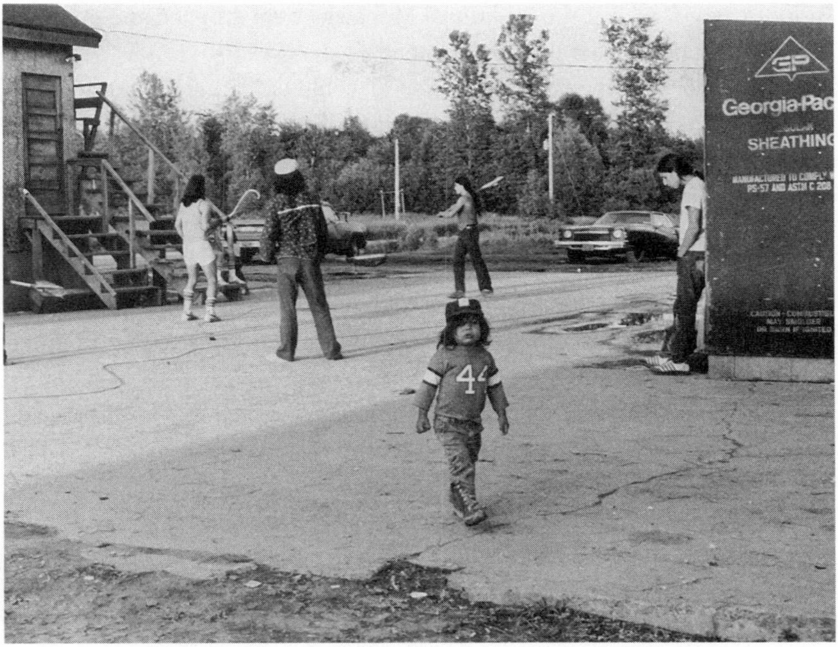

FIGURE 7. AFS children at play, around 1979–80. Tsiorasa Barreiro in foreground. Photo courtesy of Mary Rojas.

In the midst of a major crisis, Akwesasne families bonded around a common purpose. The sense of kinship this mother speaks of has contributed to the longevity and success of the school.

Ethnic Reorganization

> Animosity went on for ten years. People were just starting to forgive one another. It had split the community wide open. Families were pitted against each other. The political issues inside Akwesasne were so volatile. People are so passionate about how they believe, some born . . . of ignorance, of not knowing any better. Over time, people have changed and have become more aware of who they are and how important culture and language is.
> —*Interviewee P8: October 8, 2004*

In 1981 charges against the traditional Mohawks were dropped and everyone started going home from the encampment.

The climate was ripe during that time for community members to stand up for their rights to self-government and self-education. The conflict was an explosion of turmoil after years of oppression and gave people the motivation and energy needed to create a school that stood for the very things they were fighting for. Still, the conflict inflicted deep emotional wounds that are painful even today. A former student from the early days of the school still holds on to those wounds: "At an early age we were told that the police were bad regardless if they were good. Even to this day I tell my kids: 'don't talk to them'" (Interviewee A9: July 16, 2005).

For two years Akwesasne residents experienced conflict that tore at the fabric of the community and at the core of Mohawk identity. The "socio-political divisions in Akwesasne had become well organized, permanent, schismatic political entities in the community" (Lemelin 1997, p. 111). After generations of oppression and imperialistic policies, the conflict was the driving force behind assertions of empowerment and nationhood and pushed a community toward positive change.

Conflict and debate can create division in a community, resulting in destructive consequences. However, conflict can also have positive consequences, leading to progress and creativity. The "civil war" at Akwesasne forced Mohawks to reevaluate their beliefs, values, and identity. It led them to unify for a cause and take action, including creation of a space whereby Mohawk youth could reclaim cultural identity. The AFS was started out of necessity but quickly became a symbol of Mohawk sovereignty and self-determination. The school was also born of a form of "ethnic reorganization" of the Akwesasne community. "Ethnic" refers to minority groups who do not possess sovereign nation-to-nation relations with a federal government, but for this discussion it should be noted that the terms "ethnic" and "minority" are used in reference to marginalized groups living within nation-states and subjected to oppressive practices by them. Ethnic reorganization occurs when the group "undergoes a reorganization of its social structure, redefinition of ethnic group boundaries, or some other change in response to pressures or demands imposed by the dominant culture" (Nagel and Snipp 1993, p. 204). This restructuring (ethnic change) is a strategy whereby such groups attempt to cope with "forces of change" (p. 205).

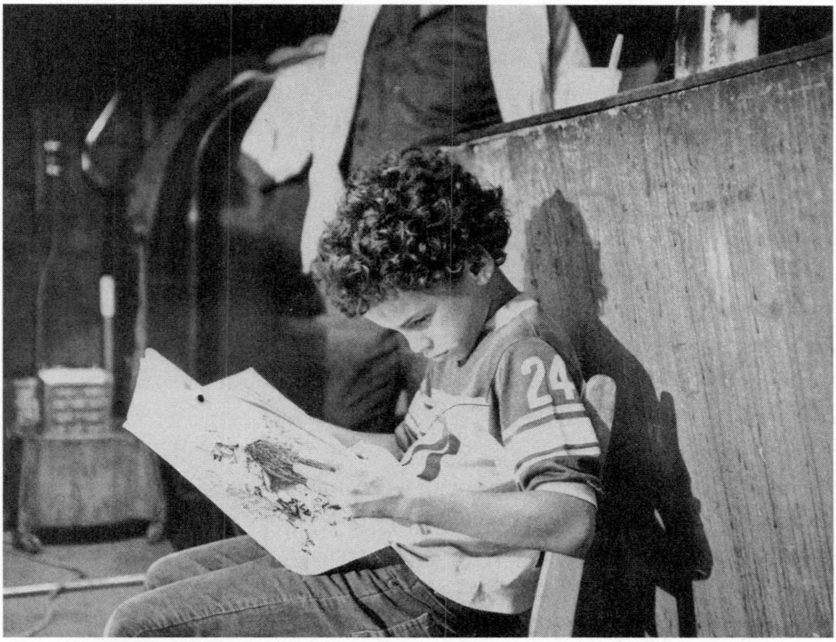

FIGURE 8. Student Joel LaFrance, around 1979–80. Photo courtesy of Mary Rojas.

To ensure cultural survival, reorganization at Akwesasne entailed a restructuring of community leadership and education. When the standoff at Raquette Point ended, political leaders of Akwesasne became "active players in the healing process of the community" (Lemelin 1997, p. 115). They agreed to a compromise in which "each side participates in the existing elected system, far different from the past when the traditionals boycotted the electoral process" (Hauptman 1986, p. 233). As a result of the conflict, the secret land claims agreement was rejected and a united land claims negotiation team was formed. In 1982 the tribal police force was dismantled (George-Kanentiio 2006). Most striking was the continuation of the Akwesasne Freedom School, an institution that stood for the beliefs and values for which the Mohawk people were fighting. The best examples of cultural revitalization are found in educational institutions and programs such as the AFS, where traditional culture, including language, is incorporated into the curriculum.

The AFS continued to face numerous challenges as its founders developed infrastructure, decided what the curricula should be, and secured adequate funding. Another challenge was added in 1980 after the AFS was moved from Thompson's land to a newly constructed school building on nearby Raquette Point. That challenge was extreme enviornmental pollution.

Contaminant Cove

> The [medicine] plants around here are polluted. We have to go somewhere else. I know they're polluted because they're always brown, with odd shapes and colors. They're polluted from the "pollution plant," Alcoa. They just let off pollution in the ground. We have to go far away to get to medicine plants now.—*Interviewee S1: October 3, 2004*

Shortly after the AFS moved into its new building, toxic levels of PCBs were found in a cove on the St. Lawrence River at Raquette Point, right next door to the school. The former General Motors (GM) plant and Alcoa Inc. (formerly Reynolds Metal Company) operate large industrial plants adjacent to Akwesasne, and the area had become known as Contaminant Cove. Toxic substances including PCBs, dioxin, and heavy metals found their way into the air, water, and land in and around Akwesasne via wastewater, spills, and illegal dumping. Akwesasne residents were told to limit their consumption of local fish and wildlife (Akwesasne Task Force on the Environment 2001). A statement by the Akwesasne Task Force on the Environment attests to the devastating effects on the community:

> By the early 1970s, cattle began showing signs of fluorosis, brittle teeth and bones, birth defects, low milk production and shortened life spans. By the mid-1980s, the Mohawk community had issued a fishing advisory limiting fish consumption in the community and warning women of childbearing age, infants, and children under the age of fifteen eat no fish from the St. Lawrence Rive due to the PCB contamination of the fishery.
>
> By the late 1980s, the amount of PCBs found in fish and wildlife at Akwesasne was astounding. Snapping turtles (the Haudenosaunee consider the turtle to be the foundation of the earth), frogs, shrews, and fish were all found to be contaminated, some with levels that would make them hazardous waste. Backyard gardens were abandoned as residents

> in the Raquette Point area (the closest to the contamination) feared the airborne contamination of their vegetables. (Akwesasne Task Force on the Environment n.d.(a))

Virtually all of the land, water, and air in the surrounding areas were affected. Enrollment at the AFS declined after toxic chemicals were discovered to be leaking into the school's water supply (Barth 1989). Relying on bottled water, the school continued.

After the Akwesasne community demanded action on the part of the polluters to address the concerns, the companies were eventually fined, the area was designated Superfund site in 1983, and cleanup began in 1990. Finally, in 2013 a $20.3 million settlement was reached with Alcoa and GM for restoration efforts, and $8.4 million was allotted to the Saint Regis Mohawk Tribe to support traditional Mohawk practices. The Akwesasne Cultural Restoration Commission was established and implemented a cultural apprenticeship program promoting language and cultural teachings, including gardening, fishing, hunting, canning, and practice with traditional medicine (Saint Regis Mohawk Tribe Environment Division, www.srmtenv.org/); $128,000 was allocated to the AFS over a five-year period to support a language nest program.

A New Era of the Akwesasne Freedom School

> The Eagle is the Creator's messenger. It soars high above the clouds, it can see the sky world and ours. What we call the Promise Land. Compared to the sky world it's not so much of a promise. Filled with pollution, we can't even swim in the rivers anymore. Two centuries ago we had all the freedom in the world. Today, we have the Akwesasne Freedom School, where we learn our language, Mohawk. — *Perkins 1994*

Despite the environmental pollution described above, the AFS has remained in its present location since 1980, when parents and other volunteers cleared the land and constructed the new building. The school had sixty-three students in its first year. By 1981 the number increased to eighty-one students, with about half coming from the Canadian side of the territory (Emery 1981; T. Foster 1981). The building was renovated in 1996 after flooding, and in 1998 a new building was constructed and now holds administrative offices and classrooms (Akwesasne Freedom School 1999). The classroom building is constructed to reflect the traditional longhouse, with doors at the east and west ends.

To escape the pollution, parents planned to build a solar-powered school building on New York State Route 37 adjacent to Akwesasne territory. In 1977 a man named Jimmy Little Turtle from Harrisburg, Pennsylvania, had established the Viola White Water Foundation to raise money for Indian education. Support from this foundation helped get the new AFS building started (Barth 1989). In the late 1980s AFS parents raised the capital to purchase 152 acres of land and began building an eight-thousand-square-foot passive solar building. A total of $100,000 was donated to build the foundation and put up the walls.

There have been periodic efforts to resume development of this site over the years, including building greenhouses and community gardens. The Cultural Apprenticeship Program that was formed out of the settlement agreement with Alcoa and GM contributed to reviving the site by installing flooring and a wood stove. The site is now a partnership between three community programs promoting language and culture: the AFS, the Cultural Apprenticeship Program, and Ohero:kon (Under the Husk), a rites-of-passage initiative (Elvera Sargent, personal communication, January 22, 2015).

Despite these developments, the school continues to struggle maintaining the current site and operates on limited funds. The main building houses prekindergarten through sixth-grade classrooms with cramped conditions. There is a small kitchen, the building is not energy-efficient and thus is cold in the winter, and the bathrooms are regularly out of service. However, parents and other community members and volunteers built the AFS with their own hands. They became carpenters, teachers, janitors, cooks, nurses, and bus drivers. The parents continue to run the school today and have exclusive decision-making authority. Having complete control over the school was and continues to be of paramount importance.

FIGURE 9. AFS main classroom building. Photo by L. White, 2005.

Figure 10. Main classroom building. Photo by L. White, 2005.

TIMELINE OF THE AKWESASNE FREEDOM SCHOOL

1979	School began for pre-K through twelfth grade during encampment on Loran Thompson's property.
1980	School, now pre-K through sixth grade, moved to current Raquette Point site.
1984–85	Classes reduced to pre-K through fourth grade. Mohawk language immersion initiated.
1990	Construction began at Route 37 site
1991–92	AFS enters tuition agreement with the Akwesasne Mohawk Board of Education for students enrolled on the Canadian side of the reservation.
1992	Mohawk language immersion extends through fifth grade. Sixth and seventh grades are added, with classes taught in English.
1993	Mohawk language immersion extends through sixth grade. Seventh- and eighth-grade classes are taught in English.
1996	Building renovated.
1998	Year-round school calendar implemented, with six weeks on and two weeks off.
2003	Adult Fluency/Literacy Project begins as a three-year funded program.
2003–4	Schedule changes to six weeks on, one week off, with two weeks off midyear and four weeks off during July and August.
2011	Mohawk language immersion extends through seventh grade. Eighth-grade classes are taught in English.
2014	Mohawk language immersion extends through ninth grade.
2014	Language Nest program begins.

(Compiled from Montour 1992; Akwesasne Freedom School 1999, 2002–2004)

Fund-Raising Activities

> When you operate on a shoestring budget, you learn to adapt.
> We used to pull straws to see who's getting paid this week.
> —*Interviewee V2: September 4, 2004*

Asserting their sovereign right to self-education and adhering to the traditions of the Mohawk Nation Council of Chiefs as a sovereign entity, the AFS has never requested or received direct funding from state, provincial, or federal governments. Parents agreed from the inception of the school that to do so would undermine their right to decide the type of education their children would receive. Although obtaining adequate funding has been an issue over the years, parents hold tenaciously to their decision to avoid direct government funding and its attendant regulations and bureaucracy. The school operates thanks to various fund-raising activities, grants, donations, and tuition. In the beginning, the school relied primarily on donations and volunteers and either charged minimal tuition or none at all (Ciborski 1990). Parents paid twenty-five dollar per week for tuition after moving into the new building in 1980 (Interviewee P12: July 16, 2005). Some years no tuition was charged. During the 1986–87 school year, the parental governing committee decided to begin charging parents one thousand dollars per year for tuition. The cost proved prohibitive and was reduced to five hundred dollars in 1991. In 2003 this was increased to six hundred dollars a year or 120 hours of volunteer time (Ciborski 1990; Akwesasne Freedom School 2002–2004).

Teachers at first volunteered their time and expertise and then began receiving a modest salary: "We weren't paid right away, but after a while we got twenty-five dollars a week for gas, so we were pretty poor" (Interviewee T4: July 18, 2005). In 1985 all staff, including teachers, aides, bus drivers, and administrative staff, regardless of experience or length of employment, were paid the same amount: five thousand dollars annually (Ciborski 1990). The school was attempting to implement a unified and noncompetitive environment, which did not always seem fair, especially to some who had worked at the school for a number of years. Continually challenged to meet payroll, some weeks teachers were not paid at all and had to wait for incoming funds to receive a check. In 1991 the school had to close for a week because it had run out of money (Warloski 1991).

The school used to host bingo games but ended that activity in 1989. According to Ciborski: "In the 1985–1986 school year, 75% of the budget was met through the approximately $50,000 [garnered] in bingos." Donations made up 20 percent of the budget while monthly fund-raising dinners at the school raised 5 percent (Ciborski 1990, p. 148). The school's dependency on gambling, however, conflicted with the anti-gambling morals of Longhouse traditionalists, thus bingo was abandoned.

Since that time, an innovative way to raise desperately needed funds has replaced bingo. What started in the 1980s as a silent auction of donated goods,

FIGURE 11. Quilt by Marie Girard, "Sun Sisters," 2008.

such as artwork and boxes of motor oil, has evolved into an annual quilt auction and dinner. At first the quilts were donated by nearby Amish communities and Native nations from western states, but soon AFS parents began making their own. The quilts eventually became more sophisticated and a creative way for parents to pay for their children's tuition. Parents became expert quilters and began incorporating Haudenosaunee designs into their work. They are busy all year preparing their next contribution to the event held every summer now at the school. The elaborate quilts are a greatly anticipated highlight of the two-day event and are auctioned off for amounts ranging from two hundred dollars to five thousand dollars. In 2004 the school raised thirty-eight thousand dollars from a single event with a chicken dinner, silent auction, and quilt auction. The same event raised twenty-eight thousand dollars the following year.

Other such events include a fund-raiser hosted by the local radio station CKON, walk-a-thons, raffles, and the sale of calendars and T-shirts. A payroll contribution plan allows employees of local tribal governments to donate to the school. This source provided six thousand dollars one year. Volunteers and summer student employees have helped repair buildings, paint, fix plumbing, and provide tutoring for AFS students.

FIGURE 12. Quilt by Shelley Greener, "To Everything There Is a Season," 2003.

A 1991–92 tuition agreement with the Canadian Akwesasne Mohawk Board of Education (AMBE) began providing funding for AFS students living on the Canadian side of the community. Mohawk educator Barry Montour writes, "Since the board did not offer a comparable Mohawk language immersion program at the time they decided to provide funding to the Ahkwesahsne Freedom School in order to allow parents and students a great choice of programmes and services. Students are added to the nominal roll and receive funding from the Department of Indian Affairs" (Montour 2000).[8] The agreement, however, allows the school to remain autonomous, with no direct regulation by the Canadian federal or provincial governments. When I asked AFS office manager Elvera Sargent if AMBE had any oversight, she replied: "No, we have an agreement to meet a couple of times a year, we share resources, but they leave us alone" (Sargent, personal communication, September 4, 2004).

In 1994 the Friends of the Akwesasne Freedom School was formed by parents of AFS students as a nonprofit volunteer organization to pursue funding on behalf of the school. Friends of the AFS directors also serve on the steering committee of the school. The Friends of the AFS has garnered funding from the Administration for Native Americans, Lannan Foundation and the Nihewan

Foundation. The Akwesasne Area Management Board has also provided funding for building construction and has contributed computers and printers. The Mohawk Nation Council of Chiefs has also provided funds to the school. In 2013 the SRMT donated $100,000 to the school. Sub-chief and AFS alum Eric Thompson said, "Since 1979 the quality and quantity of people coming out of the school speaks volumes for the foundation of our community" (www.srmt-nsn.gov/). While these contributions are certainly helpful, the school's annual budget in 2015 was approximately $700,000 in salaries, overhead, renovations, and the like (Elvera Sargent, personal communication, January 22, 2015).

However, financial independence from the US and Canadian governments allows the school flexibility in organizational structure, policies, curricula, and teacher training. Through hard work and perseverance, parents and community have built a sustainable educational program. As one volunteer says, "The Akwesasne Freedom School shows Native people that we can do for ourselves, we can take care of ourselves. This was started by our people, run by our people. We don't have to rely on others; we can make things happen ourselves. We've existed for twenty-five years. That says something about our fortitude, our perseverance" (Interviewee V4: August 23, 2004). The school may not always have sufficient funds to pay teachers adequately, acquire teaching materials, or offer similar programs to those of public schools, but the longevity of the school is attributed to its independence. A parent says, "They don't have to be afraid that their programs are going to get cut. If there was no money, it would still be there. People want to see the language survive. Commitment to the language, the parents, community members, students, the people who work there, it has a spirit. I've seen other programs that don't have that—they're too administrative. It can be free. The name is perfect" (Interviewee P3: July 12, 2005).

Other schools like the Rough Rock Demonstration School in Arizona are funded largely by the federal bureaucracy—specifically the BIA (McCarty 2002)—and differ significantly from the AFS, where, despite financial challenges, parents control the curriculum, teacher selection, and overall school operations. The AFS does not have the same "power relations" with authorities who regulate funding.

Regardless of the level of tribal control, however, there is no guarantee of the success of Native educational programs (Senese 1986). Tribal control brings on the burdens of management, funding, training, and maintaining adequate facilities. Members of many Native communities may feel that they do not have adequate infrastructure or resources to manage such a task. The AFS has continually struggled. But one parent explains: "In comparison to public schools, the AFS may seem lacking to some parents who choose not to send their children there, but to parents who have chosen the AFS, the benefits are well worth it" (Sue Ellen Herne, personal communication, October 25, 2009).

Committed and Dedicated Parents

> Parental involvement in the school is not superficial; it is deliberately an in-depth process of total commitment of the parents to the students and for the community.—*LaFrance 1982, p. 6*

As this book demonstrates, students can excel academically when home, school, and community are more closely connected. According to renowned bilingual educator and researcher Jim Cummins (1992), "Students can become empowered only when education becomes a true community enterprise involving an equal partnership between educators in the school and educators in the home" (p. 7). Children demonstrate a positive attitude toward education when their parents have some investment in it, although not all parents may have the time or desire to be as involved as AFS parents.

Parents provide the glue that has held the Akwesasne Freedom School together. Since its beginning, students' parents have taken on every possible responsibility involved with the AFS and have been the school's driving force. They offer whatever skills they possess, acting as teachers and tutors, janitors and maintenance workers, bus drivers and car-poolers, painters and plumbers, carpenters and cooks, secretaries, grant writers, and curriculum developers. Parents continue to serve on hiring committees and make all decisions regarding new teachers. Weekly cleaning committees are responsible for the school buildings and grounds.

Parents are also allowed and even encouraged to attend classes with their children to learn and improve their Mohawk language skills. Because it is the foundation of the AFS, they are also responsible for learning the Ohenton Kariwahtekwen and may be found reciting it with the students. Parental involvement reinforces the unity of the home and school and facilitates socialization.

Parents spend more time with their children, are aware of what their children are learning, have opportunities to reinforce language retention, and have input into all aspects of the school's functioning.

As already suggested, fund-raising is one of the biggest responsibilities of AFS parents, who help organize bottle and can collection drives, fishing derbies, raffles, and pie sales. In 1995 one parent-teacher led a fund-raising project in which children wrote and illustrated storybooks and sold them to make money for school supplies, using a computer to compile tales of Mohawk traditions, animals, and ceremonies. The children had high hopes for raising enough funds to build a new school with a gym (Foster 1995).

Adequate money for a new school never became a reality, and in 2007 financial struggles caused some teachers to be let go because of budget cuts; the school found itself without an office manager. A parent took over the responsibilities for a time but soon resigned. The position was then split among a few parents, and continues to be a position of high turnover with the exception of Elvera Sargent, former office manager, who still volunteers her time. Although parents ultimately control the school, the office manager is responsible for fund-raising and overseeing daily operations. An advertisement for the position read: "The job of the office manager is to work with the parents, not for them; to work with the teachers, not above them" (*Indian Time*, Akwesasne, November 12, 1993, Employment section, p. 8).

Some parents have a positive attitude about the lack of funding: "It helped to keep the school united. We were required to do so much more because of the lack of funding. You couldn't hire a janitor. You had to do it" (Interviewee P9: July 15, 2005). The school had a bus for a short period of time, but the expense became prohibitive. Looking at it in a positive light, a parent explains: "If we had school buses we wouldn't be able to go to school in the morning and see our kids off and interact with the people who are with our kids all day" (Interviewee AP3: July 14, 2005). Although these responsibilities are overwhelming at times, without the commitment and dedication of the parents the school would cease to exist.

When parents and community members are involved in the creation of a school, curricula, and instruction, they have an investment in the success of the school. Tribally controlled schools can create such opportunities for parental and community involvement (Swisher and Tippeconnic 1999). For example,

FIGURE 13. AFS logo used in the 1980s. Drawing courtesy of John Kahionhes Fadden.

among the Navajo nation, the Rough Rock Board of Education reported that the involvement of parents and community in the school led to a "feeling of pride in the people—pride in what they are doing for their community, pride in what they are doing for their school, and pride in what they are doing for their children" (Szasz 1999, p. 173). Cummins (1995) emphasizes the impact that parents and communities can have on student success through their active engagement with the school: "Students from dominated communities will be empowered in the school context to the extent that the communities themselves are empowered through their interactions with the school" (p. 3). Cummins further believes that children's school failure "can be attributed to the combined effects of parental illiteracy and lack of interest in their children's education" (p. 108). Through their continued commitment and active involvement, parents of AFS students have positively contributed to their children's education and the overall success of the school. This dedication has forged a unique educational institution based on the sovereign right to self-education. Prior to its founding, Akwesasne formal education was limited to public schools that disregarded Mohawk culture.

Schooling at Akwesasne

> The right to determine educational policy and to actively participate in the teaching of classes is essential if a Nation of Native people are to produce their own "citizens" who benefit themselves and the community. Their form of [colonial] education was not benefitting our community because we lost our young people. We are preparing our students to be good citizens of the Mohawk Nation just as the public school prepares their children to be good U.S. citizens. We have the right to do that. . . . The whole concept of Nationhood is strong in the school. If we're going to be a strong Nation we have to keep our young people and build educational, political, and economic sovereignty. That's our goal.—*LaFrance 1982*

Tom Porter (Sakowenionkwas), former traditional chief of the Mohawk Nation Council of Chiefs, one of the founders of the Akwesasne Freedom School, and former parent of AFS students, has a lot say about Western education, having attended the St. Regis Mohawk School (SRMS), a public school located in the community in Hogansburg.[9] He talks about his encounters with nuns who wore "those just-face-sticking-out clothes" (Porter 2008, p. 28) and smacked his hands with a ruler for talking Mohawk.[10] Porter cautions: "They call it St. Regis Mohawk Indian School, but there was nothing Mohawk about that school" (p. 120). He recalls the time he saw his grandfather's photo in his textbook while he was in elementary school. Excited at the possibility that his teacher would finally pay Mohawk people some respect, he waited for months to get to the chapter with his grandfather in it: "I got cold chills on myself, and I felt wonderful that now Grandpa's story was gonna be told" (p. 131). But the teacher had other plans. She said that they would skip over the chapter on Indian people because there were "much more important things to cover." Porter remembers her saying, "The sooner you Mohawk Indians realize that that Indian stuff is like water over the dam, and you must get yourself educated, the less you will be on the welfare rolls, and the less problems you will have with alcoholism amongst you" (p. 132).

Porter is just as determined today as he must have been then and once marched into the SRMS principal's office and made a declaration:

> Mr. Stanley, let's start at the beginning. In the kindergarten, they give us the stick when we couldn't speak your language. You know what that means? The Mohawk is no good, and English is. You know what it means when they play Yankee Doodle Went to Town? It means water drum, Rabbit Dance, Fish Dance is no good. Yankee Doodle Went to Town is the best. All through these years, you told me I was no good. Your teachers, your school, everybody told me I was no good. Every day since I was in kindergarten, you made me feel like I was a *nothing*, a nobody. And you wanted me to be ashamed of my own people. And I had enough, Mr. Stanley. I had enough. That's why you're not gonna do that to my kids. (p. 135)

Porter left the SRMS and never went on to high school. In return, he says, he received "liberation." He also kept his promise and as a cofounder of the AFS sent his kids to a place where they could speak their own language, sing their own songs, and be proud to be Mohawk.

Fortunately, since the time Porter was a student, parents of Akwesasne children have had choices of where to send their children to school, regardless of where they live in the community. As of 2012, four other schools besides the AFS, all public schools, serve children from pre-kindergarten through eighth grade. One is located on the US side of the international border and the other three lie on the Canadian side. The St. Regis Mohawk School has implemented Mohawk language and cultural instruction, but all of Akwesasne's public schools are driven by curricula mandated by either New York State or the Canadian provinces of Quebec and Ontario. Since there are no secondary schools in Akwesasne, students attend nearby high schools such as the one operated by the Upper Canada District School Board in Cornwall, Ontario; the public high school in Massena, New York; and the Salmon River High School in Fort Covington, New York.

Public education in New York is funded by the state and by the federal Office of Indian Education. New York assumed responsibility for educating Indians in the state in 1846, when it enacted a law providing for school buildings and annual education appropriations (Hauptman 1999). However, as AFS cofounder Ron LaFrance states: "The Iroquois believed then and now that New

York State has no jurisdiction over Indian education" (R. LaFrance 1982). Similar to many Native communities, there was little input from the Mohawk community until 1968, when after much frustration and a boycott of the school, the Salmon River Central School District (SRCSD) allowed Mohawk members on its school board (R. LaFrance 1995).

The St. Regis Mohawk Tribe has a contract with the SRCSD and the New York State Education Department. The latter funds the school 100 percent (Barry Montour, personal communication, January 7, 2009). The SRCSD also operates a K–12 school (locally known as "Salmon"), where many Akwesasne residents, including AFS alumni, attend high school. The population of students at Salmon River High School is approximately 67 percent Mohawk, but 90 percent of the teachers are non-Native (Agbo 2001; Barry Montour, personal communication, January 7, 2009). The SRMS is an elementary school (pre-kindergarten through sixth grade), where all of the approximately five hundred students are Mohawk but most teachers are non-Native (Agbo 2001; Montour, personal communication, January 7, 2009). At the SRMS, there is a Mohawk language and cultural curricular component. For forty minutes, twice a week, students draw pictographs and read Haudenosaunee legends, rarely going "beyond superficial exploration of the heritage culture" (Bates 2001, p. 100). Bates (2001) notes that this curriculum "exists nearly in an instructional vacuum and is in addition to, rather than incorporated into the overall school curriculum" (p. 86).

Some parents find the St. Regis Mohawk School to be desirable because of the programs offered. It has subsidized breakfasts and lunches, libraries, computer labs, gyms, and music programs, and its staff includes aides, school nurses, psychologists, and art and speech therapists (Montour 2000). However, one parent had very strong negative feelings about the school:

> I walked into that hallway to get my son out of class, and they had just started the day, and you could hear the whole multiple singsong of voices of young children . . . echoing and reverberating through the hallway. . . . Walking down the hallway, I could hear it all in unison: "I Pledge Allegiance to the Flag of the United States of America." And when I heard that, I almost cried. . . . I thought, what are we doing to our kids? It's one thing if [our children] were to grow to be adults and choose to pledge allegiance to the flag of the United States and they made that choice as

> grown adults. I could respect that, with them fully knowing what that meant. But fully knowing who they were first, that's what was important. My god, I knew I had to save them. I had to save my kids. So that next semester I signed them to go to the AFS. (Interviewee P11: July 20, 2005)

For this parent, the Pledge of Allegiance represented a history of colonial Western education that dismissed Native experiences and perspectives. The choice to send her children to the AFS was made on the basis that they would learn what it meant to be Mohawk.

Aboriginal Affairs and Northern Development Canada (AANDC), under the Indian Act of 1951, administers education for students from Akwesasne who attend Canadian schools. Integration of Native students into federal Indian "day schools" became the policy as residential schools began to be phased out. Unsurprisingly, Indian parents and leaders were not included in any discussions or planning. This integration was a "process of assimilation where Indians were absorbed into the non-Indian society" (Kirkness 1999, p. 5). In 1971 the Manitoba Indian Brotherhood published a report highlighting conditions of Indian education, including high dropout rates, poorly trained teachers, and culturally and historically inaccurate curricula regarding Indians (Indian Tribes of Manitoba 1971). The National Indian Brotherhood (now the Assembly of First Nations) followed with a report calling for "Indian control of Indian education" (National Indian Brotherhood 1972).

In Canada, Indian control over education has had its share of difficulties. Cree scholar and activist Verna Kirkness writes: "For many of our communities that have taken over their own schools and other educational institutions, much time has been lost either emulating the federal or public school systems or merely band-aiding, adapting, supplementing when they should have been creating a unique and meaningful education. At the base of this attitude is the difficulty to overcome colonial domination" (1999, p. 19).

Native control of schooling at Akwesasne had its start in 1957 when parents formed education committees for the districts on the Canadian side of the territory, Barry Montour writes. This was the beginning of "local control of education processes and programmes for the people of Ahkwesahsne" (Montour 2000, p. 45). It was not until 1984, however, that Akwesasne residents began to exert increased control over public education. That year a newly elected Mohawk council began negotiating with AANDC and set up the Akwesasne Mohawk Board of Education (AMBE). A year later the first director of the board was hired. Financial concerns and lingering micro-management by AANDC did not make the transition to local control easy. Montour says that "management of the newly created School Board aroused suspicions from the community, which was not yet used to the idea of a School Board separate from the Council" (2000, p. 76). The board officially took control in 1987, when the Mohawk Council of Akwesasne passed a resolution and signed an agreement with AANDC "to assume control over the local elementary school system" (Montour 2000, p. 85).

The three schools at Akwesasne on the Canadian side of the territory are administered by the AMBE, ultimately regulated by the Mohawk Council of Akwesasne (MCA). The Tsi Snaihne School comprises preschool for ages four and five ("K4" and "K5"), as well as second and third grades. Also located within the borders of Quebec, the school in Kanatakon (St. Regis Village) includes Head Start through sixth grade. Kawennokowanenne (Ahkwesahsne Mohawk School), located on Cornwall Island within the borders of Ontario, includes Head Start, K4, K5, and grades four through six.

Akwesasne Mohawk Board of Education schools all emphasize Mohawk culture in the curriculum, and the French language is nowhere to be found, unlike in most Canadian schools. AMBE has been operating Mohawk language immersion classrooms since 1984 in all district schools. In 2012 AMBE started the Skhawatsi:ra (One Family, One Nation) Mohawk language immersion school in Kanatakon that encompasses Head Start and pre-K through fourth grade. Fifth and sixth grades are English transition (Personal communication, Margaret Cook-Peters, January 17, 2015).

A New Paradigm

Although parents at Akwesasne now have choices for their children's education, many challenges remain. Parents who wish their children to learn the Mohawk language must make sacrifices if they chose the AFS. For some parents, the school's positive attributes outweigh its having no cafeteria, gymnasium, and extracurricular sports, while others choose schools where they have such options. If parents choose an AMBE-operated school, the immersion methods may not be adequate to gain real proficiency in the Mohawk language. Culturally appropriate curricula have improved in the community's schools, but state and provincial regulations along with standardized testing do not reflect Mohawk culture and history.

The move from mainstream public schooling to an independent, Native-controlled situation at the Akwesasne Freedom School did not happen overnight, nor was it an easy and smooth transition. With the AFS as a socializing institution, its founders' goal at first was "to produce Mohawk citizens to participate as Mohawks in a world community" (R. LaFrance 1982, p. 5) through a method whereby parents and community members would be self-empowered and self-reliant. The late Ron LaFrance, cofounder and former director of the school, recalled that although parents agreed on the structure and approach of the school and its decolonizing process of returning to traditional ways of educating, they could not always internalize this and go travel the same route as their children. He attributed this to the fact that most parents had been educated in public schools and knew no other way. According to LaFrance: "If the Native American is to survive as a distinct people, then critical thought must be paid to the construction of a new and exciting paradigm that will last another five centuries. With this paradigm, we must take the next intellectual step, consciously, and with the thought that our generations will evolve by our own planning and devices" (1982, p. 7).

Indeed, the AFS has served as an exciting new paradigm in education for the Akwesasne community (Montour 1992). The Akwesasne Freedom School was founded in response to a long history of colonizing forces imposing Western ideals of education and schooling upon the community. It grew out of a struggle for self-determination and efforts to keep the powers that be from suppressing and distorting "local Indigenous authority" (McCarty 2002, p. 176). Indigenous peoples have long struggled for their sovereign rights and should remember that the fight for control over education, as articulated in critical pedagogy, "must be engaged alongside other revolutionary struggles, specifically those that seek to end economic exploitation, political domination, and cultural dependency" (Grande 2004, p. 20).

The conflict of 1979 still lives on in memory of many at Akwesasne, while the AFS serves as a healing ground, bringing together community members in a common purpose. Against long odds, the AFS endures because of its committed parents, community support, and a devotion to upholding Indigenous sovereignty and self-determination.

THREE

The Akwesasne Freedom School

An Indigenous Model of Holistic Education

It takes the entire cosmology of a people to raise a child.

—*R. LaFrance 1995, p. 20*

When the Peacemaker came to the Onondaga Nation carrying his message of peace and unity, he planted the Tree of Peace and called it Tsioneratasekowa, the Great White Pine. He instructed the Five Nations to lay down their weapons of war and accept his message of Kaianerekowa (the Great Law of Peace). The roots of the Tree of Peace spread out in all directions, inviting the Haudenosaunee to join and unite under the confederacy. The Great White Roots, whose nature was peace and strength, were firmly planted in the soil, providing the Haudenosaunee with a spiritual foundation (Wallace, 1994). This is the foundation for holistic education at the Akwesasne Freedom School.

Holistic Education[1]

Throughout this book I draw from the following definitions by Rupert Collister:

> *Wholistic* refers to the whole person, mind, body and spirit including the idea that the whole is greater than the sum of its parts. Inferring human behavior cannot be broken down into its constituent parts of skills, attitudes, behavior, emotions, etc.
>
> *Holistic* includes the wholistic but is much more. It refers to the idea

> that the *whole of reality* is an interconnected whole—holism. Holism means to me that *everything* is connected. No action occurs in isolation. Each movement, each change, each response to stimulus of everything on Earth affects everything else not only on the Earth but in the universe. (Collister 2001, p. 6)

In this definition of "holistic," all aspects of a person are central to understanding human behavior, and the interrelationship of all living things is recognized. This type of education focuses on values like cooperation, reciprocity, and respect, while emphasizing a connection to the natural world. Additionally, holistic education is not about parceling out aspects of culture into thirty-minute or one-hour classroom sessions but is rather about having one's own Indigenous culture as the foundation for the curriculum so it is integrated into all aspects of teaching and learning. Verna Kirkness (1999) argues: "The major drawback currently facing us is that we have reversed our traditional holistic psychology to one wherein we are going from the parts to the whole" (p. 15). But in a "systems approach," there is understanding in relation to wholes: "To understand anything necessarily involves understanding its relationship to larger wholes—the larger the whole and the more extensive the relationships that are understood, the truer the understanding" (Forbes 1996, p. 4). Fragments, therefore, do not lend themselves to greater understanding of the world. Understanding comes from seeing the whole and the connections within the entire system. Essentially, holistic education equals education of the whole child, and the whole child includes physical, mental, emotional, and spiritual aspects.

Similar to the AFS, most holistic schools are structured with mixed-ability and mixed-age small classes and are highly flexible in their approach. Holistic educators emphasize open, honest, and respectful communication in the classroom. Mutual support and cooperation rather than competition and hierarchy are the norm (Forbes 1996).

Ron Miller (1990), a leader in the holistic education movement, identifies the following as fundamental themes in a holistic worldview of education: wholeness of human experience (education must address physical, emotional, social, creative, intellectual and spiritual qualities), spirituality and ecology (a reverence and connection to all forms of life), individual integrity (emphasis on unique potential of individual), and learning through experience (active engagement in the learning process). Miller finds that while western modes of education are limited by conservatism, capitalism, nationalism, and scientific reductionism, a holistic education paradigm has the potential to shift the consciousness of society as it strives for "peace, cooperation, and justice based on our reverence for life" (p. 159). These components are echoed by the model of Indigenous education at the Akwesasne Freedom School.

The AFS curriculum is firmly grounded in Haudenosaunee culture as it is based on the Kaianerekowa (the Great Law of Peace), the Ohenton Kariwahtekwen (the Thanksgiving Address), the Creation Story, and the Karihwi:io (the Code of Handsome Lake). Thus, the curriculum provides a foundation for Mohawk identity and for how to live as a "good Mohawk."

An Indigenous Model of Holistic Education

> It is imperative that our children take up the cause of our languages and cultures because therein lies Aboriginal epistemology, which speaks of holism.—*Ermine 1995, p. 111*

My interpretative model of holistic education at the Akwesasne Freedom School curriculum is shaped like a pine tree (see fig. 14), similar to the Tsioneratasekowa. Each component of the model is discussed throughout this book. The roots of the tree serve as the base for all learning. Through the Creation Story, students learn where they come from and their connection to the universe. Students learn about traditional and contemporary Haudenosaunee governance as articulated in the Kaianere:kowa (Great Law of Peace). Also serving as part of the curricular foundation is the message of the Karihwi:io, Handsome Lake's message. A tradition rooted in the everyday practices of the AFS students is the recitation of the Ohenton Kariwahtekwen at the start and end of each day. This reminds students to be thankful and expresses gratitude to all living things. The elements of the Ohenton Kariwahtekwen provide structure to the curriculum and points of embarkation from which students can explore topics such as botany, fishing, astronomy, and agriculture.

Since 2012, all classes at the AFS have been taught using the Mohawk language, Kanienke:ha. In my model, the language acts as the trunk of the tree, a vital lifeline to all of the branches, as discussed in chapter 4. Knowledge and understanding of the language are acquired through interactions with teachers, parents, and elders. (The role of parents was discussed in chapter 2.) All

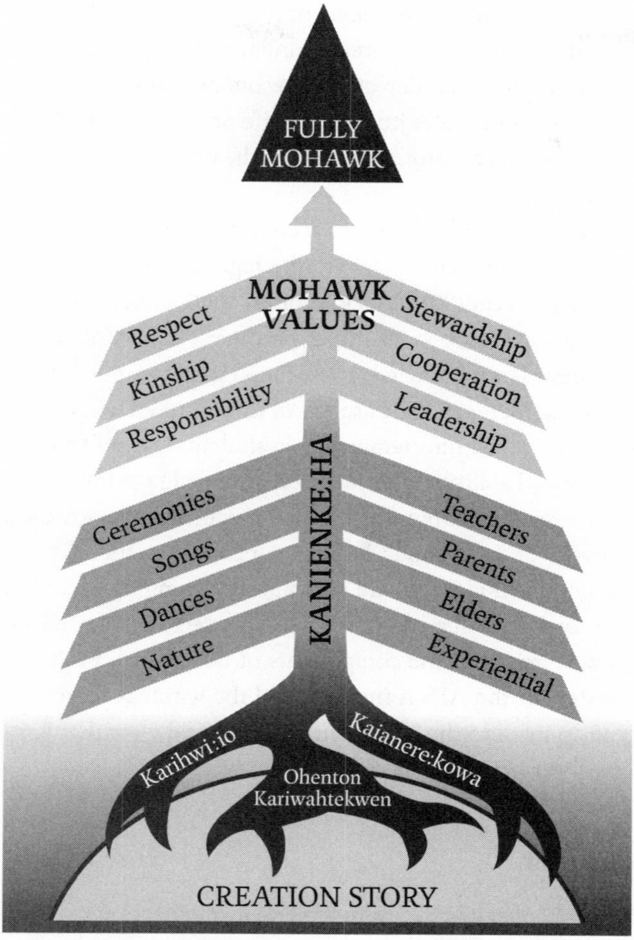

FIGURE 14. An Indigenous model of holistic education. By L. White.

play integral roles in the transmission of knowledge. Other branches of the tree are the curricular components, which include dances, songs, and ceremonial knowledge and practice. These provide content knowledge and serve as methods for learning. Through experiential means, often involving the natural world, knowledge and understanding are achieved.

Through knowledge and understanding of the Haudenosaunee worldview, students develop specific Mohawk values, such as respect, kinship, responsibility, stewardship, cooperation, and leadership (see chapter 6 for an in-depth discussion of these values). A new level of the tree is reached as students build on prior knowledge and achieve greater understanding. At the top of the tree, positive identity formation is depicted as becoming "fully Mohawk" or a whole human being. Becoming fully human is a lifelong process, with the ultimate goal of returning to the Creator, indicated by the upward-pointing arrow at the top of the tree.

As mirrored by the AFS, holistic education reflects and responds to a view of "what it means to be human," where the highest level of human existence, what Scott H. Forbes calls "Ultimacy" (Forbes 1996, p. 1), is akin to enlightenment, self-actualization, or, in this case, becoming fully Mohawk. To achieve this state one must learn knowledge associated with "wisdom" or what Forbes calls "sagacious competence." The aspects of this acquired wisdom are freedom, good judgment, meta-learning (emphasis on students learning *how* they as individuals learn), social ability, values, and self-knowledge (Forbes 2003). Holistic education nurtures human potential so that students can reach these goals.

In this model of Indigenous holistic education at the AFS, exploration and affirmation of self-identity and community belonging occur. As all of the elements of a real pine tree are connected and necessary for its survival and growth—and so are all of the components of this model. Each aspect of the education system at the AFS is integral, and the whole is more than the sum of its parts, in contrast to the "fragmentary self-world view that permeates the western world" (Ermine 1995, p. 111).

The Whole Person

The AFS not only operates as a holistic system of education; it is holistic in acknowledging and connecting with the various realms of each whole individual. As students move toward becoming "fully Mohawk," each realm is integral to their growth, as depicted in the four interrelated circles of figure 15. In the intellectual realm, students learn the history of the Haudenosaunee, including the Creation Story, the story of the coming of the Peacemaker and the formation of the Confederacy, and various treaties and the history of relationships with various outside governments. They also learn academic subjects such as math, language arts, and science. In the emotional realm, the AFS provides a nurturing environment in which self-esteem and confidence are enhanced.

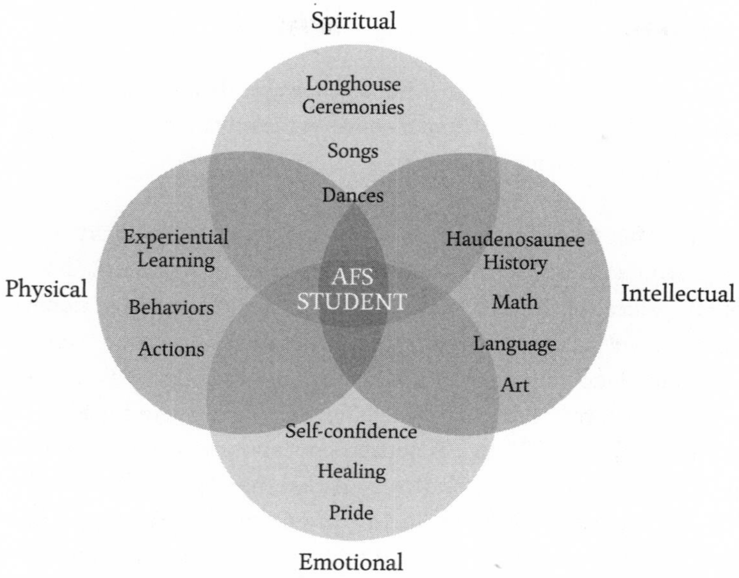

FIGURE 15. The whole person in the holistic education framework of the Akwesasne Freedom School. By L. White.

From what I have witnessed, students have little trouble speaking in public both at the school and in the larger community. Alumni who leave Akwesasne for post-secondary education possess a self-assuredness that helps guide them through their studies. The AFS also has the potential to facilitate healing historical trauma and breaking cycles of oppression that have faced Mohawk people for centuries, allowing students to take pride in their individual and cultural identities. Many of the grandparents of AFS students attended Indian residential schools or public schools where they were humiliated and taught self-hatred for being Mohawk. In the physical realm, teachers use experiential methods: students learn by doing. Behavior and actions are also a part of the physical realm as value systems are acted out. For example, students may take on leadership roles in the community by attending Longhouse ceremonies to deliver ceremonial speeches. Finally, each student's spiritual growth is encouraged. Students learn about and participate in Longhouse ceremonies, sing traditional songs, and learn traditional dances. The physical, emotional, spiritual, and intellectual realms do not occur in isolation but are connected and overlap.

Traditional Native Education

> And throughout their lives, wherever and however their journeys take them, they will carry within themselves the way home.
> —*Jennings and Montour 1992, p. 14*

Examining what traditional education was for Native people, particularly the Haudenosaunee, helps to articulate its connection to contemporary holistic education. Education at the AFS is based on Haudenosaunee traditional teachings and follows many of the principles of traditional education. Students are connected to Haudenosaunee history and to the teachings of their ancestors, forming lasting connections that will guide them throughout their lives.

Traditional forms of Native American education was quite different from Western forms of schooling (Cajete 1994; Skinner 1999). The foundational themes of traditional education in Gregory Cajete's *Look to the Mountain* (1994) include art, language, myth, spirituality, and interconnectedness. Cajete explains traditional education in Native American communities:

> American Indian education historically occurred in a holistic social context that developed the importance of each individual as a contributing member of the social group. Tribal education sustained a wholesome life process. It was an educational process that unfolded through mutual, reciprocal relationships between one's social group and the natural world. This relationship involved all dimensions of one's being, while providing both personal development and technical skills through *participation* in community life. It was essentially a communally integrated expression of environmental education. (p. 26)

Other traditional aspects of Native education include elders as teachers, emphasis on oral tradition, involvement of the entire community, and focus on the values of balance, generosity, respect, and cooperation (Skinner 1999). For some, the community was the school, instruction was developmentally appropriate, and there was an interrelationship between subjects (Evans 2001).

Alaskan Native traditional education processes were developed around "observing natural processes, adapting modes of survival, obtaining sustenance from the plant and animal world, and using natural materials to make their tools and implements" (Barnhardt and Kawagley 1999, p. 2). Young people learned these processes through stories and demonstrations, ensuring the perpetuation of culture and community survival. Other patterns in Indigenous education systems encompassed education specific to traits like gender, age, leadership, and clan or rank.

Autobiographical accounts provide glimpses of what community life and upbringing were like prior to Western schooling. Training for young boys often involved hunting, warriorship and knowledge of local plants and animals (Eastman 1971; Johnston 1989; Standing Bear 1988). Important traits in building character were self-control, reticence, honesty, bravery, and respect. One also had to learn to transmit stories and legends in order to be an "apt scholar" (Eastman 1971, p. 51).

While seen by some as primitive and informal, traditional forms of knowledge were critical to cultural survival and adhered to rigorous standards. As Charles Eastman wrote in *Indian Boyhood*, "It is commonly supposed that there is no systematic education of their children among the aborigines of this country. Nothing could be further from the truth. All the customs of this primitive people were held to be divinely instituted, and those in connection with the training of children were scrupulously adhered to and transmitted from one generation to the next" (Eastman 1971, p. 46). And Lomawaima and McCarty (2006) point out, "Formal education means more than schools" (p. 27). Indigenous education traditionally took place outside of a school building, which meant that outsiders often viewed it as "informal," unplanned, and unconscious, without rules or structure. Calling traditional education "informal," in contrast to "formal" Westernized institutional ideas of schooling, was a "one-dimensional strategy used to denigrate and marginalize Native education," Lomawaima and McCarty write (p. 27).

For the Haudenosaunee, formal training often took place in the Longhouse, where knowledge was passed down by elders (Wall 2001). Haudenosaunee oral tradition developed young people's capacity for remembering long, involved speeches and songs, "which were transmitted from one generation to the next by word of mouth, by certain hieroglyphic records cut or painted on staves of wood or on strips of skin, and by the wampum belts" (Greene 1972, p. 89). In traditional Haudenosaunee education, "children learned through observation of and participation in the ongoing life on the community. . . . Elders educated the young by continuously providing unstructured and non-coercive guidance" (Abate 1985, p. 8).

Observation, community connection, and involvement of elders are important aspects of traditional education for the Haudenosaunee that continue today. Reflecting on his youth, a Mohawk elder recounted, "We didn't have radio, TV—we had story time. I learned a lot that way. We used to play bingo—that's how I learned numbers. I knew a lot of things before I started school" (Interviewee T3: July 19, 2005). Traditional Haudenosaunee education was a lifelong process of "developing the individual for a society that was closely integrated with nature" (Abate 1985, p. 8). Education prepared young people for productive roles in Haudenosaunee society and "provided the growing child with opportunities to acquire abilities and skills and knowledge directly related to the economic, social and cultural bases of their culture" (Abate 1985, p. 8). Education was a part of everyday life and included formal periods of training—"for performance of certain specialized roles and professions having to do with, for instance: religion, health, fortification for security purposes and house-construction" (Abate 1985, p. 9).

Haudenosaunee culture is largely based on oral tradition, and storytelling "would have been a main [feature] of instruction, particularly for those with a natural gift for it" (Herne, personal communication, October 25, 2009). Traditional forms of education served individual and community purposes and were an essential aspect of physical and cultural survival.

Western forms of schooling were thought by some to have little purpose in the traditional lifestyle of Native peoples. During proceedings for the Lancaster Treaty in 1744, Onondaga leader Canassatego expressed:

> You told us likewise, you had a great House provided for the Education of Youth, and that there were several white People and Indians Children there to learn Languages, and to write and read, and invited us to send some of our Children amongst you. We must let you know we love our Children too well to send them so great a Way, and the Indians are not inclined to give their Children Learning. We allow it to be good, and we thank you for your Invitation; but our Customs differing from yours, you will be so good as to excuse us. (Merrell 2008, p. 84)

AFS parents demonstrate the same tenacity as Canassatego in their perpetuation of Mohawk culture through an education system based on Haudenosaunee tradition.

The Ohenton Kariwahtekwen

> *Iethinistenha Onhwéntsia (Mother Earth)*
> May we now gather our minds together as one and greet and give our thanks to our mother the earth for all that she gives us so we may live.
> —*Akwesasne Freedom School, n.d.*

Specific examples from the AFS pedagogical structure further demonstrate the holistic education model. Although the curriculum is also based on the Great Law of Peace, the Code of Handsome Lake, and the Creation Story, primary focus is placed on the Thanksgiving Address, the Ohenton Kariwahtekwen, which can be seen as part of the roots in the tree model. The Great Law of Peace states that whenever the Haudenosaunee are gathered together in council or assembly, they shall offer gratitude

> to the earth where men dwell, to the streams of water, the pools, the springs and the lakes, to the maize and the fruits, to the medicinal herbs and trees, to the forest trees for their usefulness, to the animals that serve as food and give their pelts for clothing, to the great winds and the lesser winds, to the Thunderers, to the Sun, the mighty warrior, to the moon, to the messengers of the Creator who reveal his wishes and to the Great Creator who dwells in the heavens above, who gives all the things useful to men, and who is the source and the ruler of health and life. (White Roots of Peace 1970, p. 5)

The Ohenton Kariwahtekwen begins with the words "*Tho niiohtonhak ne onkwa'nikon:ra*" (Let's bring our minds together as one), in sync with how the school began as a united effort by the Akwesasne community: "Our whole mission was *Tho niiohtonhak ne onkwa'nikon:ra,* let's bring our minds together as one. And with that, that's how we built the rest of it" (Interviewee P11: July 20, 2005). The philosophy of uniting in respect, peace, and gratitude is central to the Ohenton Kariwahtekwen. It teaches us to be thankful for all living things, to revere, respect, and understand our relationship to the universe and to take responsibility for carrying the message of gratitude to the future generations. It reminds children of their relationships to one another as brothers and sisters in the same creation. As they give thanks to the earth, the water, all life upon the earth, children remind themselves that they are a part of nature. As they give thanks to Grandfather Thunderers, Eldest Brother Sun, and Grandmother Moon, children remind themselves of their part in the universal order, and as they give thanks to the Creator, they remind themselves, individually and collectively, of the spiritual core of their culture as Onkwehonwe, "the real people" or the "original human beings" (Jennings and Montour 1992, p. 6).

The Ohenton Kariwahtekwen contributes to positive identity development in AFS students by instilling a sense of cultural pride and what it means to be a good human being. It is an important pedagogical tool helping young people develop a sense of responsibility and maturity and is used as a curriculum base for teaching reading, writing, math, science, history, and the Mohawk ceremonial cycle. Important Mohawk values of self-respect, peace, community, and connection to the natural world are nurtured in the students. For example, AFS teachers may take elements of the Ohenton Kariwahtekwen and use them as part of a science lesson. A walk in the woods to look for medicine plants, which are recognized in the Ohenton Kariwahtekwen, can turn into a weeklong lesson on botany and human impacts on the environment. Teachers may also extend a science lesson into a social studies lesson on the history of the land and the formation of the Akwesasne community. Giving thanks to the water may lead to lessons about the nearby St. Lawrence River or local wetlands. This mirrors what educators in Alaskan Native communities have found: that through incorporation of traditional knowledge and culture, a curriculum can integrate natural sciences, social sciences, language arts, and math "in a way in which the learning can be recognized as having legitimate meaning in life" (Kawagley, Norris-Tull, and Norris-Tull 1998, p. 142).

There are many other examples of how the Ohenton Kariwahtekwen provides a curricular framework (see table 1). A science lesson focusing on trees first acknowledges the living spirit of a tree and then examines the role trees play in the cycle of life and considers differing Indigenous views of various trees. Students begin to respect and understand the interconnectedness of trees with other life. Black ash trees are used in Mohawk basket making and continue the lesson in the utility of trees for traditional purposes. While studying the concept of energy, lessons cover the Four Winds, Ratiweras (the Thunder Beings), lightning, and the sun. The cosmos provides experiential lessons on the Creation Story and the connection to all things: "The moon, stars, and other galaxies are intertwined with Indigenous cosmos mythology to demon-

TABLE 1. Unit on birds

Topic	*Bird Life (Otsi'ten'okon:'A)*
Spiritual	The Ohenton Kariwahtekwen tells us: "The Creator instructed the birds to sing upon the arrival of each new day, and to sing so that all life will not know boredom"
Language Arts	"The Hermit Thrush" by Tehanetorens
Science	Local bird-watching and seasonal activities
Art	String art bird's nests
Mathematics	Classification, comparison, and computation of local bird species
Social Studies	Societal factors affecting local bird populations; for example, how humans affect birds and how birds affect humans

Source: Adapted from Jennings and Montour 1992, pp. 17–18.

strate the intricate thought of Haudenosaunee ancestors relative to cosmology" (Johansen, 2000, p. 12).

The long hallway in the main AFS building, decorated with murals and student artwork, is lined with benches where students sit when reciting the Ohenton Kariwahtekwen, which they do at the start and end of each day to bring their minds together as one. Students must understand the language to fully comprehend the Ohenton Kariwahtekwen, and it is meant to be understood and lived, not merely memorized. Connections with all living things are real and acted upon and acknowledged every day as demonstrated in a line from the AFS newsletter (Early Spring 1991): "Spring is here and everyone is patiently waiting for *Ratiweras* to return. *Ratiweras* is the Thunder People." Expressing gratitude to the Thunder Beings acknowledges the interconnectedness between human beings and the forces of nature:

> Indigenous people have long understood that education is a life-long continuum of experience gleaned from interaction with each other and all of nature, seen and unseen, including all of the cosmos. For *Kanienkeha:ka* (Mohawk) people of the *Rotinonhson:ni* (Iroquois) culture, this is reflected in the Thanksgiving Address which reminds us of the role assigned by the Creator to all living entities, as well as offering our thanksgiving that the

> cycle continues. The underlying philosophy of this simple address forms the basis of our approach to life and its experiences. (B. LaFrance 1994, p. 20)

LaFrance further explains that historically "the Rotinonhson:ni people considered themselves only one part of nature and observe[d] their surroundings from the smallest unseen living organism to the cosmos in order to gain intense understanding of the natural world. The Thanksgiving Address, recited for centuries, not only acknowledges and expresses appreciation for all the natural world, but also the duties that are fulfilled in order to maintain existence" (p. 20). While the Ohenton Kariwahtekwen is in essence a ceremonial practice in itself, students may also choose to participate in more formal ceremonies that take place in the Longhouse.

Traditional Ceremonies, Songs, and Dances

> Sometimes people say, "Isn't the Longhouse just church?" No, because we don't go there just on Sundays, we take those things home. We talk about those things. Those stories are a part of our life. The Creation story, it makes you feel stronger. . . . It makes you feel stronger about the way you raise your children, the love that you have for the people around you. The way you love your culture, it makes you feel stronger that way.
> —*Interviewee A12: July 14, 2005*

Continuing upward with the model of Indigenous holistic education, traditional ceremonies, songs, and dances comprise distinct branches of the tree. The Kanien'kehaka Aohsera or Cycle of Ceremonies follows the seasons and the AFS encourages students to participate with their parents. Sometimes the entire school attends the ceremonies at the longhouse. The ceremonies are held depending on the natural cycle. For example, the thunder ceremony is held when the very first sound of thunder of the year is heard and again at the last sound of thunder, and the strawberry ceremony is held when the berries are ripe. Some ceremonies, such as Midwinter, last for several days. The ceremonies that the school participates in include:

1. Satekohsehne (Midwinter) includes Sha'tekohsehra—Stirring of the Ashes (ashes are stirred to revive life), Ohstonwa'ko:wa—Great Feather Dance (to honor the Creator), Wa'therara:ken—White Dog Sacrifice

(today the white dog is replaced by a white basket burned as an offering to the Creator for supporting life), Aton:wa—Personal Thanksgiving Chant (men sing to the Creator and all living beings, thanking and requesting assistance for the new year) and Name Confirmation (babies receive Kanienke:ha names), Oheho:ron—Drum Dance (a recitation about creation), and the Kaientow:nen—Peach Stone Game (in which clans play against each other by putting up their favorite possessions, and the winners conduct the ceremonies for the rest of the year).

2. Ohki:weh (Dead Feast) honors deceased relatives.
3. Enatihseta:ta (Tobacco Burning) requests protection for maple sap gathering.
4. Wahta (Maple Tree Ceremony) thanks the maple trees.
5. Ratiweras (Spring Thunder Dance) thanks the Thunderers for returning to replenish the waters.
6. Hato:wi (Medicine Masks) is a healing society in which the grandfathers come together to help heal the sick. Hato:wi ceremonies are also held to give thanks to the grandfathers, to ask for protection, and for cleansing.
7. Ka:nen (Seed Ceremony) entails men and women competing at the Peach Stone Game to determine who will do the planting.
8. Ken niionhontesha (Strawberry Festival) thanks the Creator with strawberry juice.
9. Skanekwen tara:ne (Raspberry Ceremony) is combined with Strawberry Festival.
10. O rhotseri (Bean) thanks the Three Sisters (corn, beans, and squash).
11. Okasero:ta (Green Corn) involves a dance to honor corn.
12. Kaientho kwen Enhontekwaro:roke (Harvest) gives thanks for all that was asked for at Midwinter over four days of dancing, tobacco burning, Aton:wa, and Kaientow:nen.
13. Ratiweras (Autumn Thunder) thanks the Thunderers for the year's replenishing waters.
14. Ohki:weh (Dead Feast)—honors deceased relatives again.
15. Ontkenhnhokten (End of Seasons) entails chanting personal songs and giving thanks for the entire year.—*(Gibson, n.d.)*

Ceremonies, socials, funerals, weddings, and council meetings also take place in the Longhouse. During these events students sing traditional songs and practice traditional dances. Ceremonial practices are a critical part of students' education process that helps them in becoming fully Mohawk. An former student reports: "The Longhouse seems to tie into who you are. [I] want to go to give thanks, to continue traditions, to make sure the culture survives" (Interviewee A1: October 18, 2004). Perpetuating Mohawk culture through ceremonies may also entail fasting and purification ceremonies.

By participating in ceremonies, students take on the responsibility to carry out instructions and live according to the Great Law of Peace. Those instructions are to give thanks, conduct ceremonies, and be grateful for life given to us by the Creator. Ceremonies and dances reflect the Skyworld that has been re-created here on earth. They are necessary to keep balance in the world and for continuing Mohawk culture and way of life (Mohawk 2005, p. xiii). In this Indigenized approach to education, ceremonies are "integral and vital to the learning experience" (Four Arrows 2013, p. 65).

Elders and Traditional Knowledge of the Haudenosaunee

When teachers at the AFS have questions regarding cultural components of the curriculum, they ask an elder to come into the classroom to tell the Creation Story or to explain the Great Law of Peace. Elders are not necessarily aged but are carriers of traditional knowledge and Haudenosaunee culture. They may be faithkeepers and may also help prepare students for ceremonies.

Elders at the AFS transmit traditional knowledge through a variety of means, including storytelling, an important method to validate Aboriginal knowledge, which is critical to forming strong identities (Brown 2004). Calling upon the Haudenosaunee oral tradition is an important way of getting students to deal with "the whole—the physical, intellectual, emotional, and spiritual inner and outer ecologies. The Native person realizes that he/she is a microcosm of the whole, the universe" (Barnhardt and Kawagley 1999, p. 39). The holistic education model of the AFS encourages students to explore and understand their connections to the universe. As traditional knowledge bearers and an integral branch on the tree model of Indigenous holistic education, faithkeepers and elders help AFS teachers pass on important cultural information to the next generation.

Touching the Heart: The Teachers of the Akwesasne Freedom School

> To send them to school, you're giving somebody power with your children.
> —*Interviewee A12: July 14, 2005*

The success of the AFS is due in large part to the efforts of its teachers. In the pre-K classroom, Iawentas Nanticote teaches students in much the same way as she was taught as a student at the AFS many years earlier. She spends much of her time taking students outside on walks to identify medicine plants.

Most of the teachers at the AFS in pre-K through sixth grade are women, while male teachers have regularly instructed seventh and eighth grades. The teachers serve as parent figures, and, unlike in most public school systems, they are a part of a small community and known outside of the classroom. This major difference from standard Western education models becomes important when parents consider where to send their children to school. One parent explains: "I know the women that teach there. They are either mothers or grandmothers from within the community . . . so there's a related community connec-

FIGURE 16. AFS teacher Nancy Davis with students (*left to right*: Michelle George, Wahienhawi Cook-Barreiro, Karoniahawi Thomas), around 1983. Photo courtesy of the Akwesasne Cultural Center.

tion to knowing the woman that's teaching my child, and I see how she raised her family" (Interviewee P4: July 15, 2005). Parents have a level of trust in AFS teachers that is not always present in public schooling. AFS teachers are members of the Akwesasne community and are highly dedicated.

Some grades are co-taught by a teaching team, as is the case with two sisters who are former students. They now have children of their own attending the school. Visitors to the school are greatly impressed to hear these young teachers and their students converse on an everyday basis.

Because Mohawk language resources are scarce, teachers have to create much of their own classroom material. One sixth-grade teacher explained to me how she covered up the English sections in a math textbook and provided her own translation in the Mohawk language. A student reflected: "They erased all the English and they wrote it in Mohawk, and that's how they taught us" (Interviewee S2: November 3, 2004). Teachers are constantly translating English texts into Mohawk and verbally instructing their students. For a while a curriculum coordinator organized and gathered teaching materials, but typically teachers gather their own resources and share ideas and themes with one another.

The AFS does not require its teachers to be certified or to have received teacher training. A few have a college education, some have worked as language translators, and most were hired because they are fluent in the Mohawk language. Some teachers grew up in the Longhouse religion and have extensive knowledge of ceremonies and traditional teachings. In 2009 three teachers enrolled in an Ontario-based teacher education program designed to accommodate immersion teachers from the AFS and the area's public schools. What all teachers have in common is their fluency in the language. Although not consistently held over the years, professional development days have provided opportunities for local experts to visit and discuss topics such as wampum, nutrition, and mental health (Akwesasne Freedom School 1999).

Teaching at the AFS is not an easy job. Salaries are well below teacher salaries in public schools, and AFS teachers receive no health or retirement benefits. One must have an extremely high level of commitment to teach at the AFS. While there has been high turnover in recent years, a core group of teachers has remained. A parent explains her perception of the AFS teachers: "It's teaching from a different level, at a level that's truly from the heart. It's teaching from a level that's truly connected. It's teaching from a level that's not just a number.

The public schools will never be able to do that because ultimately a number is the important value in those schools. It will never touch the heart" (Interviewee P11: July 20, 2005). AFS teachers are devoted to creating a space where Mohawk students are nurtured and cared for and where they learn through active participation. Thus, they play a crucial role as a branch of the tree in the Indigenous holistic education model.

Experiential and Nature-Based Education

> We did outdoor things, environmental things, gardening, and we used art as a learning tool because we didn't have too many things.
> —*(Interviewee T4: July 18, 2005)*

On a late summer day, several eighth- and ninth-grade students gathered on the front lawn of the AFS to make a large corn grinder. They took turns carving out the inside of a large log and sanding another piece for a pounder. Their teacher had salvaged timber after a tree fell on someone's lawn. Seeing a teaching opportunity, he'd brought the wood to the school for the project. Using experiential methods, AFS students learn from activities that have purpose and meaning: "Chopping wood is an education for these kids. They [have] learned you can't chop wood when wet. Everything is a lesson, like gardening. They learn why we plant corn, beans, and squash, and on top of that is a Mohawk [language] lesson" (Interviewee V1: October 6, 2004). Education at the AFS is centered on such experiential activities that provide meaningful life lessons for students.

Philosopher and educator John Dewey first articulated the concept of experiential education through his "theory of experience," whereby students make meaning of their experiences (Dewey 1938). Itin (1999) draws clear distinctions between "experiential education," in which transactions between teacher and learner are present, and "experiential learning" which "rests within the student and does not necessarily require a teacher" (p. 92). Freire (1993) also placed value on experiences as part of learning. He described Western forms of education as embodying a "banking" approach—the teacher merely deposits information into the passive student. Freire advocated for a democratic process of education that would allow for critical thought, by explicitly addressing the power relations between students and teacher. In the "banking" style

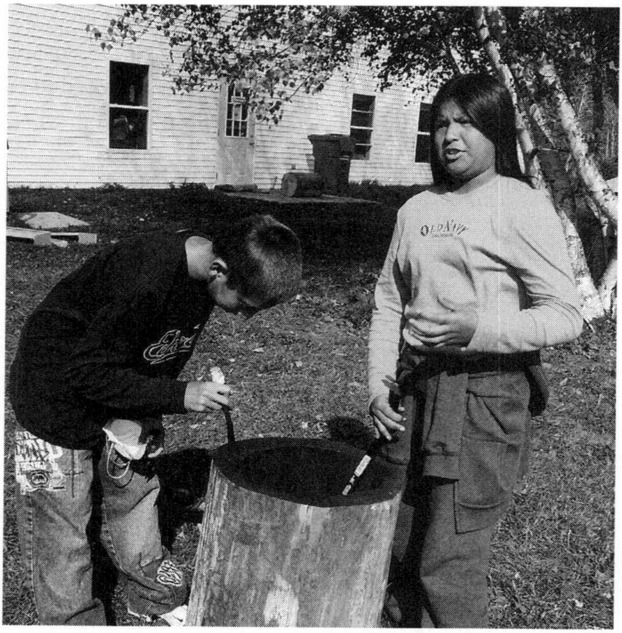

FIGURE 17. Seventh- and eighth-grade students carving a corn grinder. Iotore Wheesk (*left*) and Kahentawaks Perkins. Photo by L. White, 2005.

education, scholar Ray Barnhardt says, "knowledge and learning can become disassociated from the experiential realities outside the school, and potentially interfere with the student's own process of inquiry" (Barnhardt 1981, p. 101). He asserts, "What we need then is a way to link the content of a process oriented curriculum to the experiential and situational framework of everyday life, so that what is learned and how it is learned can be more effectively merged into a meaningful whole" (p. 105).

Cummins (1992) asserts, "An experiential-interactive model of instruction focuses on giving students hands-on (context-embedded) classroom experiences that provide students with a basis for understanding more abstract (context-reduced) academic curricula" (p. 8). This hands-on type of learning is collaborative, with the student and teacher interacting in such a way that students are empowered. Learning in this way is an active process that is enhanced by interactions and collaboration (Piaget 1954; Vygotsky 1978).

While teachers at the AFS may not be familiar with the work of Freire and Dewey or the philosophy of experiential education, they embody the basic principles in development and implementation of a curriculum that "makes sense" according to Haudenosaunee philosophy and practice. Even a trip to a local big-box store can be a positive learning experience. A teacher described how she takes her students on field trips to the nearby Walmart and, on the way there, uses the opportunity to teach about the geography and the history of the area as well as place names. Once at the store students learn about counting money, adding and subtracting, and they practice new vocabulary. Back at school, students write stories about the field trip—in the Mohawk language, of course—or conduct presentations to demonstrate what they have learned. Whether going on a field trip, making their own traditional clothing, or fishing, the point is that students learn by doing rather than by reading a book.

Contrary to most public schooling, many of the educational activities at the AFS take place outdoors, in the natural world, which may involve finding medicine plants or planting traditional gardens. Kirkness (1999) explains why Native people have moved away from the practice of teaching in the natural world: "We are uncomfortable when too much time is spent outdoors learning from the land because we have been conditioned to believe that education occurs in the classroom" (p. 22). With the Ohenton Kariwahtekwen as a foundation for the AFS curriculum, learning takes place outdoors, where students are exposed to elements of the natural world. Experiential and nature-based education are integrated as tree branches in the Indigenous model of holistic education.

A Guide to the Curriculum

The curriculum at the AFS is not rigid. In fact it is rarely set to paper with the exception of a curriculum guide that was prepared by a parent in 1992. Teachers may modify that guide to meet the needs of their particular classrooms, and some choose not to use to the guide at all. It does, however, provide some idea about how the curriculum is structured at the AFS. The goals of the Onkwehonewe:neha (curriculum guide) are to:

> Produce and maintain fluent Mohawk speakers; instill responsibility, independence, and a positive self-concept; foster respect for the Elders and the knowledge they possess; develop pride in and understanding and practice of Haudenosaunee customs and values; ensure the continuation of the Haudenosaunee Seven Generations philosophy (all decisions must be considered in light of the consequences for the future seven generations);

> [and] develop the skills required to function effectively in the over culture Western society. (Jennings and Montour, 1992, p. 7)

The five components of the Onkwehonwe:neha address spirituality, language and literacy, analytic ability, social affective development, and identity (AFS 1992). Spiritual goals are to instill respect and understanding for Sonkwaiatison (the Creator), creation, and the spiritual world, to foster respect for Mother Earth, and to provide for the continuation of ceremonies, spiritual practices and beliefs, songs, and other traditions to provide a firm foundation of values, pride, and personal contentment. These are achieved through the Ohenton Kariwahtekwen, the Creation Story, the Cycle of Ceremonies, and the Karihwi:io (the Code of Handsome Lake), and through teaching about Mohawk names, healing societies, traditional medicines, prophecies, the clan system, and the traditional role of women in Iroquois society (Akwesasne Freedom School 1992).

The language and literacy component of the curriculum addresses a student's ability to speak, read, and write in Mohawk and in English, and it also includes the arts and communications in general. Students learn to make sense of wampum belts and traditional Iroquoian symbols such as the pine tree, the four roots, the eagle, the five bound arrows, buried weapons of war, and the circle. They gain skills in painting, drawing, and traditional pottery-making, beadwork, and clothing-making, learn traditional songs and dances, and even make water drums and deer horn rattles (Jennings and Montour 1992, p. 8). By attending ceremonies, festivals, Great Law readings, and community meetings, students practice listening skills (Akwesasne Freedom School 1992). After eighth grade, students may depart for a public high school located away from the community, but students and their parents may request that they remain at the AFS for a year or two when it is in their best interest to delay entry to a public high school.

Under the analytical component of the curriculum guide come science, math, problem solving, and critical thinking. Under social affective development fall education in Haudenosaunee, Mohawk and Akwesasne history. This entails Haudenosaunee confederacy formation and organization, governing systems, the life and journey of the Peacemaker, European arrival (Christianity, missionaries, residential schools, land encroachment, treaties, and the influence of the confederacy on American democracy), global awareness, and the impact of modernism and industrialization (Akwesasne Freedom School 1992; Jennings and Montour 1992, p. 9). As an AFS staff member explains, students are prepared to represent their nation: "They'll go through and tell you where they fit in with the Longhouse and with the nation, and where they fit in with the Confederacy, and where the Confederacy fits in with general white society . . . instead of giving [a] short little two-minute answer, they'll give you a twenty-minute answer. . . . They know where they're going" (Interviewee V1: October 6, 2004).

Learning one's own cultural history helps to instill a sense of pride and self-confidence. A parent states of a daughter: "She gained a lot. I think what she gained was more than just the language. I think it helped her to frame her thought process . . . how she treats other people . . . her understanding of our history" (Interviewee P9: July 15, 2005). An understanding of Haudenosaunee history shapes student's worldviews, grounding them in a shared identity as members of the Mohawk Nation and the Haudenosaunee Confederacy.

Identity development in the AFS curriculum is a conscious effort, not just a by-product: "The building of a strong self-concept and positive identity occurs through the educational process. This component addresses the socialization process of each child into the traditional community at Akwesasne and of the *Kanienkeha:ka* (Mohawk people). This strong and positive self-development will insure that our children are content and succeed in both worlds, as well as ensuring our survival as Hotinoshonni 'seven generations' into the future" (Akwesasne Freedom School 1992). Through socialization at the Longhouse and in the community, students develop an understanding of their place in Mohawk society, building a strong sense of identity.

Evaluation and Assessment

> Language education is holistic in nature, learning is an active constructive process, every child is unique . . . [and] evaluation must be coherent and consistent with our *Kanienkeha:ka* (Mohawk) and Hotinoshonni culture.
> —*Akwesasne Freedom School 1992*

The creativity and flexibility the AFS curriculum allows is reflected in how student progress is evaluated at the school. Since the AFS is not government-funded, it is not required to abide by public school standards and therefore does not administer standardized tests as evaluation measures. Financial independence has allowed the AFS tremendous flexibility and freedom in its curriculum and in the methods used to evaluate student progress.

At first it was difficult for me to determine exactly how evaluations occur at the AFS, and it seemed as though there was little consistency between teachers, just as lesson plans appeared to develop informally as teachers shared ideas. There is no single standard evaluation procedure at AFS—each teacher appears to grade his or her students differently—but evaluation, I would find out, is done consciously. Through interviews with teachers and classroom observation I learned that most student evaluation takes place as teachers listen and observe, paying attention to students' use of the Mohawk language. Some teachers use portfolios to evaluate their students because AFS teachers feel a portfolio reflects the individuality of each student, is noncompetitive and qualitative, and encourages a kind of consensus by allowing students and parents to participate in assessment. Teres Cook, who taught at the AFS for fourteen years, followed this method. Using them as main source for grading, she gave out portfolios containing students' written work, notes on presentations, and various projects at quarterly meetings with parents to help facilitate the discussion of student progress (Teres Cook, personal communication, December 19, 2014). Portfolios are often used in conjunction with report cards that are created with heavy input from parents. Not all teachers use the same type of report card, although they all emphasize oral skills and the basic cultural content, including "*Iekewennaie':ri*" (I speak in sentences) and "*Wakatahonhsata'tskon*" (I listen well during Mohawk language class). Students are generally rated "Very Good," "Good," or "Improving" in math (for example, counting in Kanienkeh:a), science (recognizing and naming water animals and sky beings), language arts (basic vocabulary, following instructions), and social studies (showing respect for others, learning the seasonal calendar), as well as participation, attitude, socialization (how they get along with others), and how, when, and where they use the Mohawk language. Another teacher may use the same ratings and the same basic areas of evaluation but also evaluate "traditional forms of expression," which includes singing traditional songs. All students are evaluated on their ability to recite the Ohenton Kariwahtekwen.

When students participate in community activities, this may be evaluated as it shows socialization development. Important activities such as singing, dancing, and participating in traditional ceremonies may be noted on a student's progress reports. When a student made an announcement during a social dance at the Longhouse, the teacher noted this as part of the student's learning process. Teachers of the younger children may check comprehension after storytelling by having students draw pictures. Language arts are assessed as students learn traditional stories and identify Mohawk words, grammar, and phonics. Students participate in parent- teacher meetings a few times each year to discuss how they are doing in school.

Teachers at the AFS realize that students do not all learn alike. Holistic educators also recognize that there are multiple ways of knowing. Drawing from Gardner's (1983) theory of multiple intelligences, which proposes that learning is different for every learner, Forbes (1996) states: "If education is a process of discovery and uncovering and every child is unique, how could the traditional educational judging of children be anything other than inherently wrong? How could a child be a slow learner if he was learning at a pace that was right for her/him? If a child doesn't learn . . . words and numbers, is that child unintelligent or can that child be learning from other intelligences?" (p. 7). AFS teachers recognize the learning process as one of discovery and see each student as having unique skills and abilities.

Discovering Gifts and Talents

> The elders know all about the children. They could always see how the children would turn out. That's why they would help to guide the children in the right direction. Some would become singers of the sacred songs. Others would be Faithkeepers. They knew the trades they'd be best at. They could see the artist in each one. Then, the elders could see which ones would be strong in the Longhouse and the ones who would "go over the hill" to get away from their teachings.—*Wall 2001, p. 42*

In traditional Haudenosaunee education, elders played a significant role in identifying and nurturing the special talents of children. When students are supported and nurtured they have the freedom to develop their natural gifts and abilities. If a particular student comes to the AFS with certain talents, the teachers make an effort to help identify and nurture them. Haudenosaunee traditional teachings instruct adults to watch children carefully to see what special skills, gifts, talents, or strengths they may have. One parent says of her daughter, "She had gifts of singing and as an artist . . . these were enhanced at the Freedom School. . . . If she [had attended] a public school, her gifts [might] have not been recognized. . . . She learned how to be a good parent at the Freedom School . . . she's an excellent mother. . . . The Akwesasne Freedom School helped to bring out her gifts" (Interviewee P3: October 8, 2004). The daughter, now an AFS alumna, pursued her gift of singing and now participates in a traditional group, the Akwesasne Women Singers. She travels to regional events, has produced CDs of her music, and has also become a good parent.

A teacher explains about her students: "One girl is an artist. I have a singer—her mother takes to her contests. She plays the piano. I have one child that knows history, and one hyper child—he'll be my gym instructor. I look for what they're good at, and that's what I work on" (Interviewee T6: July 20, 2005). The AFS helps its students develop by identifying and nurturing their strengths. Students who may be seen as difficult by some are not ignored: "There was this one girl, they said 'she's so mean, so terrible,' *she's always this* and *she's always that*, and I said, hold on. . . . She's going to be our leader because she has that strong spirit. I said, 'Don't take that out of her. We're going to need her to stand up and speak for us someday'" (Interviewee P11: July 20, 2005). These beliefs and practices are consistent with the Haudenosaunee philosophy of seven generations. Everything we do today has an impact on the future: our children, our grandchildren, and seven generations beyond. Every decision and action made today must take this into account. By honoring and nurturing children's natural abilities, the community is ensuring cultural survival.

Achieving Quality Education

> Western schooling separates "education" from living: the experience alienates us from our surroundings and, therefore, our culture.—*B. LaFrance 1994*

Schooling at the AFS does not separate education from Mohawk culture. The AFS is not merely an institution for learning. Its holistic educational process grounded in the traditional worldview prepares students to have strong Mohawk identities and equips them for life inside and outside the community.

Critical theorist Henry Giroux (2001) suggests that schools need "forms of teaching that are inclusive, caring, respectful, economically equitable, and whose aim, in part, is to undermine those repressive modes of education that produce social hierarchies and legitimate inequality while simultaneously providing students with the knowledge and skills needed to become well-rounded critical actors and social agents" (p. xxvi). In holistic education, writes Ron Miller, "human development must be served before the economic and political goals of those in power" (R. Miller 1990, p. 17). Students, particularly those from marginalized groups, can be empowered through such a system that acknowledges historical injustices their people have known. When learning "is connected to the imperatives of social responsibility and political agency" (Giroux,2001, p. xxiv), such as how learning occurs at the AFS, students are equipped to contribute positively to society.

Students at the AFS have greater potential, thanks to a holistic Indigenous education model, to become agents of social change in their own communities. They demonstrate self-confidence, high self-esteem, and pride in their identities as Mohawk people. Kirkness (1999) writes: "You will know you have achieved your goal of quality education when your children are enjoying the challenge of school/learning, when their self-esteem and self-confidence is evident, when your children are proud of who they are, when their links with the older generations are made" (p. 26).

FOUR

Kanienke:ha and the Akwesasne Freedom School

Tohsa ne tentewatka:neren tsi naho:ten iah thaetewakwe:ni. Ohen:ton iteweht tanon ne:e tetewatka:neren oh naho:ten entewakwe:ni. Tahatikonhsontonkie raotiwen:na ne Kanienke:ha (The language belongs to the future Seven Generations and we are the generation who will continue to give it to them).

—*Cook-Peters 2003, p. 12*

On a warm summer day in 2006, local bands gathered for the AFS annual fundraiser. A temporary stage had been constructed on the school grounds for singers and local bands to perform. At the start of the day a group of AFS students stood on the stage to recite the Ohenton Kariwahtekwen. One first-grade boy stepped up to the microphone and began reciting the Ohenton Kariwahtekwen in his ancestral language. Not a fluent speaker, he struggled with some of the words but kept a big smile and, with concerted effort, continued on. When he stumbled over a word, he glanced over to his peers for help and they whispered the word to him. He quickly carried on with a quiet confidence, fulfilling his duties as a member of Mohawk society. Parents, teachers, and other community members listened to the students with anticipation and hope that the future generations will carry on these traditions and perpetuate Haudenosaunee culture and way of life.

Kanienke:ha, the Mohawk language, is the central component of the curriculum at the AFS. In the Indigenous holistic model of education proposed in the last chapter (see fig. 14), Kanienke:ha is the trunk of the tree, the component that connects everything else in the curriculum. Students begin and end each day by reciting the Ohenton Kariwahtekwen to acknowledge the coming together of their minds, their thoughts and intentions. Although the Ohenton Kariwahtekwen has been translated into numerous English versions, knowledge of the Mohawk language is necessary to fully understand the depth of its meaning.

Indigenous languages, virtually outlawed at North American residential schools, have been overwhelmed by majority languages used in mass media, public schools, and elsewhere. Danish scholar Tove Skutnabb-Kangas writes that education in majority languages has been the "most powerful assimilating force for indigenous children, immigrants, and refugee minority children" and thus has "a homogenizing function" (Skutnabb-Kangas 2000, p. 202). Skutnabb-Kangas asserts that language can also be an important tool in gaining self-determination. When communities have control over their own education, language renewal initiatives can be at the forefront. When Indigenous communities decide to resist dominant power structures and choose to adopt an Indigenous form of schooling, including the teaching and learning of their own languages, they are engaging in a form of critical pedagogy. In the AFS the Akwesasne community has created an institution that is a "point of resistance" against "linguistic and cultural assimilation . . . the center of the arena in which the politics of language are worked out" (McCarty 1998, p. 38).

Status of Kanienke:ha

> If it weren't for the AFS pointing out how at risk our language is, maybe it would have been too late to save our language. The Freedom School kept . . . it alive when people didn't realize how important it was. Now people are beginning to realize that.—*Interviewee V4: August 23, 2004*

Akwesasne is similar to many Indigenous communities in that there are no longer any monolingual speakers of the Native language and English is predominant. Quebec is a French-speaking province, and some Mohawks choose to learn French in their post-secondary education or for jobs in Canada, but only a very small portion of Akwesasne is located in a rural area of Quebec, and French is rarely heard in the community.

Prior to European contact, the Mohawk language was recorded in wampum belts that conveyed stories, histories, and eventually treaties with Europeans. Kanienke:ha was first put into written form in the seventeenth century by Dutch explorers who learned the language for trading purposes. Then, in the early eighteenth century, French Jesuit priests learned the language and translated bibles and hymnals for Mohawks who had converted to Christianity. Some Mohawks at Akwesasne still use these texts. The Jesuits also created the eleven-letter alphabet that is still in use today.[1] Diacritical marks were added and orthography created in the early 1970s by Mohawk educators from the territory of Kahnawà:ke. Variations remained between all of the Mohawk reserves since speakers of Mohawk did not agree on a standard writing system. It was not until the early 1990s that a group of educators, elders, and linguists from all of the Mohawk reserves attempted to standardize orthography for all dialects. They created an accepted form of the written Mohawk language spoken by people in all eight Mohawk communities (D. Lazore 1993) (see map 2). Despite the standardized orthography, there are dialectical differences between Mohawk community, and pronunciation can differ. For example, the word "Ratiweras" (Thunder Beings) has a standard spelling, but at Akwesasne it is pronounced "la dee way las." At Kahnawà:ke and Six Nations it is pronounced "ra dee way ras." Slight differences in spelling still occur within the Akwesasne community.

It is difficult to ascertain the exact number of fluent speakers of Kanienke:ha. In an informal survey completed in 2004, a language instructor guessed the number of fluent speakers within each household by looking at a detailed map of Akwesasne. This survey suggested approximately seven hundred fluent speakers, most over the age of fifty. Language instructor and fluent speaker Kaweieinón:ni (Margaret) Cook-Peters estimates that because of the increase in immersion programs there may be approximately twelve hundred fluent speakers where the majority are young families (Cook-Peters, personal communication, December 19, 2014). Tom Porter guessed that in of all the Mohawk communities there are five thousand fluent speakers (Porter 2008). Freeman, Stairs, Corbiere, and Lazore (1995) caution that the "variable definitions of language use and the subjectivity of self-report add to the uncertainty of statistical interpretation" (p. 40). No formal studies have assessed the language status at Akwesasne, and all numbers are estimates.[2]

One sign of vitality in a language is adaptability to social and technological changes. Kanienke:ha has this, allowing for the possibility of new words to be created. As one community member notes, "We haven't found a good Mohawk word for snowmobile, but we have words for airplane and TV" (Interviewee

T2: July 19, 2005). As an active language, Kanienke:ha is also spoken by all generations. Krauss's (1998) classification system for Native languages categorizes speakers as follows:

Class A: speakers in all generations
Class B: speakers only in parent generation and older
Class C: speakers only in grandparent generation and older
Class D: speakers only among a few elders

In Akwesasne many of the fluent speakers are in the older generations, but a recent development puts it in the Class A category. There are at least three families (possibly more), who are making a conscientious effort to teach Kanienke:ha to their children from birth. Unsurprisingly, the parents of these families are alumni of the AFS.

The difficulty in assessing the status and fluency of speakers is not unique to Akwesasne. Dauenhauer and Dauenhauer (1998) describe this among Tlingit groups in Alaska: "[Assessing language status] is obscured by the reality of people who speak but choose not to. And by the often large category of people who understand the language but who cannot speak it. Then there are speakers who can handle everyday situations but who are not literary or ceremonial stylists. Fluency is often a matter of impression or opinion; many non-speaking parents [wrongly] assume their children are fluent in the ancestral language after a few weeks of language instruction or immersion in a cultural camp" (71–72). This scenario plays out in Akwesasne families where there is a wide range of language proficiency among parents and children.

The Battle between English and Kanienke:ha

> We'll have no Nation if we have no Mohawk language.
> —*Interviewee S2: November 3, 2004*

One evening I sat at the kitchen table of Kaweienón:ni (Margaret) and Teddy Peters, former AFS teachers and parents and now grandparents of AFS students. Kaweienón:ni and I had become friends over the years, beginning when I first began learning Kanienke:ha at Kanatsiohareke. Kaweienón:ni and Teddy's three children, all of whom had attended the AFS, were home and going about their daily routine. As Kaweienón:ni and Teddy and I talked in English about Teddy's radio show broadcast in Kanienke:ha, Kaweienón:ni's work at the Akwesasne Mohawk Board of Education (AMBE) creating language materials, and struggles to save the Mohawk language, I noted that the Peters children were speaking to each other in Kanienke:ha. I had no idea what they were saying but they appeared to be using the language naturally and comfortably. They were not speaking it to impress me and did not seem to pay much attention to my presence. Kanienke:ha is their preferred language at home, in school, and throughout their daily lives. However, things were not always this way. Kaweienón:ni confessed: "Me and my husband were fluent. Other parents were paying money to send [their] kids to school and paying me to teach them when I wasn't even teaching my own kids to speak Mohawk. I saw the commitment to language. . . . I began to feel ashamed for not teaching my own kids" (October 8, 2004).

Kaweienón:ni and Teddy's first language is Kanienke:ha. Their children however, were highly influenced by English in the home and—at first—in public schools. Kaweienón:ni and Teddy realized that they needed to speak the language more often in the home in order for their children to become fluent. And they also made the decision to send their children to Akwesasne Freedom School. Their children eventually attained fluency because of the Mohawk language immersion at the AFS and the exposure they received at home. It is now the language of choice for the entire family, as a result of a conscious decision made by their parents. They knew the language was in danger of disappearing unless they, as speakers, passed it down to their children. Kaweienón:ni and Teddy are now grandparents, teaching their grandchildren from birth to speak and understand Kanienke:ha. Their grandchildren are growing up bilingual, speaking and understanding English too. The oldest grandson now attends the AFS, where his language skills are continually strengthened.[3]

The English language is a powerful force that is seen and heard everywhere in Akwesasne. In homes like that of the Peters family, children are more likely to maintain Kanienke:ha as their primary language. However, other parents who spoke Kanienke:ha as their first language no longer speak it or chose not to pass it down to their children. As one person said, "None of my kids are speakers. Teaching was a job. I got home and thought, *I don't want to do that anymore.* So my kids are not speakers. The parents got lazy. They're learning English at school, it's easier. . . . It's my fault my kids don't speak [Kanienke:ha]. It's because I made my husband speak English" (Interviewee T6: July 20, 2005).

The reasons members of the AFS community choose not to speak Kanienke:ha are varied and complex. Overwhelming exposure to and pressure to speak English are more likely causes than simple laziness. One AFS student has a fluent parent who chooses not to speak to him in the language. The student says, "Just my dad speaks at home, but not often. [He] will ask me to get him something in Mohawk. . . . [My] grandmother always speaks to me. . . . She gets mad if I don't speak back to her. . . . I use mostly English now" (Interviewee S2: November 3, 2004).

Children are exposed to English through television and everywhere outside of the AFS, so it takes a conscious effort to maintain Kanienke:ha in the home. Children and parents both come to prefer English because that is the language they are most exposed to and English becomes easier. One student told me, "I feel more comfortable speaking English. Don't know why—English is just easier. [I] understand Mohawk, but if they ask me a question, [I] can answer back in Mohawk, but usually I speak English" (Interviewee S2: November 3, 2004). This same student also expressed the dilemma he faced when trying to maintain his Mohawk language ability while facing constant pressure to speak English: "Over there [in immersion classrooms] I answered back in Mohawk. When you see the big kids speak Mohawk, you want to speak it too. Little kids want to be like the big kids. . . . When I'm over there [in the seventh- and eighth-grade building], they always speak English. I just don't talk to them. . . . I say it quietly if I do. . . . My nieces and sisters over there [in immersion classes], I want them to learn. . . . Language is our culture, religion" (Interviewee S2: November 3, 2004).

English and Kanienke:ha are in a perpetual struggle, and pressures to speak English can seem insurmountable. However, unwavering efforts on the part of teachers, parents, and the community can tip the balance in favor of Kanienke:ha. Since the AFS is a Mohawk language immersion school, it follows that AFS parents support language learning and immersion strategies. However, not all community members are so supportive.

Language Ideologies

Assessing language ideologies and attitudes of the Akwesasne community is beyond the scope of this book, but I do want to present a glimpse of what may shape such ideologies and attitudes in Native communities in general. First, however, a discussion of what constitutes language ideologies and how they compare to language attitudes is in order. The terms are often used interchangeably, but, according to Colin Baker, "attitude is a hypothetical construct used to explain the direction and persistence of human behavior" (Baker 1992, p. 10). Thus, assessing attitudes is useful in measuring language vitality and can aid in determining the health of a language as they indicate "community thoughts and beliefs, preferences, and desires." Language attitudes provide "social indicators of changing beliefs and the chances of success in policy implementation" and can measure "the status, value, and importance of a language" (Baker 1992, p. 9, 10). Ideologies, however, are about "consciousness, subjective representations, beliefs, ideas" (Woolard 1998, p. 5), and a community's language ideology is about more than language. It is tied to identity, aesthetics, morality, and epistemology as well as notions of "religious ritual, child socialization, gender relations, the nation-state, schooling, and law" (Kroskrity and Field 2009, p. 3).

Beliefs about language are also multiple, diverse, and sometimes contradictory. As Kroskrity and Field write, "There are local language ideologies for language socialization, for interpersonal communication, for constructing local identity, for linguistic representation, and for storytelling" (Kroskrity and Field 2009, p. 9). These beliefs are also directly linked to positions of social, political, and economic power. Linguistic anthropologist Kathryn Woolard concurs: "Ideology is seen as ideas, discourse, or signifying practices in the service of the struggle to acquire or maintain power" (Woolard 1998, p. 7).

In some Indigenous communities, beliefs surrounding language may prevent parents from passing their language to their children. Parents who are fluent in the Native language have various conscious and subconscious reasons for not passing it on, including their experiences in residential or public school, where they were punished for speaking their language; fears of their children not becoming literate in English and therefore falling behind in school; fears that their children will not fit in with the rest of society; and fears that they will not be able to find a job and become successful members of their community.

Resistance to dominant languages can be rooted in ideologies about religion, as in expressing the need to preserve Native languages in order to communicate with the Creator. "The power of this spiritual meaning and value orientation, expressed collectively through the Longhouse ceremonies—their high forms of traditional language, can cause some resistance when language teaching—often initiated by Longhouse people—is construed in terms of 'evangelism'" (Freeman, Stairs, Corbiere, and Lazore 1995, p. 48). However, according to a Mohawk language advocate from Tyendinaga, Jan Hill, "The Mohawk language is not religion but a way of life in all its aspects" (qtd. in ibid.).

Kaweienón:ni Cook-Peters is a strong advocate for the Mohawk language, and when inquiring about my initial plans to research this book she stated: "I hope that part of your research will focus on the reason why our own people have a hard time supporting their own language being taught" (personal communication, November 15, 2001). Kaweienón:ni's two daughters attended the AFS, and when one was having academic difficulties after transitioning to a local public high school (Salmon River Central School), some people attributed her falling behind to having been in an immersion school. Kaweienón:ni disagrees: "Many students never having been in immersion have the same difficulties and sometimes even more so" (personal communication, November 18, 2001). Persuading community members to support language initiatives is often an uphill battle. Community members' beliefs about language can impede or help language revitalization efforts. Christopher Loether writes, "The acceptance or rejection of language revitalization efforts may depend more on a community's beliefs and feelings about language than on seemingly more substantive issues regarding language structure or the practical concerns of implementation" (Loether 2009, p. 238).

Young people may choose not to pursue learning their Indigenous language because of influences from mainstream society, a society that continues to devalue their language and culture. Due to overwhelming exposure to pop culture and mass culture via media and in public schools, a mainstream lifestyle is difficult to resist. Dauenhauer and Dauenhauer (1998) found that assessments of language status needed to include an understanding of the attitudes of speakers and nonspeakers. They warned that people may respond with denial and anger when facing linguistic and cultural loss. "Psychosocial consequences" of colonization, oppression, genocide and linguistic repression include feelings of shame, guilt, and fear (McCarty, Romero-Little, and Zepeda 2006, p. 671). These varied and often contradictory language ideologies may be one reason why parents in Native communities are increasingly turning to educational institutions for language revitalization rather than attempting to teach their children at home.

Schools as Agents of Change

> If school-based resources for linguistic educational self-determination are not used, the remaining, largely negative forces at work will only speed the rate of language loss. Further, schools and their participants will be complicit in the loss.—*McCarty 2002, p. 190*

If we agree that Indigenous languages are worth saving, then what role does the school play? If schools were powerful enough to eradicate Native languages, is it "reasonable to expect they can play a powerful role in restoring languages?" (Peacock and Day 1999). Francis and Reyhner (2002) write that "the school represents one of the central institutions at the community level that can play such an active role since, potentially, educational and language policy can be subject to some degree of control by the community itself" (p. 13).

Although historically assimilative, schools, with community involvement, can function as effective agents of change. McCarty and Watahomigie (1998) declare that if language efforts are left to individuals and families alone, "the crisis of language loss will go unchecked" because the traditional contexts of language learning in the family have been vastly disrupted by "colonizing and linguicidal policies" (p. 5).[4] But school-based programs alone are not sufficient to reverse language shift, and they are not without their problems. McCarty (2003) draws attention to the criticism that school-based language programs have faced because they "transfer responsibility for mother-tongue transmission from its natural and necessary domain—the home and the family—to a secondary institution" (p. 28). While acknowledging the importance of community initiatives, McCarty (1998) asserts: "To dismiss schools as insignificant underrates the destructive effects on Indigenous languages of past schooling and of current educational practices that neglect those languages; ignores the singular social, economic, and political importance of schools in many American Indian communities; and tosses aside the enormous language-maintenance resources produced by school-based native-language programs" (p. 28).

How effective schools can be in language revitalization efforts depends on the school. The AFS is an extreme example of cultural continuity between home and school. Mohawk language, ceremonial protocols, and traditional values that are taught in the home are reinforced at school and vice versa. The AFS is an extension of the wider community and bridges the gap between home and school. Saving Indigenous languages takes the concerted and unified effort of young people, parents, and communities.

Language Learning in the Home and in the School

While Native language learning used to take place primarily in the home, Native nations are becoming increasingly dependent on schools to provide language instruction (Holm and Holm, 1995; Hornberger 1996; Kamanā and Wilson 1996; McCarty 2002; McCarty and Watahomigie 1998; Stairs, Peters, and Perkins 1999). Problems with school-based efforts in language revitalization occur when parents agree that their children should learn the language in the school but believe that the school is enough and leave it up to the institution. Schools alone have been consistently ineffective in language revitalization, and scholars advocate for the family and community as the primary routes for Indigenous language learning (Freeman, Stairs, Corbiere, and Lazore 1995). Krauss (1998, p. 19) adheres to this position: "School programs can do more harm than good, insofar as they shift the responsibility for transmitting the language in the home, where it is still possible, to the school." The position that children learn language in the home assumes, however, that the parents know the language well enough to teach their children and that they are willing to teach it to them. A bilingual educator sheds light on this dilemma as she tells Krauss, "No, we don't need linguists, what we need is psychiatrists" (p. 20). Inherent in this statement are the varied and complex language ideologies in Native communities that are rooted in centuries of colonization, including residential school experiences and colonial education systems that shut out Native languages. For some Native Americans, the shame they experienced associated with their language has continued to be a strong factor in their language ideology.

According to Fishman (1991), "reversing language shift" (RLS) cannot be accomplished if it is not accomplished at the intimate family and local community levels. RLS efforts should concentrate here while avoiding risky conflict with the "powers that be" until there is a strengthening of resources within the community. By focusing on them in the family and local community, RLS efforts can be successful, otherwise they risk being lost in "the process of ever expanding and prematurely competitive aspirations for political power and economic success" (p. 6). Fishman is not advocating that communities ignore or remain complacent in their quest for social justice, acknowledging that "language shift is a by-product of unequal rates of social change and of growth of econotechnical powers and therefore, of self-regulation" (p. 6). He sees RLS efforts comprising a foundation for dealing with "problems that are greater than the one that is first on its own agenda" (p. 7).

Hinton and Hale (2001) agree that language revitalization must occur in the broader community and in the home as well as in school.[5] For families of the AFS, oral proficiency in Kanienke:ha is influenced by whether or not the language are reinforced in the home. The AFS alone cannot produce fluent speakers of the language. The students from the AFS who come from Mohawk-speaking families are more likely to become fluent. If Kanienke:ha is not spoken in the home, AFS students are less likely to achieve fluency, even when in a full immersion program. Parents, however, should not be discouraged if their children do not quickly reach a level of oral fluency. They must make long-term commitments and understand that proficiency in speech and comprehension are difficult to achieve. Those students who begin using Kanienke:ha early, however, will have the language base that may enable them to eventually reach oral proficiency (Fortune and Tedick, 2003).

The goal at the AFS is for students to achieve oral fluency in Mohawk, but without constant use of the language in a variety of situations including the home, they may only reach a functional speaking level. Home and school are therefore each critical settings for reversing language shift.

Language Immersion

There are various types of language immersion programs, and the structuring of those programs is an important factor in achieving proficiency in the target language. Typical foreign language immersion programs teach in the target language for at least half of the school day. Partial immersion programs equally divide time between English and the target language, while full immersion programs do not use English at all until second, third, or fourth grade, when English is introduced for one period per day. In full immersion programs, there is an eventual balance between teaching in English and the immersion language (Fortune and Tedick (2003).

Skutnabb-Kangas (1984) draws distinctions between language immersion, which she calls a "language bath," and language submersion, which she calls "language drowning" (p. xiv). An example of language submersion occurred in government-sponsored residential schools for Native students where Native languages were forbidden and replaced with English as the dominant language. Assimilation was the goal in this "sink or swim" type of language learning (p. 139). During the residential school era, Native students were submersed in the English language and in European-American values. The goal for language submersion initiatives is monolingualism in the second language rather than bilingualism.

The goals of language immersion, however, are to provide educational experiences that "support academic and linguistic development in two languages and that develop students' appreciation of their own and other cultures" (Fortune and Tedick 2003). When immersion programs are carefully planned and teachers are properly trained, immersion schools can provide the language exposure needed to produce fluent speakers and provide situations that lend themselves to real communication. For students to learn their Native language, it must make sense to them. They must practice it throughout the day—increasing language proficiency and furthering efforts to decolonize Indigenous education is almost impossible to achieve through one-hour-per-week language classes (Krashen and Terrell, 1983). And they must use the language in meaningful ways (Genessee 1994; Hinton and Hale 2001). Reyhner (2010) states: "Just translating a non-Native curriculum into the Native language and focusing on vocabulary and grammar is in no way part of a decolonizing agenda" (p. 142). Immersion programs can therefore be vital in "healing the negative effects of colonialism and assimilationist schooling" (p. 137).

Hinton and Hale (2001) outline some key factors in successful immersion language teaching, including emphasis on oral rather than written learning; use of the target language without translation into English, repetition rather than repetitiveness; use of active physical lessons; and the use of praise and positive reinforcement.[6] Additionally, successful language immersion programs begin at a young age when children are developing linguistic and communication skills (Francis and Reyhner 2002; Dejong 1998).

Many attempts to teach a Native language have been ineffective because of poor teaching methodology, including a small range of vocabulary, too much time spent on explaining the language in English rather than actually using the language, too much emphasis on writing rather than speaking, and students' failure to learn to communicate in a way that is useful to them (Hinton and Hale 2001). However, in recent years, immersion has gained attention worldwide as one of the most effective methods in teaching a second language within certain contexts (Genessee 1994; Harrison 1998; Hinton and Hale 2001; Holm and Holm 1995; Kamanā and Wilson, 1996; Kipp 2000). Immersion has been effective with minority languages that have been threatened and marginalized by the dominant society.

"But What if My Child Falls Behind?"

> There's a fear of immersion. A fear of the unknown. The residential school experience affected our kids, our parents, our grandparents. They carried that mentality when they left that they weren't as good. Today a majority of people feel that kids need to learn English and get a Western education and follow New York State guidelines. They don't realize they can do both. They can learn these subjects in the language. They believe if they learn in the language, they'll be behind and won't be academically successful. But these kids are on the honor rolls and are showing there's nothing to be afraid of.
> —*Interviewee P3: July 12, 2005*

Research shows that students in immersion programs often perform better or as well academically as students in public mainstream settings (Barik and Swain, 1976; Genessee, 1994; Holm and Holm 1995; Slaughter 1997; Yamauchi 2003). Likewise, language instruction that is integrated with instruction in academics is more effective than teaching language alone (Genessee 1994). In Hawaii, children performed at least as well, and sometimes better, on standardized tests than their counterparts in non-culture-based and conventional public school settings (Kana'iaupuni and Ishibashi 2005). In cases where Navajo students entered school with their mother tongue, they performed significantly better academically when they received consistent and cumulative academic support in that language (Holm and Holm 1995; McCarty 2003).

Anglophone students in French immersion programs across Canada learned French without detriment to their academic skills. Students caught up quickly on standardized test scores, and no differences were found in "English test performance between immersion students and comparison groups whose instruction has been totally through English" (Cummins 1998). These sociolinguistic scenarios are quite different from Native communities where Native languages are threatened and marginalized. Anglophone students are mainly middle-class and are "relatively privileged majority language L2 speakers" who learn French as an enrichment program (May and Hill 2008, p. 69). Scholars refer to students' first language, their mother tongue, as "L1" and their second language as "L2." Although the language base at the AFS is mixed, most students are L1 speakers of English and L2 speakers of Mohawk. There are very few students whose first language is Mohawk. A closely related linguistic situation to AFS students is the example of Māori students. Māori students in L1 English and L2 Māori language programs performed significantly better in academic areas than their English-only counterparts (May and Hill 2008). The Māori programs operate at 81–100 percent language immersion, while the AFS has 100 percent immersion. Level-1 immersion programs are critical to successful bilingualism and school achievement (Genessee 2008; McCarty 2008). In summarizing the effectiveness of Indigenous immersion programs, Romero-Little and McCarty (2006) find that "time spent learning the Indigenous language is *not* time lost in developing English; over a period of several years, students in Indigenous-language immersion programs perform as well as or better than their peers in mainstream classes on academically rigorous tasks" (p. 24).

Parents should know that academic delay among immersion students is to be expected but is likely temporary (Fortune and Tedick 2003). As Cummins notes, there can be "academic and intellectual benefits for bilingual children" (Cummins 1998, p. 6), and Wilson and Kamanā give examples, writing that Hawaiian language immersion students have won several academic, artistic, and athletic awards, received prestigious college scholarships, and attended the local university (Wilson and Kamanā 2001). Similarly, AFS alumni have been on honor rolls and in national honor societies while in high school and in college. They have won academic awards, attend Ivy League colleges, and become teachers and tribal leaders. One alumna, Kawennehente Cook, daughter of Kaweienón:ni and Teddy Peters, attended the AFS, went on to the Salmon River Central School starting in ninth grade, and graduated in 2006. During high school she received academic awards and was on the honor roll and a member of the National Honor Society. Her proud mother explains: "She graduated with high honors, was in the top thirteen of her class, and she also won the Title VII Culture and Language Excellence Award" (personal communication, July 12, 2005). Kawennehente attended a language immersion school, had high academic success, and is fluent in Kanienke:ha. After high school graduation she returned to AFS as a teacher, a position she holds today alongside her two siblings. Although this case is not representative of all students who attend the AFS, it stands as an example of what AFS students are capable of achieving.

Immersion at the Akwesasne Freedom School

"*Nahoten iesaiats*?" (What's your name?), they all shouted when I walked into the pre-K classroom. I told the students my name and repeated my newly acquired phrase—"*Nahoten iesaiats*?"—to several of the students. They were all very eager to tell me their names and teach me the names of trees and animals and other things pictured in their drawings. I was very conscious to not use English and uttered the few words and phrases I knew in Kanienke:ha. While I quietly observed these children I had the distinct feeling that I was in a special space, where English was left behind and Kanienke:ha was as alive and vibrant as it might have been hundreds of years ago. Listening to and watching these young children was a very personal and emotional experience. One can go to Germany to hear German and Italy to hear Italian, but few Native people have a geographic space where their ancestral language is dominant. Kanienke:ha is primarily an oral language, and there are few places where one can be surrounded by it and immersed in it. The AFS provides this space for hearing, using, and gaining proficiency in the Mohawk language.

Kanienke:ha is heard almost everywhere at the AFS. Literacy is conveyed through Mohawk books, postings of the eleven-letter Mohawk alphabet, and various pictures of animals and plants captioned with their Mohawk names. Upon my first visit to a second-grade classroom I was astonished to hear the sound of the language being spoken by such young children. I had heard my own teachers speak to each other in Kanienke:ha and had heard it spoken in homes like that of the Peters family, but this was different. I rarely heard English used in the classroom. When students would occasionally slip into English they were quickly corrected by fellow students in Kanienke:ha. During one classroom observation, a friendly little girl came over to me and whispered in my ear, "See that boy over there? Well, he's smelly!" I suppose she recognized my limited Mohawk language ability but her whispering also indicated her consciousness of the necessity of staying in the Mohawk language while in this immersion setting.

I observed similar language use in a sixth-grade classroom when students

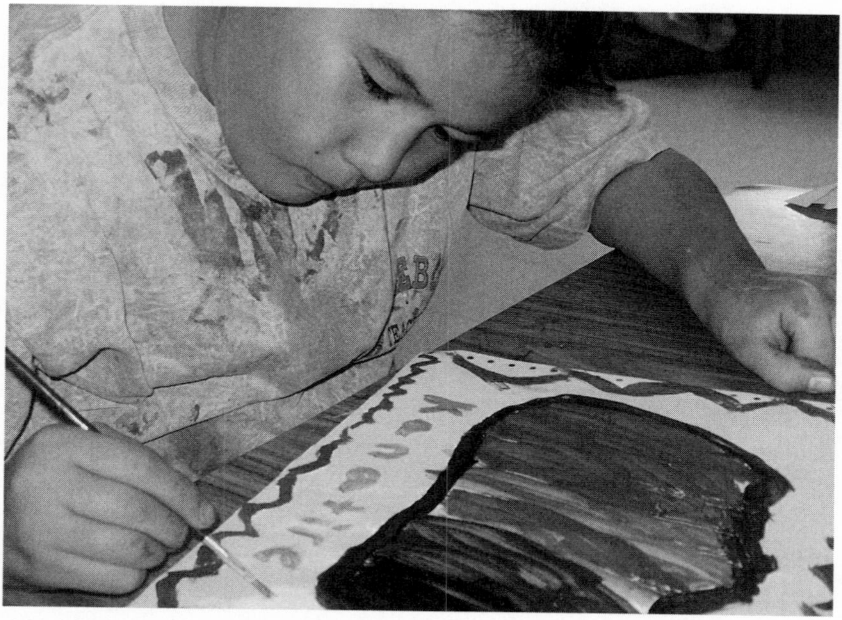

FIGURE 18. Second-grade student Kanatires. Photo by L. White, 2004.

took turns reading Mohawk stories aloud. When a student stumbled over a Kanienke:ha word, others quickly helped out by quietly saying the word. Occasionally students in these classrooms would slip into English, but they quickly reverted back to Kanienke:ha on their own or when another student or the teacher spoke back to them in the Mohawk language. Teachers almost always spoke to each other in Kanienke:ha, even when students were not around. After all, for most of them, it is their first language.

Parents and teachers for whom Kanienke:ha is their first language are likely the last generation to learn the oral language naturally in the home. Some AFS teachers however, had to gain literacy skills while working at the school. When Kaweienón:ni Cook-Peters began teaching at the AFS, she could not read or write in Kanienke:ha. Somewhat embarrassed and insecure, at first she pretended she could read, following along in the book the students were reading. She called on the students to read to get through each lesson. To her surprise, after two weeks, she began to learning to read: "The kids were teaching me and I didn't even realize it" (personal communication, October 8, 2004).

Dauenhauer and Dauenhauer (1998) note some interesting differences between literacy and speech. They state, "It is understandable that beginning teachers with limited training may feel insecure with literacy, but the problem is that rather than use genuinely oral methods of instruction, they almost always end up spelling" (p. 90). Dauenhauer and Dauenhauer also note technical problems with the Tlingit language in that many sounds have no equivalent English letters: "For learners, the problem is twofold: to learn to hear and pronounce the differences, and to learn to read and spell the differences. For the older generations that already speak Tlingit, literacy is not very important; for them the language survived without writing since time immemorial" (p. 90).

The students at the AFS are exposed to Kanienke:ha throughout the school day, English is rarely heard or seen, and students learn academics through the Mohawk language. They are not merely learning Mohawk words and phrases through repetition and rote memory. They are actively using the language to gain speaking proficiency and learning literacy skills only in Kanienke:ha. At the same time, they are learning their own history and culture as well as academic subjects such as math and writing. An alumna states: "The only place that taught me the language was the Freedom School" (Interviewee A12: July 14, 2005). While a student at the AFS, she brought her language lessons home and taught what she was learning to her mother. Now she has her own children at the school, and they continue the tradition of carrying language lessons back into the home.

Community Language Initiatives

Akwesasne has made other efforts in language renewal, including summer weekly language classes for adults at a local campground; language lessons through CKON, a local radio station; singing societies; and advanced Kanienke:ha classes at Salmon River Central High School. The Akwesasne Mohawk Board of Education also produces language materials for use in its schools. Kaweienón:ni Cook-Peters develops the material and shares language books, CD-ROMs, music, and other language-teaching material with the AFS and other Mohawk communities.

In 2003 the AFS implemented a three-year language-teacher-training program to build adult Kanienke:ha fluency and literacy. The program also covered teaching methodology, immersion training in specialized areas such as math and science, and the incorporation of cultural foundations in the classroom. Finally, a practicum component allowed trainees to rotate among AFS classrooms. The project was funded by the Administration for Native Americans and the Akwesasne Area Management Board. Of the twelve graduates, four went on to work as AFS teachers, one went to work at the St. Regis Mohawk School, and another went to the Salmon River High School (Sargent, personal communication, August 21, 2012).

An exciting Mohawk language nest program was added to the school in 2014. Approximately nine children ages eighteen months to three years are immersed in the language and culture throughout their day, aided by three teachers and an elder serving as tota (grandparent). Like the rest of the school, the language nest follows a holistic cultural model as well as drawing from the Waldorf education model, which allows for learning to be meaningful and purposeful.[7] The children are given the freedom to use their imaginations and are allowed to naturally progress at their own pace. A double-wide trailer was added to the property to provide adequate space for napping and playing. The curriculum is hands-on, and in the facilities' homelike setting the children learn singing and dancing as well as skills like cooking and cleaning (Kanerahtens Tara Skidders, personal communication, January 21, 2015).

Despite the community's and the school's conscious efforts to produce speakers of Kanienke:ha, the language is not out of danger of disappearing. There is concern that traditional ceremonies may one day have to be conducted in English because there are not enough Mohawk language speakers with the knowledge needed to carry out them out. The AFS provides hope that Mohawk language and culture will survive for the next seven generations.

Finding Our Talk

During the Indian residential school era, Native students were forced to speak English and suffered severe punishment if they spoke their Native language. During this period of aggressive assimilation policy in the United States and Canada, the colonialist agenda was overt. English-only schools threatened to extinguish students' language and in many cases accomplished their goal. Overall, however, authorities failed to achieve 100 percent English-only speakers among Native students, due to the resistance of Native students and their families (Adams 1995; Johnston 1989; Lomawaima 1995, 1999; Lomawaima and McCarty 2002, 2006; Standing Bear 1988). The US government underestimated the "life-sustaining strength of linguistic and tribal identity" (Spack 2002, p. 42).

Currently tribes are choosing to use immersion techniques to reverse generations of linguistic loss. Spack states (2002, p. 7) that "because language can be used to justify or resist oppression . . . it is a site of struggle over power, meaning, and representation." Tribal education departments are attempting to regain some of this power, but because of English-only educational regulations, immersion schools are uncommon (Hinton and Hale 2001). However, immersion strategies for teaching Indigenous languages are the most effective way to obtain fluent speakers and ensure that these languages remain for future generations. "Given the gravity of the current state of language loss, anything less than full immersion is likely to be too little, too late" (McCarty 2003).

Akwesasne Freedom School students, teachers, and parents have varied and complex Mohawk language speaking and literacy abilities. Not everyone becomes fluent at the AFS. Language ideologies, attitudes, and reasons for not speaking or transmitting the language are equally complex. Contradictory behaviors and negative attitudes toward language learning and use reflect a history of cultural genocide that has left the Mohawk people confused on many levels regarding their "talk." AFS Students have to navigate between a world of being immersed in Mohawk culture, showered with Mohawk words, phrases, and songs, and trying to make meaning of their experiences in Kanienke:ha, while at the same time being bombarded with English from television, newspapers, radio, the Internet, and other media throughout their daily lives. One has to wonder if it is worth the effort to combat such powerful forces that have succeeded in eradicating ancestral languages and ways of life in a multitude of Native communities. However, the people at the AFS have a tenacious spirit and are not ready to give up. As they move back and forth between these opposing forces, they forge new ground and create an even stronger foundation.

FIVE

Language and Identity

"What Kind of Indian Are You if You Don't Speak Mohawk?"

> I always had my language, but I didn't know where we came from as Haudenosaunee. I didn't know my culture, my background, or who I was. It wasn't until I learned about it that my language meant something to me.
>
> —*Interviewee P3, July 12, 2005*

"What kind of Indian are you if you don't even speak Mohawk?" the elderly gentleman asked my father. My father, Louis J. White, was living at Iakhisohtha (The Grandparents), an Akwesasne nursing home where the majority of the residents grew up speaking the Mohawk language. After suffering a severe stroke, my father was spending the winter of 2005–2006 at the home. "It's their place, their language, their home, and I don't belong here," my father later said to me. Suddenly he felt like a man without a home. A resident had virtually told my father he wasn't Indian because he didn't speak or understand the Mohawk language. My father's sense of belonging was deeply affected by his lack of competence in the language of his ancestors. I naively hoped that he would permanently move from his home in Ilion, New York, and make Akwesasne his home again, that he would return to his roots and live the rest of his life among his people. But I was wrong. Already confused from his stroke, at age eighty-four he was still negotiating a search for belonging that had spanned his lifetime.

My father grew up in Ilion, a small town in central New York, in the traditional homelands of his ancestors, the Mohawk Valley. He spent most of his childhood summers on his grandfather's farm in Akwesasne and grew up with a limited knowledge of the Mohawk language. His father had attended Carlisle Indian Industrial School and rarely spoke Mohawk as an adult. His mother had attended a convent school in Quebec as a child and spoke French and Mohawk but had not passed the Mohawk language on to her children. My grandparents married in Akwesasne and then moved to the Mohawk Valley, where my grandfather found a job at the Remington Arms factory in Ilion. There they raised their children, although they visited Akwesasne frequently.

My father sometimes spoke his own version of the Mohawk language. He knew the basic greetings and a few phrases and would also make up his own words, especially when giving out "Indian names" to kids in his neighborhood. With his wry sense of humor he gave them "Mohawk" names like Ó'ta and Soniskatsia. Of course he never told them that "ó'ta" is an actual Mohawk word meaning "feces" and "soniskatsia" was his made-up word meaning "to defecate." They never knew what meaning he attached to them, and each went about their merry way quite proud to have his or her new "Indian name" given by the only Indian in town, "Chief Louie."

When I began taking Mohawk language classes as an adult, my father, in his eighties at the time, also took an interest in learning more of the language. I shared the language materials I received, gave him a Mohawk dictionary, and taught him some of what I was learning. Together we began using Mohawk words and phrases on a regular basis, always remembering every time we parted ways to say *konnonronhkhwa* (I love you). Many times while he was recovering from his stroke my father uttered words and phrases in Kanienke:ha that I had never heard him say before. It was as if the stroke had reactivated the part of his brain that held long-lost memories and caused linguistic knowledge to surface. It is possible that he was remembering pieces of his childhood, when he had heard Kanienke:ha spoken by his parents and grandparents and other family. Having some knowledge of the Mohawk language connected my father to his identity as a member of a distinct group of people. The language authenticated that claim for him as an identity marker because the Mohawk language is a symbol of solidarity among the Mohawk people (Mar-Molinero 2000, p. 185). Gaining this "sense of belonging" is a lifelong developmental process for many Mohawks, including my father and myself.

As I talked with members of the Akwesasne Freedom School community about language use, language status, immersion, and revitalization, two of my worlds began to converge: my professional academic life and my personal family life. Here I was—as an academic researcher—trying to understand something that also affected me personally. I began to ask myself some of the same questions I was asking others regarding the Mohawk language and cultural identity. Speaking Kanienke:ha connects us to Sonkwaiatison (the Creator), but if I cannot pray in my language, how can I speak to my ancestors or to the Creator? Can I be Mohawk without my language? I am one-half Mohawk according to my blood quantum, and although I'm fully cognizant of the issues surrounding the colonial imposition of measuring Indians by their blood, I still internalized this colonial mentality and questioned whether I was really less than half because I am not proficient in the Mohawk language.

During an interview one precocious eighth-grader asked me, "Do you know Mohawk? Do you consider yourself Mohawk?" There are different types of Mohawk people and ways of being Mohawk. Some live on their reserves, know the language fluently, follow traditional ceremonies, sing traditional songs, and are knowledgeable about traditional teachings. There are also Mohawk people who live within their community but who don't know their language, though they participate in traditional practices. There are some who know the language but follow Christian beliefs and practices. Others don't speak Mohawk but can understand it when others speak it. Are they still Mohawk? Some live in their community and do not speak the language and do not follow the ways of the Longhouse religion but still identify as Mohawk. Still other Mohawks live away from their community and may or may not speak the language yet still identify as Mohawk. At the time, I did not know how to answer this student's question. After writing this book, spending time at Akwesasne with my family, and doing a lot of reflecting, I would now answer, "Yes, I am Mohawk. But I may not yet be fully Mohawk."

While language certainly plays an important role in identity, it is never as simple as "You know your language, so you are Mohawk," or the more sinister "If you don't know your language, then you are not Mohawk." There are far too many other factors that comprise identity besides language. Attitudes toward language and identity vary between nations, communities, families, and individuals. For the Inuit of Nunavut, language alone is not essential to identity. What is important is the *power* that language holds as an agent and a symbol of identity (Dorais 1995). For the Inuit, Inuktitut (the Inuit language) is important to identity because it is a *tool* for maintaining identity. Inuktitut is used as a marker of identity and for building relationships and social networks. Inuktitut is one component of identity among many other aspects of Inuit culture, including hunting and survival on the land. Tulloch (1999) warns that there are negative consequences of adhering to the position that language is essential to identity, that "if you lose your language, then you lose your identity" (p. 7). When Tulloch questioned Inuit informants she discovered a more "qualified and pragmatic relationship between language and identity" (ibid.). She explains: "The importance of Inuktitut to Inuit identity is perhaps not found so much in the language itself . . . but rather in the role that Inuktitut plays in society. The loss of Inuktitut may not categorically lead to the loss of Inuit identity, but it does represent the loss of an important element of identity in and of itself, as well as the loss of the mainstay to other elements of Inuit identity" (p. 8). The loss of Inuktitut then is the loss of a tool for maintaining other aspects of Inuit identity.

Who Is a Mohawk?

Defining who is an Indian is a complex task, and there are numerous definitions (Garroutte 2003; Snipp 1989). Within the Akwesasne territory encompassed by the United States, the St. Regis Tribal Council determines eligibility for tribal membership based on blood quantum. The federal government originally mandated membership by blood quantum to keep track of Indian people, but today individual tribes determine their own membership rules and depend on their membership rolls to allocate services such as health care, housing, landholdings, and education. Membership in the St. Regis Tribe entitles Mohawks to receive these kinds of benefits and to vote in tribal elections. Where Akwesasne territory overlaps into Canada, the Mohawk Council of Akwesasne (MCA) determines membership based on mandates following the passage of Bill C-31 in 1985. This amendment to the Indian Act of 1876 restored status to members who lost it under previous legislation (Innes 2007; Venne 1981) and allowed the MCA to determine its own membership. The MCA states: "There is a distinct difference between Membership and Indian Registration in Akwesasne. The Community in accordance with the Akwesasne Membership Code determines membership. Indian Status is still determined by the Federal Government of Canada in accordance with the Indian Act" (http://www.akwesasne.ca/membership).

For the MCA, membership is based on commitment to Mohawk culture and traditions, knowledge of language and customs, family ties, clan membership, birth in the community, and degree of involvement in community affairs, as well as blood quantum. Benefits include residency privileges, land ownership, housing assistance, voting rights, education, and social assistance (Ciborski 1990).

Aboriginal Affairs and Northern Development Canada (AANDC), a Canadian federal agency, also maintains a register of those who have Indian status.[1] The Indian Act of 1876 determined the qualifications, which defined someone as an Indian under Canadian federal authority based on blood quantum and prior federal rolls. Before the amendment in 1985 with Bill C-31, Indian women lost status when marrying a non-status Indian (Fiske 1995). Today those persons can have their status restored through application to AANDC (Innes 2007).

Equating cultural authenticity with a measure of blood, however, is hardly an accurate way to determine one's identity. The Mohawk Nation Council of Chiefs, the traditional council that does not align itself with either the Canadian or the US government, recognizes membership through matrilineal descent. The Haudenosaunee, like many other Indigenous groups, used to practice adoption as a method for ensuring the survival of the population. In their "mourning wars," the Haudenosaunee sought captives from other tribes and even newly arrived Europeans to replace their members who had died during battle. This practice not only renewed population and ensured social continuity, it provided a means to deal with death, according to historian Daniel Richter (1983). When it came to Haudenosaunee identity, ethnic background was of little if any importance. Often today, however, authentication of Indian identity means being federally registered as an Indian and thus holding a US Certificate of Degree of Indian Blood. Because of the complexities created by an international border, created by the Treaty of Paris in 1783 (Fenton and Tooker 1978; Frisch 1970), Akwesasne residents can obtain dual US and Canadian citizenship and can carry four identification cards issued by the St. Regis Tribal Council, the Mohawk Council of Akwesasne, the Mohawk Nation Council of Chiefs, and Aboriginal Affairs and Northern Development (C. Lazore 2006).

The politics of identity can create divisions within communities and tribal nations and cause inner turmoil for those seeking to belong. Mi'kmaq scholar Palmater (2011) discusses the legal challenges in regard to determining "individual and communal Indigenous identity and belonging." Grande (2004) finds that identity politics obscures the real sources of oppression, "colonialism and global capitalism," while undermining tribal sovereignty and self-determination (p. 92). She also says that dominant modes of educational theory, including critical pedagogy, have "failed to construct models of identity that effectively interrogate and disrupt the project of colonialism" (p. 95). Grande calls for an indigenous theory of identity that is emancipatory, grounded in struggles for self-determination, centered in issues of sovereignty, and spiritually guided.

Ethnic Identity Development

As psychology professor David Moshman writes, "Identity is constructed; it is a creation constrained but not determined by a complex interaction of inner and outer realities" (Moshman 1999, p. 96). He defines ethnic identity as a construction that is part of the general process of "identity formation" (p. 94). Phinney (1996) develops this notion further in describing ethnic identity as "an enduring fundamental aspect of the self that includes a sense of membership in an ethnic group and the attitudes and feelings associated with that membership" (p. 922). Ethnicity can be determined by self-categorization, descent, specific cultural traits, and social organization (Skutnabb-Kangas 1990).

Identity is also fluid, dynamic, always evolving and changing throughout one's life (Phinney 1996; Toohey 2000), and it is dependent upon social relations (Vygotsky 1986; Wertsch 1991). A strong foundation in one's cultural identity is essential to a sense of well-being, feelings of belonging, and self-acceptance. Phinney (1989), who developed a measure of ethnic identity among minorities, calls the final stage of ethnic identity development "Ethnic identity achieved." In this stage subjects explore their identities and commit to their particular ethnic group. Phinney found high scores on ego identity and psychological adjustment to be associated with positive identity development. Later studies find an association between ethnic identity achievement and higher levels of self-esteem (Phinney and Alipuria 1996). Furthermore, security in one's ethnicity leads to better overall adjustment. Conversely, "those who fail to achieve a secure identity are faced with identity confusion, a lack of clarity about who they are and what their role is in life" (Phinney 1993, p. 62).

Exposed to both "mainstream" culture and that of their own ethnic minority group, adolescents integrate their "ethnic identity into a self-identity" (Phinney and Rosenthal 1992, p. 145). It then becomes understood that "if minority youth are to construct a strong, positive stable self-identity, then they must be able to incorporate into that sense of self, a positively valued ethnic identity" (p. 145). Phinney (1996) further states: "For ethnic minorities of color, identity formation has to do with developing an understanding and acceptance of one's own group in the face of lower status and prestige in society and the presence of stereotypes and racism" (p. 144).

Most young Indigenous people in North America are situated within a dominant English-speaking Western culture and face unrelenting pressures to assume identities other than those of their own ethnic group. They face temptations and also must be armed to react to discrimination and racism. For many the pressures are too great. They are not equipped to deal with such forces. Studies show, however, that adolescents with high ethnic identity and self-esteem are equipped with more strategies to dealing with discrimination and stereotypes than those with low ethnic identity (Chavira and Phinney 1991).

In William Cross's examination of stages of racial and identity development in African Americans (1991), he identifies the encounter stage as one in which the individual begins understanding what it is like to be part of a racially targeted minority group. The students at the AFS are equipped to deal with discrimination and racism. I have not met a more confident student than the one who stated: "I have a grip on where I come from . . . [but] see other students who don't know. People ask me 'Do Indians still live in teepees?' I can explain and I don't get offended. I just try and make sure they understand. It's important that I know who I am" (Interviewee A1: October 18, 2004). The AFS has prepared its students to cope with such outside forces. Developing a Mohawk identity becomes, in part, a reaction to them.

The Role of the Home and School in Identity Development

> Right now are their formative years. They're going to learn who they are.
> —*Interviewee A12: July 14, 2005*

At the Akwesasne Freedom School, a sense of Mohawk identity is cultivated through language learning; participation in ceremonies, songs, and dances; kinship ties; knowledge of Haudenosaunee history; and transmission of Haudenosaunee beliefs and values via in-depth understanding of the Creation Story, the Great Law of Peace, the Ohenton Kariwahtekwen, and the Code of Handsome Lake. As a result of these traditional teachings, students develop ethnic pride and self-confidence. Little research has examined the topic, but it has been found that "one very important dimension affecting ethnic identity development in Native Americans, and presumably other ethnic minorities, may be school context" (Lysne and Levy 1997, p. 384). After all, during their developmental years children spend a great deal of time away from home in the care of others, studying academic subjects but also exploring where they fit in the world. Lysne and Levy found that "Native American adolescents from the high school with a predominantly Native American student body demonstrated significantly greater ethnic identity exploration and commitment than Native American adolescents from the high school with a predominantly White student body" (p. 381).

Although AFS students spend a great deal of time at school where this identity exploration and development occur, what is learned in the home is as important. One alumna describes how what she learned at home was solidified when it was congruent with what she had been taught at school:

> It gave me a sense of who I was, and that was instilled in me, not just [by] the AFS but my grandfather too. What was taught at home was taught at school. It was cemented in me. At Massena [a high school located outside of Akwesasne] it was a little different. How to look at creation—there was nothing like that, nobody that thought like that. Be aware of your creation and be appreciative of that. I would see roadkill and feel bad. . . . As a mother I'm proud to say I went to AFS and to have that to share with my son and daughter. I remember there's something instilled inside of me. Part of my identity, I think. (Interviewee A6: October 13, 2004)

Feeling and Thinking Mohawk

Ethnic identity development, whether at home or at school, has affective and cognitive aspects. When AFS students say that they "feel" Mohawk or say "it's just a feeling you have," they are integrating the group identity of being Mohawk with their self-identity. Those feelings are an important aspect of identity exploration. As psychologist Denise Newman writes, "Affirmation and belonging, a sense that one is part of a group or feels like part of a group is an affectively charged measure of ethnic identity" (Newman 2005, p. 740). But on the other hand, Newman says, "Ethnic identity achievement has a more cognitive content because it involves items that describe thinking, considering, or even inquiring about what it means to be of a particular ethnic group" (p. 740). Similarly, an AFS parent reflects on her identity: "Somehow I'm between worlds. When I had my child I quit going to church. I felt better not going. I didn't want my child to be confused. I don't go to the Longhouse regularly. I'm still not comfortable because I was brought up not going. I think people wonder, 'Who is she? Who's her family?' I feel like an outsider. Identity is partly formed by who your family is." (Interviewee P7: October 7, 2004).

Constantly negotiating between mainstream culture and traditional Longhouse teachings is a process of ethnic identity development, and while there is the potential for identity confusion, there is also the opportunity for growth. As scholar Kelli Zaytoun writes, "Living between and among identities can keep one intensely aware and constantly in mental motion, making transitions back and forth between old and new ways of thinking. Such experiences promote the development of complex capacities for learning" (Zaytoun 2005, p. 13).

Speaking a language is one identifier to others and perhaps makes one feel more accepted by others, thereby strengthening ethnic identity. For Puerto Rican students, "The more fluent they became [in Spanish], the more Puerto Rican they felt" (Zavala 2000, p. 132). Sheila Nicholas writes that Hopi youths realized that language was essential to "feeling and becoming 'fully' Hopi" and to attaining "emotional and psychological well-being as a fully contributing member of Hopi society as well as personal spiritual fulfillment" (Nicholas 2008, p. 361).

Ethnolinguistic theorists Giles and Johnson (1987) state: "Individuals make themselves distinct using language to adhere to an ethnic group identity" (p. 142). Many AFS alumni attending high school discussed their use of the Mohawk language as "code" among themselves. This "speech divergence" (p. 142) was a useful mechanism in identifying as Mohawk, not just in not letting anyone outside the group know what was being said.

Theories of ethnic identity development in minorities help explain the general process of identifying with a cultural group and developing one's self-identity. The process for individual Mohawk identity development includes important cultural markers of Mohawk language, kinship, cultural norms, and traditional Mohawk naming practices.

Mohawk Names as Markers of Identity

> Names are profoundly linked to identity and to private as well as public declarations of self-purpose; they have considerable affective power and, however unacknowledged in daily usage, a magical role as well, the power to change people's lives.—*Kaplan and Bernays 1997, p. 22*

Most of AFS students have Mohawk first names. Traditionally, clan mothers give Mohawk names through Longhouse ceremonies. However, the traditional protocol is not always followed. Some families ask an aunt or grandmother to provide a name and have their own private family naming ceremonies. According to the Great Law of Peace, no two living people are supposed to have the same name. Either way, Mohawk names are descriptive and contribute to identity development and a sense of belonging. In Hopi practice, naming is a part of the everyday social life of being Hopi, thereby contributing to one's identity as a member of Hopi society (Nicholas 2009). Mohawk names are often tied to natural processes. For example, Kahe'ntawaks means "She sways with the grass" and Tehawerakwatsia means "He picks up the wind" (Hoffman 2001). Students hold firmly to the belief that their names are special as markers of their identity. Aronhiaies, an AFS alumnus, recalls his frustrations when people refuse to learn his name:

> Someone will ask me my name and I'll say "Aronhiaies." And then they'll say, "Don't you have another name, a shorter name, a nickname?" I say no. Later on when I see them again, they'll say, "Hey *you*. How are you doing?" It kind of defeats the whole purpose of my name and it's kind of an insult to me. That's my name, and it's very important to me. I think the only thing it needs is effort. A little bit of effort. Look at the English language. There's people that live in Japan [and speak] Japanese, but they can speak a little bit of English. Every day I . . . say, why can't we speak a little bit of Mohawk? Everybody speaks English. . . . It's a big struggle to keep the language.

When I asked Arionhiaies what his name meant, he replied: "He strikes the sky with light—I was born on the Fourth of July" (personal communication, July 15, 2005).

FIGURE 19. AFS students perform at annual fund-raiser. *Left to right*: Wahsohkwiio Graffis, Kahentenhawe Francis, Tahentishon Francis, Shatekaronhioton Fox, Ioherase Ransom, Tosakiateni McDonald, Kahontaronkwas Herne. Photo by Ceely King, 2003.

Language as Culture

According to Teresa McCarty (1998a), "There is tremendous human impoverishment when a language, with all its collective wisdom, beauty, and richness, falls silent. Then, there is the forfeiting of a community's birthright, the medium through which it constructs and reconstructs its identity" (p. 2). Jon Reyhner goes further, saying that when there is a loss of language, there is a destruction of the self (Reyhner 1999). This loss stems from the connection between language and culture, and when language is lost, culture is also lost. Culture is expressed through language. When you take away its "greetings, its curses, its praises, its laws, its literature, its songs, its riddles, its proverbs, its cures, its wisdom, its prayers . . . you are losing all those things that essentially are the way of life, the way of thought, the way of valuing, and the human reality that you are talking about" (Fishman 1996, p. 81).

Language also expresses one's spirituality and allows for communication with the Creator, medicines, plants, and the spirit world. Identity as an Indigenous person is confirmed when the spirits hear you speaking to them in your language. Tom Porter writes,

> My grandmother and different elders told us that if you're born a Mohawk, then whenever you pick tobacco up or you're gonna offer a ceremony, you should talk Mohawk. If you're Seneca then you should talk Seneca, when you talk to the Creator. If you're an Ojibway, then you talk Ojibway to the Creator. If you are a Lakota, then you talk your language, or a Cheyenne, then you talk Cheyenne to the Creator. Because that's the one that the Creator made you to be, when the world was new. And he gave you that special Seneca language or that special Ojibwa language. He gave it to you as a present, so that you would be proud to use it. And when you talk to him, he says, "I wanna hear the one I gave you." He doesn't want us to use another one. So that's the way our grandmother told us and the elders told us. And so I try to do that all the time. (Porter 2008, p. 152)

N. Scott Momaday (1969) says that even though "the Kiowa language is hard to understand . . . the storm spirit understands it. . . . Kiowa were not afraid of *Man-ka-ih,* for it understands their language" (p. 48). Similarly, one Mohawk parent states that language "connects you with the land, the environment, the space, creation. . . . And it connects you with the names, it connects you with the people of the past, it connects you with places. It's the cultural code. It's the link to everything in the culture" (Interviewee P6: July 20, 2005).

As a link to the culture, language shapes one's view of the world.

Language as Worldview

> When you can navigate in a language and understand the language, you know that the language itself encapsulates whole worldviews of who we are and why we are. It gives you a better understanding of why we need to be so connected to Iethinistenha Onhwéntsia, Mother Earth, and to our home environment and family, and to be aware of how essential that is to our constant survival.—*Interviewee P4: July 15, 2005*

Mohawk language and worldview contain nuances and meanings that are distinct from other languages and worldviews. Language shapes how we see and understand the world around us, therefore affecting our concept of self. According to the Sapir-Whorf hypothesis, "the way we respond to the world corresponds to the way our language categorizes it" (Pyles and Algeo 1993, p. 22). As a young boy, Simon Ortiz (2006) recalls, he asked his grandmother to speak to him in Acoma, "So I could feel Acoma." He feels that one's Native language is needed to be whole, to feel whole, to think, and express oneself. When English is used, it becomes a part of one's worldview. "When our language ceases to exist, our worldview is gone, and therefore, we cease to exist." Ortiz feels that to deny his language and speak only English is to be "split in half": "Only when we can feel, think, and express ourselves in our Indigenous language, can we truly be whole." He adds that the three things that make us Indigenous people are our land, our culture, and our community. The land, he feels, is a part of us. Our culture encompasses our beliefs and behavior and is the philosophical system that makes up our identity. Finally, our community consists of our clans and families, and we cannot exist as Indigenous people without them: "I am not Acoma unless I [am] a part of a community of people called Acoma."

"Lost in Translation"

As a cultural marker or code, the Mohawk language encapsulates Mohawk spirituality in its deeply expressive and highly descriptive syntax. Like many Indigenous languages, Mohawk is polysynthetic. One Mohawk word can be as long as an entire sentence in English—for example, *sahatsyahserunyahna* (He went back to prepare the fish) (M. C. Baker 1996). Linguist Marianne Mithun (1999) provides detailed examples of Mohawk word structure. "*Wa'tionkwatonhontsahrihten,*" when broken down into linguistic segments, translates as "they/me-own-earth-broken-cause-for" or "they caused my earth to be broken up for me." A free translation would be "they plowed my garden" (p. 11). Another linguist, M. C. Baker (1996), asserts, "It is obvious that much more can be expressed within the Mohawk verb than within the English verb" (p. 11). The Mohawk language is filled with cultural nuances too, and translation from Mohawk to English is complex and can be painstaking. Mohawk scholar Christopher Jocks (1998) relays a Native language speaker's frustration when trying to translate a traditional ceremonial event in English:

> He began to grope for words as he tried to explain important implications of the coming evening to the teenage woman-to-be. There were extended

> pauses. Frequently the singer lapsed into his own language, then abruptly he stopped, clearly frustrated with the attempt. I remember him staring for a moment into the trees or sky, a look of unmistakable pain in his face. "I can't do it," he said. "I can't say it right in English." I could only guess at the mental work he had been engaged in, crossing back and forth between very different conceptual worlds. He was drained and distraught; there would be much the young woman would have to do without.[2] (p. 219)

Translation may be possible, but when the language carries so much of the culture, much can be lost. Jocks writes, "Perhaps the perfect translation could be achieved between two languages. . . . In real life, however, in a kind of conceptual entropy, something significant always seems to be 'lost in the translation'" (Jocks 1998, p. 231). When relying on English versions of ceremonial practices, those practices become "rote and formalistic," Jocks says, and "it becomes easy for us to adopt and incorporate alien images and understandings of ourselves, without knowing it" (p. 219). The traditional teachings—the Ohenton Kariwahtekwen or the Kaianerekowa, for example—entail a complex interplay between "cosmology, metaphysics, and ethics," that may not survive translation, "especially when the original and target languages embody such significant conceptual differences as between, say, English and Mohawk" (Jocks 1998, p. 228). A Mohawk elder shares his concerns regarding the translation of the Ohenton Kariwahtekwen:

> There's some difficult parts in there that I've never heard . . . translated adequately. At the end of each thought . . . there's a word [or] sentence in Mohawk that is almost impossible to translate to English. Something like "our minds will continue to be thankful" [or] "we put our minds together and now continue to be thankful"—that's close. "Our minds will continue to be so." Some will say, "Now our minds are together." It's difficult to get the entire meaning in English. (Interviewee T2: July 19, 2005)

While translation into English may be possible, "a language long associated with the culture is best able to express most easily, most exactly, most richly, with more appropriate overtones, the concerns, artifacts, values, and interests of that culture," linguist Joshua Fishman writes (1996, p. 81).

Jocks (1998) ultimately feels that Native culture can be expressed in English, to some degree. After all, traditional ceremonies are sometimes in the English language. "Language is not the only carrier of culture," he writes. "One need not speak a traditional language in order to engage in traditional dance or traditional social exchanges or other non-verbal expressions of culture. For another thing, in places where a sizable number of English-speaking people are nonetheless determined to forge some kind of traditional identity, a body of traditional discourse in *English* can arise that is related—though not identical—to discourse in the original, traditional language" (p. 230).

Dauenhauer and Dauenhauer (1998) disagree with Fishman's (1996) notion that "culture could not be expressed and handled in any other way" (p. 81) than the heritage language. They note that there are Tlingits who speak only English and have succeeded in contemporary European-American economic life. Dauenhauer and Dauenhauer write, "Like other Tlingits, they identify with certain selected elements of culture as 'badges of ethnicity', and do not identify with other components of the culture (such as language)" (p. 75). They find many Tlingits who speak only English but participate in traditional Tlingit culture, including subsistence activities, and they write, "All of this demonstrates that language and 'culture' are in fact to some extent separable, and that English and Tlingit language use are two of many cultural components that interact in very complex patterns. It also reminds us that culture is not absolute but is dynamic and constantly renegotiated" (p. 76). Dauenhauer and Dauenhauer believe that "it is wrong, unrealistic and mentally unhealthy to insist or expect that all Native American persons speak and appreciate the ancestral language. . . . Just as no one should feel guilty for speaking Tlingit, no one should feel guilty for not speaking it" (ibid.). These points are often overlooked regarding expectations surrounding Native language speech ability and ideology.

One difficulty that many students face in terms of learning the Mohawk language is how much it differs from any other language. An AFS parent expressed the challenges of learning a language that is based on a completely different worldview and set of constructs than English (L1). "For many who want to learn Mohawk, this is a leap that is too far too breach. Learning a second European language like Spanish or German might be much easier since it is related to L1" (Herne, personal communication, October 25, 2009). Many parents have expressed a desire for more day-care provision by Mohawk language speakers so their children could learn the language during their early years of language formation.

Do You Have to Know the Language to Be Mohawk?

> Language is important but not the only thing. We have to know *why* we do things.—*Interviewee A1: October 18, 2004*

Native languages are rapidly declining, and desperate measures are needed to reverse this process, but just how language is connected to identity is complex and worth exploring further. So I return to the question that started this chapter: "What kind of Indian are you if you don't speak Mohawk?" And "Do you have to know your language to be Indigenous?" These are not easy questions and they have no simple, straightforward answers. What do we say to Native people who are struggling with their efforts to learn their language but are not fluent, or to those who lack opportunities to learn the language, or to communities where there are no speakers to pass on their linguistic heritage? Do we tell them that they are not Indigenous unless they speak their ancestors' language? Sheilah Nicholas's research on contemporary Hopi youths and Hopi language loss, language shift, and identity (2008, 2009, 2010) led her to the same question about identity: "How can you be Hopi if you don't speak it?" In fact, the name of any Indigenous language can be inserted in this question to illustrate the undeniable link between language and identity and the tensions between speakers and nonspeakers.

There is more to one's identity than the language one speaks. Just as language is not the only carrier of culture, Kanienke:ha does not equal Mohawk culture or identity. One nonspeaker of Kanienke:ha stated: "I think I equated it [Mohawk language] with identity, cultural identity . . . something that specifically means that I'm from Akwesasne" (Interviewee A3: July 19, 2005). For her, the language was important as a marker to locate her in a particular community. However, language learning became a dilemma for her and she later realized that she could still belong to the community as a Mohawk even though she did not know the language. She says: "I think now in my life for some reason I don't feel like the language is the same thing as identity. I think it's important . . . but I don't equate the two now. . . . I just thought that maybe I needed a way into the community. But now I don't think I replace that with something else. I think I just feel like part of the community" (Interviewee A3: July 19, 2005).

Perhaps unsurprisingly, many fluent speakers of the Mohawk language seem to feel that language is critical to being a true Mohawk, while non-fluent speakers generally feel that language proficiency is not the most important aspect of being Mohawk. One who insists that a person cannot be Mohawk without speaking Kanienke:ha says, "If you're going to get benefits and live on the reservation, then you should know your language" (Interviewee A2: July 14, 2005). Inherent in this statement is the belief that the language is critical to nationhood and cultural survival.

Similar to Jocks (1998) and Dauenhauer and Dauenhauer (1998), Freeman, Stairs, Corbiere, and Lazore (1995) recognize that "a range of alternative options are accepted by others—including more specific and unique community uses of the oral and written language." While some members attempt to learn the language, they also advocate for a "simultaneous deep mastery of English as one response enabling people to more subtly express Mohawk ideas even if they do not have the language" (p. 53).

Valuing the Mohawk Language

While Mohawk language is central to AFS teachings and to one's identity, there are other important cultural components to being Mohawk that are conveyed at the school, including cultural values of respect, responsibility, cooperation, stewardship, leadership, and kinship. The students at the AFS understand and value these aspects of their culture and are strongly rooted in their identities as Mohawk people, even though they may not be fluent speakers of the Mohawk language. A former student says, "Even though I'm not a speaker, I knew who I was and where I came from, my culture—I knew a lot. In seventh or eighth grade the kids in class were all Native but they didn't know anything about being Mohawk. They didn't sing, dance, speak the language, attend the Longhouse. Kids my own age who grew up here still don't know anything, because [while] I went here [AFS], they went to public school" (Interviewee A10: October 12, 2004).

Alumni have reported that the most important aspect of their AFS experience was gaining a strong foundation in their identity formation as Mohawk. It is important to emphasize the value and "ethnolinguistic pride" (McCarty, Romero-Little, and Zepeda 2006, p. 668) students place on knowing and learning Mohawk language and in perpetuating the language in Mohawk society. Students may not have the ability to speak the language fluently, but they still highly value it. Conversely, one parent believes, "just because people speak it,

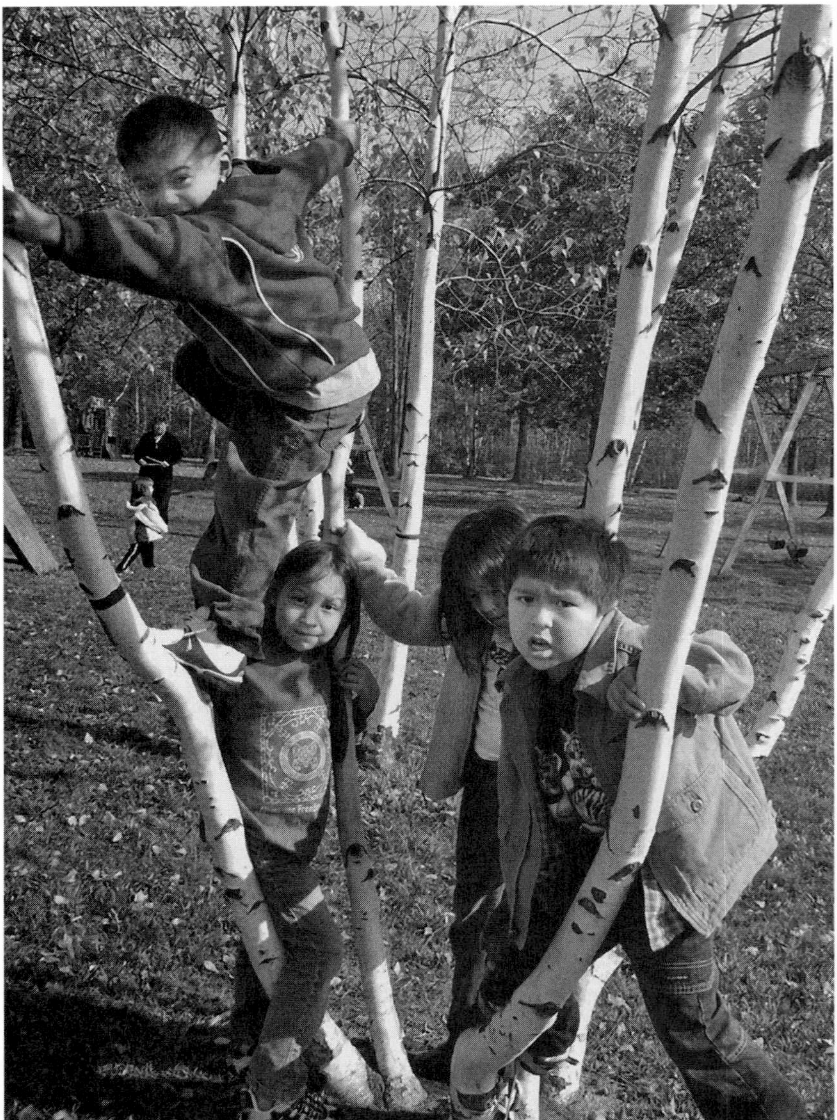

FIGURE 20. Children on school playground. *Clockwise from left*: Sewenonko, Kanonkwenhawi, Kariwaiens Perkins, Koiahre Perkins. Photo by L. White, 2004.

doesn't mean they value it" (Interviewee P7: October 7, 2004). The attitudes and ideologies of teachers and schools may be more critical to student achievement than students' ability to master the language (Nieto 1992). Karmela Liebkind (1999) states, "Although language can be the most significant criterion of social identification, it is not the only one, nor is it necessarily the most significant one for all social groups" (p. 144). The importance of language to ethnic identity varies with the situation, individual, and group.

It is evident that AFS youth have positive attachments to the Mohawk language, whether they speak it fluently or not. Fluency is the goal at AFS, but equally important is that these youths have an interest in learning their language, take pride in it, and value it. These three factors constitute "critical resources for Indigenous language revitalization and maintenance efforts" (McCarty, Romero-Little, Zepeda, 2006, p. 673).

Content Matters

> I would say teach the culture. That is actually more important than the language. . . . It's important *what* you say. It's not as important *how* you say what you say. They need to know *what* they're saying. In order for them to know what they're saying, they need to know who they are. They need to know where they come from. Like I said, when they want the language as much as they want air, they'll have it.—*Interviewee P11: July 20, 2005*

An Indigenous language provides a foundation for a unique worldview and way of thinking, and it is important that language speakers and second language learners understand the deep cultural content that is conveyed through the Native language. But the content of what is said may be more important than how it is said. One can be skilled in speaking Mohawk without understanding the deep cultural meaning embedded in the language. Both the content (the *what*) and the language itself (the *how*) are important to Mohawk identity formation and continuance of Mohawk culture. It follows then that "if attitude towards the language is 'purely instrumental' the second language is viewed only as a tool for communication and does not affect identity" (Liebkind 1999, p. 148). But learning to communicate in Kanienke:ha does not automatically bring an understanding of deep cultural meaning, Mohawk values, or what it means to be Mohawk. Ojibwe language instructor Mary Hermes expresses her concerns about language including cultural content: "How do we know we are not just teaching white kids to speak Ojibwe?" Her concern was that even though she was teaching Ojibwe students, without cultural context "even fluent Ojibwe could be appropriated to reflect an English way of thinking" (Hermes 2005, p. 53). This suggests the need for teaching language in a cultural context like immersion at the AFS rather than in fifty-minute class periods a few times a week.

When ceremonial life is threatened by loss of language, there are significant consequences. Jocks (1998) writes, "When the most deep and far-reaching forms of expression the people possess—and the critical relationships they enliven, especially with Other-than-human beings—grow pale, lose significance and coherence, and begin to die," we experience "cartooning" (p. 231). Without a deep cultural understanding of the language to continue ceremonial traditions, culture is merely preserved in "fossil form, in articles and reports and proceedings and field notes"— "the loss of performability, from a Native perspective, renders such knowledge moot" (ibid.). To use a specific example that can stand for any Indigenous people, for the Hopis a distinct cultural identity is conveyed through language, and an understanding of Hopi is necessary for full comprehension of cultural meaning (Nicholas 2010). But while most Hopi youths living in contemporary Hopi villages actively participate in traditional activities (Nicholas 2009), many Mohawk youths in Akwesasne do not follow traditional Longhouse practices. The AFS seeks to provide an avenue for its students to be active participants in traditional practices, thus strengthening their cultural understanding and identity as Mohawks. For young Hopis, the Hopi language is still essential for a deeper understanding of their people's history and culture, including religious knowledge (Nicholas 2010).

Likewise, meanings of traditional songs and dances as well as ceremonies in the Mohawk language convey a deep meaning about the Mohawk way of life. Ceremonial language is specific to Longhouse practices and not used in daily interactions. Unfortunately, many Longhouse participants do not understand what is being said during ceremonies due to their lack of proficiency in Mohawk. Tom Porter writes, "What they're saying and what they're praying about in their Midwinter talk is renewal of all the things that gave us life for all the people. Yet the people don't know what they're saying" (Porter 2008, p. 153). To rectify this situation, Porter and others gather people for a meeting prior to the ceremony and explain it in English: "At least they know what that day is for. And that's the best we can do. That's why it's sad. We are supposed to know that. And that's how much we've lost our language, in Mohawk country" (p. 153). For several years, no one was in training to recite ceremonial speeches, until a grant from the Administration for Native Americans allowed for a program in which seventh- and eighth-grade students teamed up with a faithkeeper to learn Longhouse speeches (Konwanahtotani (Elvera) Sargent, personal communication, 2008).

Traditional stories, including the Creation Story, carry deep cultural meaning that can only be understood in the Mohawk language. Porter says that "people can speak Mohawk fluently, but they're not always associating the meaning with what they're really saying" (Porter, 2008, p. 94). Porter cites counting as an example:

> Counting from one to ten for the Iroquois is our chronological telling of the major events of our Creation. . . . Now as Skywoman, *Atsi'tsiaka:ion,* was falling she was pregnant already, remember? . . . And now she's gonna give birth. And this is the one where we call it *enska.* That means *one.* So number one is attributed to her. And the Senecas and Onondagas, they call it *ska.* . . . So when you say one, it came from the lady who fell. . . . The beginning of life; that's why we begin, when we count, with her. *Enska.*
>
> When we say in Mohawk, *tékeni,* that word comes from the word *tehníkhen. Tehníkhen* means twins, two. And that's what that young girl when she was pregnant, had—twins. And so our word that we use for two, *tékeni,* comes from the word "twin" because of those two boys that were gonna be born. (Porter 2008, p. 81–82)

One might have thought counting to ten in Kanienke:ha entirely equivalent to counting in English, but it is far more than that, carrying aspects of the Haudenosaunee Creation Story within it. Porter says he's lucky to understand the root words and their meanings—not everyone who speaks Mohawk understands them. Language learners can go one step further than memorizing how to count and also learn the deeper cultural content of a language. "*Tekeni*" as simply "two" is not the same as "*tekeni*" that is not only "two" but also refers to the twins in the Creation story. It is in these profound spaces of meaning and understanding that language and culture come together to provide a Haudenosaunee worldview that informs identity. Lack of proficiency in Kanienke:ha and lack of an understanding of the deep cultural meanings embedded in the language can create confusion.

"I Knew I Was Indian but Didn't Know What It Meant"

> "What kind of Indian are you?" . . . I thought back to the movie I had been watching the previous night and [remembered] the name that the Indians in the movie had been called. "I think I'm an Apache," I replied. . . . Many of my people grew up the same way I had, speaking our language without having the culture that goes along with it to make us whole. When you don't have your own identity, you will try to find a surrogate identity as a cloak in which to hide your shame, whether you realize it or not.—*Peters 2013, 61*

"I think I'm an Apache." These words that Akwesasne Mohawk community member Teddy Peters remembers having said as a teenager reflect the disconnection he once felt from identity as a Mohawk. Even though Kanienke:ha was his first language, his identity had been altered by his people's history of oppression.

A conscientious parent who also felt caught between different worlds of Mohawk tradition, the Christian faith, and the English and French languages decided to send her son to the AFS "so he'll be less confused and have a straighter path. He'll have a better sense of who he is from the start" (Interviewee P7: October 7, 2004). This parent and child are non-fluent speakers of Mohawk, but this type of dilemma is found among fluent speakers as well.

My assumption when I began this book was that I would find the majority of Mohawk language speakers to also be traditional Longhouse followers. I naively equated "traditional" with Mohawk language proficiency, and I assumed that the language was the sole carrier of the Longhouse tradition. This turned out not to be the case. At Akwesasne many traditionalists, those who follow the Longhouse, are not fluent Kanienke:ha speakers. Many fluent speakers are Christian churchgoers and do not participate in traditional ceremonies. And many whose first language is Mohawk are not able to read and write in Mohawk. In Tom Porter's book, *And Grandma Said: Iroquois Teachings as Passed Down through the Oral Tradition*, editor Lesley Forrester notes:

"For the purposes of this book, [Tom] asked to have *Karihwénhawe* (Dorothy Lazore) correct his written Mohawk. Yet since she was raised as a Catholic and not raised as a traditional Longhouse woman, there are spiritual references and ceremonial language that she might not be familiar with. In contrast, those more steeped in the traditional culture and the old language have not necessarily learned to write it" (Porter 2008).

When the AFS began, the school needed to find teachers who could speak the language. Those teachers happened to be Christian rather than strict followers of the Longhouse. One of them says, "I was Catholic at the time I started at AFS. We were all Catholic teachers ... [just] one, I think, was traditional. That was a concern with the clan mothers. But, in fact, the lady that was traditional talked to the clan mothers. She said their religion has nothing [to do] with it.... They're coming to teach the language. It didn't matter that they were Catholic" (Interviewee T6: July 20, 2005).

Eighteenth-century French Jesuit Missionaries learned the Mohawk language and created the alphabet that is still used today. They translated hymns and prayers and the entire bible into the Mohawk language for the purpose of converting Mohawks to Christianity (D. Lazore 1993). Thus the Catholic Church encouraged Mohawk literacy. But today that literacy is involved in moving some Mohawks back toward their ancestral traditions. Many AFS parents and teachers have found their way back to the ceremonial Longhouse and the original teachings of the Haudenosaunee. A fluent speaker says: "I grew up not knowing Mohawk culture. I knew I was Indian, but I didn't know what it meant" (Interviewee T6: July 20, 2005). As new Mohawk speakers began to understand various aspects of the Mohawk culture embedded in the language, the Creation Story, the coming of the Peacemaker, and other unifying cultural markers, everything fell into place, as one parent said.

> I started learning more about the Longhouse.... I was taken to church not understanding Christianity.... If I go to the Longhouse, it makes sense. Everything was falling into place, making sense to me.... I was learning all of this from having been at the Akwesasne Freedom School.
>
> When we started getting involved with the AFS, we had no cultural background. I was taught that the Longhouse was bad.... As a teenager I wanted to learn more—wanted to know about the clan systems [and] finally went to a social. When my brother found out, he said he would

> whip me. It was a bad thing in our family to be a part of the Longhouse. (Interviewee P3: October 8, 2004)

This fluent Mohawk speaker felt that she had "no cultural background." Thus, while serving to communicate at a superficial level, the language did not completely carry the Mohawk culture for this speaker.

Making a choice between following generations of faithful churchgoing Mohawks or returning to traditional beliefs and practices is not easy or trivial. One AFS teacher says, "After I started learning the Mohawk ways, the history, I didn't go back to the Catholic way. It wasn't for me. Some people stayed Christian. I couldn't after learning what I learned. . . . [But] a lot of people wouldn't go to the Longhouse because their parents were alive and they didn't want to hurt them" (Interviewee T4: July 18, 2005).

Another teacher likewise expresses how she found meaning in the traditional teachings when she began to understand Haudenosaunee culture and spirituality but continues to practice Christianity out of respect for her grandmother: "We were Catholic when [that meant] the punishing God. And we learned from the Creator that it wasn't like that. Things just had more meaning than the Catholic way. Couldn't say that to my grandmother, though. A lot of it [my staying in the church] was out of respect for my grandmother. . . . Kids are still being baptized and that's out of respect for my grandmother too" (Interviewee T6: July 20, 2005). The primary reason parents send their children to the AFS is for language learning. But since some families follow the Longhouse ways and others are Christian, the school has provided an opportunity for healing in the Akwesasne community. Through his involvement with the AFS as a teacher and a parent, Teddy Peters and his family eventually found their way to the Longhouse, which was a "life-changing experience" (Peters 2013, 62).

Hope for Cultural Continuance and Language Vitality

> You don't learn about the ceremonies or the witnesses. You can't go to your churches because there are so many different ones you don't know which one is the right one. The Creator's brother jumbled them up in confusion. What can you use education for when there's nothing that will work? Everything'll be coming down and there'll be a time when money will be of no use. Why work when you can't buy food? The people will be coming back and planting.

> That's what I'm seeing. It's getting nearer and nearer, and I can't say when. But as the years go on, you can tell that the people have started coming back. All the people will be coming home. They will be coming to power again. Must be something going on out there when they want to come back.
> —*Tadodaho Chief Leon Shenandoah, quoted in Wall 2001, p. 26*

To survive, languages must have meaning beyond memorization of vocabulary and rules of grammar. For the language to be a carrier of culture it must be used in cultural contexts. According to Cummins (1998), second language acquisition "will remain abstract and largely trivial unless students have the opportunity to express themselves—their identities and their intelligence—through that language" (p. 13). At the AFS, students are learning more than just speech. They are becoming culturally literate and expressing their very identities through the language as they prepare to be responsible and competent adults.

For those proficient in Kanienke:ha, language is a key element in their worldview and instrumental in defining themselves. For nonspeakers, however, language is one aspect of identity formation, and other elements of Mohawk culture such as ceremonies, songs, and stories take a larger role in making up their identity. Some knowledge of the language certainly strengthens their sense of self and makes them feel more Mohawk.

Various opinions and beliefs surround the Mohawk language, and identity and language are undeniably connected. The complex relationship is continually changing, as the culture of the Mohawk people changes over time and is renegotiated. Dorothy Lazore, fluent speaker and Kanienke:ha teacher, said in 1999: "Over the past twenty years, our Mohawk language has disappeared, our resources as Native are being depleted. Identity is lost or scattered. Ownership of who we are was placed in the hands of the government, religion, and schools." She urged people to act: "Native people need to look within themselves, to rekindle the inner depth of who we are as Native people, to recapture the wisdom of our Elders, and to re-learn our language so that we can communicate with our Creator" (qtd. in Freeman, Stairs, Corbiere, and Lazore 1995, p. 66).

SIX

Becoming "Fully Mohawk"

> The Akwesasne Freedom School teaches us who we are as Onkwehonwe.
> —*Interviewee P3: October 18, 2004*

A great brown turtle with black eyes emerged from a bright blue sea. A small creature swam in the choppy waves while large white birds carried a young woman through the sky. Second-grade students at the AFS had painted their own visions of the Creation Story, splashed with vivid colors and an occasional rainbow. Seated at their classroom tables, some covered from head to toe in paint, these children recalled how the Onkwehonwe (Original People) came into being on Iethinistenha Onhwéntsia (Mother Earth). The students sang a song to honor the earth as their brushes had re-created a story passed down for generations by their ancestors. The Creation Story teaches the students at the AFS where they come from and that their existence is tied to a spiritual force that connects them to all living things.

To refer to oneself as Mohawk also recognizes kinship with other members of the Haudenosaunee Confederacy. When we say "Onkwehonwe," it connects us back to creation and to the original humans, our ancestors. Mohawk scholar Taiaiake Alfred (2005) states that an Onkwehonwe identity is "one layer of identification among the multiplicity of layers that form people's sense of self—from the individual, to the family, to the clan, village, nation, and then on to our participation as Onkwehonwe in a more expansive conversation that links us to other indigenous peoples in other parts of the world who share our thoughts, feelings, and plans of action" (p. 140).

FIGURE 21. AFS students riding behind tractor. *Faces visible, left to right*: Tsientenhariio Herne, Kentarahtiron Arquette, Kariwaiens Perkins (*rear*), Iakoiatahawis McDonald, Ranawatsistoronkwas McDonald (*front, partially hidden behind cornstalk*), Iotariiio Smoke-Sellers (*far right*). Photo by Ceely King, 2003.

Giroux (2001) states that knowledge of the self entails a critical consciousness or "self-conscious critique" (p. 8). Ultimately, knowing one's self is to be aware of what it means to be a complete human being. One learns how to be complete based on experiences and values, and according to critical pedagogy we move toward this while learning about historic oppression and resilience of Native nations and learning to be committed to our communities, protecting culture, language, land (Lee 2006, p. 3). Freire (2000) asserts, "At all stages of their liberation, the oppressed must see themselves as women and men engaged in the ontological and historical vocation of becoming *fully human*" [emphasis added] (p. 66). Students at the AFS gain freedom by learning how to become fully human, Onkwehonwe, through service to their people.

When schools allow Indigenous children to have a solid grounding in their own histories, their own people's stories, and their own cultures, they will develop positive identities. When they have a positive identity, they will naturally develop self-esteem and self-confidence and become high achievers in all areas of education and life (Faries 2009).

What Does It Mean to Be Mohawk?

> It makes me feel not like everybody else. I have a history, a culture. I have something that not a lot of other kids have. Some kids don't want to have anything to do with their culture. They want to be like other cultures. I like that I am my own. I know my language and my history.
> —*Interviewee A7: October 14, 2005*

Does the AFS cultivate a sense of Mohawk identity among its students? More important, what is Mohawk identity? When asked what it means to be Mohawk, respondents had varied definitions, and mentioned speaking the Mohawk language, knowing traditional songs and ceremonies, maintaining strong kinship relations, and having a sense of shared history distinct from the mainstream population. Several described being Mohawk as an intangible feeling, something that is difficult to describe but "you know it when you feel it." One passionate parent explains: "If you grow up on the reserve and you're educated in the public school, you just live on reserve, you don't really get a sense of who you are. There's no cultural or spiritual attachment to who you are. You're just empty. You always feel that hole, wondering, 'Who am I really, what are my roots?'" (Interviewee P4: July 15, 2005). The roots this parent refers to are connection to the land, to ancestors, and to the history that ties the Mohawk people to one another. Haudenosaunee history is a focal point of the AFS curriculum. Students learn through the Creation Story that we come from the Skyworld. Students learn how the Peacemaker helped unite the Haudenosaunee Confederacy, and they learn the message of peace encoded in the Great Law. By learning their history before US or Canadian history, student worldviews are shaped in such a way that they take great pride in being Mohawk. As one former student says, "I feel like I really know who I am. I really respect myself and my people. It seems like a lot of other people are lost and don't know who they are. We were taught our own history and that made me feel good about myself" (Interviewee A4: October 18, 2004).

A sixth-grade student commented that being Mohawk set him apart from others. He equated "Mohawkness" with being a good person: "To have a different culture, language. You got to know your language, got to know your songs, got to know how to dance. If you can do all that, it means you're a good person" (Interview S1: October 3, 2004). A very bright AFS alum also recognizes the unique aspects of being Mohawk: "To be Mohawk means to be alive. . . . Anytime we go to a social or we have a ceremony, I think about it. We're the only people in the world that do [exactly] this. There's only us left to do this. It's just that pride. You feel that pride" (Interviewee A8: July 15, 2005).

For others, being Mohawk involves a sense of community with a common history. Another alum says, "There's a shared history. It's a community, so there's an extension of the family unit. It's a group of people that you grow up around. For those who grew up in the Longhouse, there's a common spirituality. . . . I guess it's a shared identity" (Interviewee A3: July 19, 2005). AFS alumni seem to generally have a solid sense of their individual identities as a result of their experiences at the school. However, many Mohawk adults, including teachers, who were schooled in mainstream public education systems, expressed confusion regarding their identities. One parent says, "I was trying to understand what it means to be Native. To be a good Indian you had to be tough. To drink people under the table is what I learned. . . . Some friends were traditional, and I started going to socials. My dad was brought up with that being taboo. Through high school I learned the wrong things about what it meant to be Native. The common bond was to drink—that's what brought people together" (Interviewee P7: October 7, 2004).

Through their experiences with the AFS, some adults have realized their place in Mohawk society. A teacher says, "I finally found out that I was Mohawk. . . . When I was little I didn't know what a Mohawk was. I didn't know I was a Mohawk. I lived here. I didn't know that any of my friends were either" (Interviewee T4: July 18, 2005). Another teacher finds that he learns as much as his students, saying, "I didn't know anything about Native people growing up. . . . I didn't know who I was for the longest time. Maybe I still don't, but I'm learning" (Interviewee T5: August 20, 2004). The AFS provides a unique space for cultural renewal not only for its students, but for adults: "I wanted to learn my culture and history, and that was the only place to do it. I never knew anything" (Interviewee T4: July 18, 2005).

An elder teacher eloquently described being Mohawk as a responsibility that one strives for and works toward in an effort to become a good person. In this sense being Mohawk is not a given granted by being biologically Mohawk. Rather that responsibility is to family, to community, to carrying on values, ceremonies, songs, and traditions and becoming a true Mohawk. He says: "It's a big responsibility. It's almost like a goal, something they should be working at

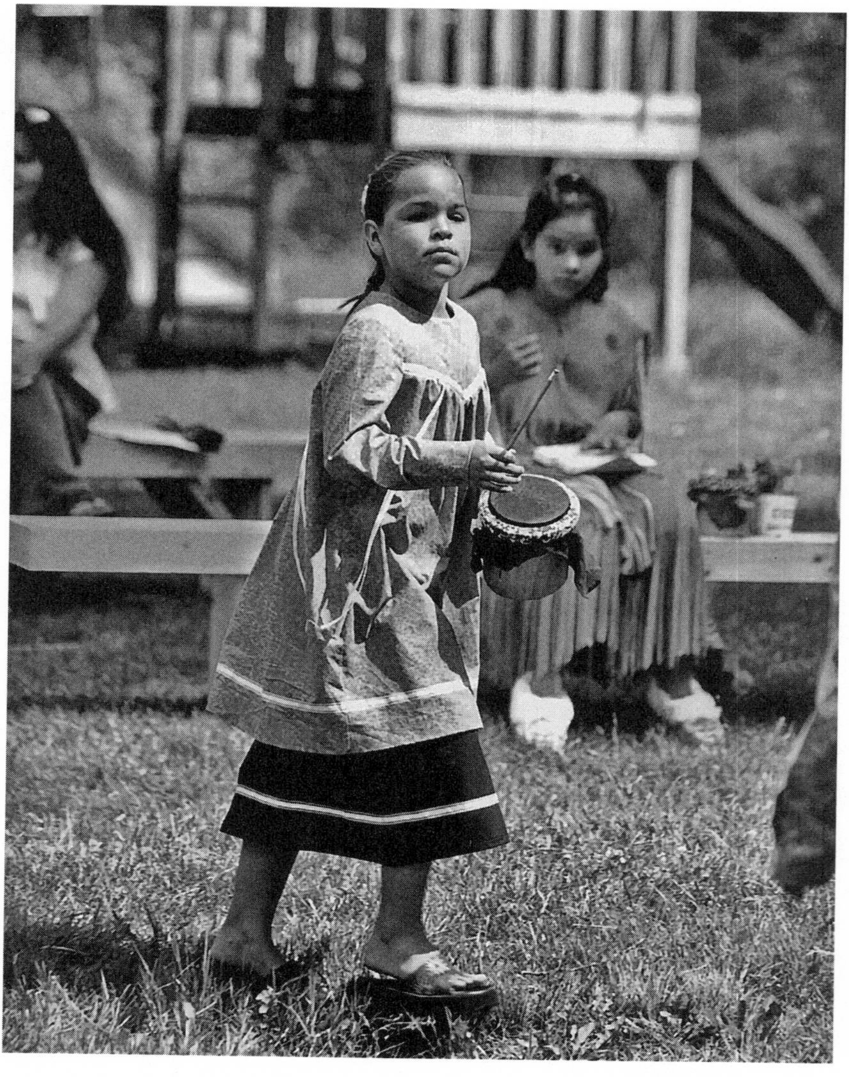

FIGURE 22. AFS students Kahontaronkwas Herne and Tsionati:io Laughing. Photo by Ceely King, 2003.

to make sure that Mohawk doesn't become something past or forgotten. Being Mohawk is almost an achievement, right at birth. . . . They [AFS students] are learning that better than any other school or institution could do for them" (Interviewee T2: July 19, 2005).

Traditional Values

> Renewal of respect for traditional values is the only lasting solution to the political, economic, and social problems that beset our people. To bring those roots to new fruition, we must reinvigorate the principles embedded in the ancient teachings, and use them to address our contemporary problems.
> —*Alfred 1999, p. 5*

Reinvigorating traditional values and principles in Native communities is necessary because, as Mohawk scholar Taiaiake Alfred declares, "without a value system that takes traditional teachings as the basis for government and politics the recovery will never be complete" (1999, p. 2). Recovering traditional values in Alaskan Native communities began with identifying what each community believed was important in their contemporary lives. The Alaska Native Knowledge Network (ANKN) produced several posters describing the cultural values of Athabascan, Tlingit, and other Alaskan Native groups. In 2002 I had the privilege of spending a summer in Alaska where I enrolled in a cross cultural studies course at the University of Alaska Fairbanks with Professor Ray Barnhardt. One week of the course was spent with elders, youth, and other visitors at Old Minto, a traditional Athabascan fish camp on the Tanana River (White 2003). I was struck by the strength and resilience of the elders, who shared stories of subsistence living and their fears that the youth would stray from their cultural traditions. These fears were somewhat assuaged when their children joined them in traditional singing and dancing during a potlatch at the end of the week. Reflecting the wishes of the elders, the community identified Athabascan values as a part of the ANKN project, stating: "Every Athabaskan is responsible to all other Athabaskan for the survival of our cultural spirit, and the values and traditions through which it survives. Through our extended family, we retain, teach, and live our Athabaskan way. With guidance and support from elders, we must teach our children Athabaskan values" ("Athabascan Cultural Values," Alaska Native Knowledge Network, http://www.ankn

.uaf.edu/ANCR/Values/athabascan.html). Among these values are knowledge of language, sharing, peace, respect for others, cooperation, respect for elders, knowledge of and responsibility to kinship relations, humility, and responsibility to tribe. Acknowledging the connection to all living things and our responsibilities to creation, the statement concludes: "Our understanding of our universe and our place in it is a belief in God and a respect for all his creations" (ibid.).

Another example of cultural values in Native education is apparent in the Navajo STAR (Service to All Relations) School, a community based charter school. The STAR School identifies its core values as service and what are known as "the 4 R's": respect, relationship, responsibility, and reasoning. The "4 R's" are incorporated into the daily lives of its students and even the school's grading system (Sorensen 2014).

Cultural values for the Haudenosaunee are embedded in the Great Law, which established not only a sociopolitical structure but a code of conduct. Students at the AFS receive the original teachings of the Haudenosaunee, including the Great Law, but more importantly they exhibit and live by cultural values I was able to identify through extensive interviews and observation: respect, responsibility, cooperation, stewardship, leadership, and kinship (see fig. 14, Indigenous model of holistic education). There is hope that the AFS can teach our youth moral codes important to Haudenosaunee society. According to Tom Porter, if the AFS were to achieve its goals: "[It] would teach a whole value system by which children could judge what they want. . . it would give them the foundation in Mohawk morals . . . it would enable them to become good Mohawk people so our Nation will flourish . . . and to be morally good human beings" (qtd. in Ciborski 1990). As Jon Reyhner writes, "Well thought out and implemented indigenous immersion programs can restore positive traditional values, develop students' reasoning ability, and teach solid academic content" (Reyhner 2010, p. 147). The AFS is reaching its goals. Giving its students a solid foundation in Mohawk identity, it helps students develop with a value system that allows them to become fully Mohawk, living with "good minds."

Identifying values, beliefs, and moral codes requires a broad perspective. Certain behaviors or ways of being are subtle and not easily identifiable or articulated. One parent, after being asked why she sent her son to the AFS, said, "I wanted him to have a certain way about him. I think that the Akwesasne Freedom School is going to give that to him. . . . It was the attitude, the way the kids are." In trying to articulate the "certain way" AFS children are, she continues: "It's hard to describe, but if you ask people, they'll notice it" (Interviewee A12: July 14, 2005).

Unlike the Navajo STAR School, the AFS community has not made its values explicit. But personal and cultural values rooted in traditional teachings are reflected in the students' behaviors and actions. They are readily identifiable and are consciously embedded into the AFS curriculum. These values are shared by the Haudenosaunee community and govern how to live life as an Onkwehonwe.

Respect for Self and Others

> [Being Mohawk means] to be nice to each other. You have to take care of your environment, your home, your family. Respect is why we're still a community.—*Interviewee T4: July 18, 2006*

Those interviewed for this book overwhelmingly reported that respect was the main value held by AFS students. Respect can mean taking into consideration another person's feelings, thoughts, and needs. It can also refer to listening to and accepting others' views. One can feel and act respectful toward self, family, community, and the environment.

When referring to student attitudes, a parent who once was an AFS student says: "They respect themselves, love themselves. They have pride in who they are" (Interviewee A12: July 14, 2005). One young woman describes how her sister cared enough about herself to abstain from sex, drugs, and smoking: "When other kids were talking about 'screwing,' my sister didn't know what that meant. . . . She was innocent. I think the AFS gave her that kind of innocence of not knowing those kinds of things. She's never smoked or drank. Her foundation is stronger than mine was" (Interviewee A6: October 13, 2004). A proud parent sees how her child acts as a positive role model for others because she also respects herself enough to refrain from using alcohol and drugs: "The AFS is part of why she's like that. She learned her culture and it helped her self-esteem. Her spirit is really strong" (Interviewee A11: October 11, 2004). When AFS alumni attend a nearby public high school located away from the community, they carry those lessons with them: "When you see the kids come into this school [Salmon River High School], they're different. They have so much respect. . . . A lot of kids coming out of AFS are less prone to peer pressure. They're strong. They know where they came from. I don't hear them talk so much about drinking, partying, and all that stuff" (Interviewee P1: October 18, 2004). These alumni recognize how they are different from other students, both Native and non-Native: "The Akwesasne Freedom School teaches you never to talk to the teacher like they do here [Salmon River High School]. There they teach you calmness, to be quiet, listen" (Interviewee A7: October 14, 2005).

Kinship: Upholding Familial Roles and Responsibilities

> I think that's part of what the Freedom School has done, and that's to keep the family together.—*Interviewee A9: July 15, 2005*

For many Indigenous people, kinship ties are just as important, if not more so, than tribal or cultural identification. Kinship roles determine one's responsibility to others, and kinship is an important aspect of Indigenous cultural and physical survival (M. W. Foster 1998; Innes 2007). The Haudenosaunee Confederacy is based on kinship principles and is bound together by a matrilineal clan system in which members of the same clan are linked with other nations in the confederacy. Kinship ties and family relations still hold an important place in the contemporary lives of the Mohawk people.

Many AFS students have kinship ties to other students and teachers, and they many attend school with their aunts and uncles or cousins or both. The familial atmosphere reflects the fact that the school's founders sent their children to the AFS, and these children grew up to send their own children to the school. Some alumni have also returned as teachers. The many intergenerational and familial relationships contribute to the longevity and success of the school.

Because parents assume the responsibilities of cleaning and doing other needed duties at the school, their presence is common. At the beginning and ending of the school day parents flood the parking area and the school's halls waiting for their children. During these socializing opportunities, parents talk with teachers, staff, and with each other. As one parent says, parental responsibilities are important: "[They] keep us close, as a family, a community" (Interviewee A12: July 14, 2005).

Responsibility to Self and Others

> The question really is, "Are we Native?" That's the question we need to ask each other. . . . Every person in this community needs to ask themselves that. . . . If the answer is yes, then they need to ask themselves, "What is my responsibility?" The answer to that question is everything the Akwesasne Freedom School does.—*Interviewee P11: July 20, 2005*

The responsibilities that this parent refers to are those that are necessary to ensure cultural survival. Passed down over generations through the Great Law of Peace and other traditional teachings, these obligations ensure that ceremonies are performed, family and governing structures are intact, and songs, stories, and dances are carried out. These duties come with being Mohawk. It is an individual's choice to uphold these responsibilities, both for oneself and for others. Students at the AFS learn their obligations and carry them out by choosing to speak the Mohawk language with their classmates, friends, and families. Some students take the responsibility of upholding the language further when they use it in the larger Akwesasne community. For example, students have been called upon to recite the Ohenton Kariwahtekwen at events like the annual Strawberry Festival at the Native North American Travelling College. Others have taken this responsibility outside of the community and continue using the language when they go on to high school and to college and university.

When students choose to participate in traditional songs, dances, and ceremonies, they are upholding their responsibility as young Mohawk citizens. Upholding one's responsibility as a Mohawk is not limited to traditional ceremonial practices, however. There are plenty of AFS students who come from nontraditional families, and while they may not participate in traditional ceremonies they still take on the responsibility of living their lives as Mohawk people. These students may also choose to speak the language both at the AFS and outside of school. They may also pass the language on to their own children along with traditional stories and songs they learned at the AFS. They may choose to live their lives nontraditionally, in the sense that they do not attend Longhouse ceremonies, but they live with "good minds" and take responsibility for upholding traditional values.

One parent says: "The AFS instills in the students a sense of who they are, and that sense is one of respect, one of responsibility, one of sharing, and I think those are exactly the qualities we need in this community" (Interviewee P9: July 15, 2005). Another responsibility is to uphold the school community. Just as parents play a large role in the continuance of the AFS, its students are called upon to assist with activities that support the school. Appreciative of this opportunity, one alumnus expresses his thoughts: "All the hardships we had, the fact that it's a small school and we had to fund-raise, it makes you stronger. You get older and even your work ethic and your ambition [are stronger because of your school experience]. You're working hard to get the things other students get for free" (Interviewee A8: July 15, 2005).

Stewardship of the Land and Natural Resources

> This is our homeland. We are definitely connected to the land, and we are home. And the language puts us at home.—*Interviewee P4: July 15, 2005*

Haudenosaunee land and the earth itself are critical to cultural and physical survival, to Haudenosaunee existence, and to the AFS teachings. The Ohenton Kariwahtekwen conveys gratitude, respect, and reverence for all living things, from the smallest blade of grass to the planet Earth, the moon, and the sun. According to Mohawk people, land is not property: "It is the bones of our ancestors, it is sacred, it is our mother" (Akwesasne Task Force on the Environment 1997, p. 11). The protection of the earth is a responsibility that must be considered seven generations into the future.

Our children and grandchildren, the generations of the future, must be ensured that they will be able to carry out cultural activities that are connected to the earth. Fishing in the local waterways has always been a way of life for Mohawk people, along with hunting and, more recently, farming. The St. Lawrence Seaway runs directly through Akwesasne territory, with tributaries providing wetlands and prime fishing. Fifty percent of the local economy was once associated with fishing, while water, plants, and turtles were seen as medicine and central to subsistence living (Akwesasne Task Force on the Environment 1997, p. 24).

Cultural activities such as fishing help maintain family and community cohesion. They also provide opportunities for the language to be used in context, which makes it real: "For young people to understand and value their language, they must see and experience it" (Akwesasne Task Force on the Environment

1997, p. 27). The land not only provides cultural opportunities, it is inextricably linked to the language. Place names in the Mohawk language are not mere markers but carry stories, instructions, and history that connect us to our ancestors. Without being able to continue the stories because of the loss of language or because of the loss of land, critical damage to the culture occurs. One student at the AFS responded eloquently when asked if he would teach his own children Mohawk one day: "Yes, so we can keep our land. [People are] trying to take our land. If we lose our language, they can take it away from us right away" (Interviewee S1: October 3, 2004).

Unfortunately, similar to the contamination from industrial plants (see chapter 2), the damming of the St. Lawrence River damaged and destroyed much of the land at Akwesasne. To the Mohawk people, waters are the "bloodlines of Mother Earth, they are sacred and very much alive" (Akwesasne Task Force on the Environment 2001, p. 3). In the 1950s, the New York Power Authority dammed the St. Lawrence River (*Kaniatarowanenne*) to create hydropower, which caused a separation of the land from people, and both the land and people have suffered. A vibrant livelihood of fishing and trapping is no longer possible.

As a consequence, many parents do not allow their children to swim, fish, or play in the rivers, and mothers have passed toxins to their babies via breast milk, causing birth defects and other complications (Grinde and Johansen 1995). The people's relationship with the natural world has come out of balance, and the "very survival of a Nation" is has been put at risk by this social and cultural destruction (Akwesasne Task Force on the Environment 1997, p. 25). Once land is destroyed and water flow is altered, responsibilities given by the Creator may no longer be fulfilled. When these responsibilities are not fulfilled, the state of harmony is put out of balance (Akwesasne Task Force on the Environment 2001).

AFS students, however, have been involved in projects to restore wetland ecosystems, and they planted three thousand trees to help restore a forest ecosystem on and around school grounds. In 2001 students in the eighth and ninth grades were honored with the President's Environmental Youth Award for a project they had worked on with the Akwesasne Task Force on the Environment to restore fifty acres of wetlands around the school. A teacher says, "We followed the Thanksgiving Address. . . . [Students] found out about the different kinds of wetlands, and a medicine person showed us medicine plants" (Interviewee T4: July 18, 2005). Five students got to travel to Washington, D.C., to receive the award from President George W. Bush.

Through traditional teachings that focus on caring for and giving thanks for all living things, a sense of stewardship is instilled in AFS students, who then set an example for others.

Cooperation: Working Together for the Benefit of the Group

> The other schools in the area asked if we wanted to participate in their science fairs. I always said no because it's a competition, and someone is always left out, and there's a lot of hurt feelings. Besides, if we did it, we'd win every year, and they'd get mad at us!—*Interviewee T4: July 18, 2005*

During one of my visits to the Akwesasne Freedom School, I spent time outside during recess with a group of first graders. One of them managed to throw her book bag up into a tree where it stuck. Concerned and eager to help, another young girl grabbed my wrist and brought me over to the tree. She rallied her fellow students, grabbed the lower branch, and said, "Everyone pull! Everyone has to help!" I grabbed the branch, and then several students lined up behind me holding onto each other and onto me. Through this joint effort we managed to knock the bag loose, and I managed to keep from being pulled over by a group of very small Mohawk children. To ensure that a culture, nation, or community survives, its people must work together cooperatively, just as the students on the playground demonstrated that day. The teachers at AFS try to encourage a noncompetitive atmosphere where all students are treated equally and cooperation is nurtured. Students help each other in the classroom and on the playground.

Public schools tend to cultivate competition in academics, sports, and popularity. Socio-economic differences can be evident through clothing, footwear, and the latest technological gadgets. One AFS alumna expressed her disdain for this, saying, "I hated public school. I dreaded it every day. The people were just so into material things, and over there [at the AFS], some of us were into having possessions and stuff but the majority of us didn't care" (Interviewee A9: July 15, 2005).

As an observer at the AFS I didn't notice anyone sporting designer clothes or competing to be the most popular. Some parents described how their children left fancy clothes at home when they attended the AFS. They were allowed to be children at the AFS without the pressures of fitting into a materialistic mold designed by the dominant culture. A teacher described one of the reasons why she sent her daughters to the school: "When the hairdos were real high, in the eighties, we sent them to the AFS for grade seven and eight. The hair came down. The Barbie dolls came back out. It didn't matter if their clothes matched. They came right back down to being little girls. It changed them completely" (Interviewee T6: July 20, 2005). In an environment lacking competitiveness, students appear more relaxed and not worried about outdoing each other. They generally work together for the common good.

Leadership through Language and Cultural Knowledge

> We need more leaders who are grounded in who they are if we're going to continue to not only survive but thrive as a community. We have all kinds of other problems here [but] by having a strong cultural identity we can address them, and that's where the value of the school comes in.
> —*Interviewee P9: July 15, 2005*

One of the clearest examples of leadership coming out of the AFS is an alumnus, Aronhiaies Herne, who was recently named a traditional chief of the Mohawk Nation Council of Chiefs. Herne describes how the AFS prepared him for that role: "The Freedom School not only teaches the language but it also teaches leadership. Even the language itself—you have to be a leader to enforce that language. If you can choose the Mohawk language over English, automatically that's a leadership role. They teach a lot of cultural stuff there that helped me a lot to be a leader. It helped me to stand up and use my voice, to take part in [the community], to reach out and make changes" (Aronhiaies Herne, personal communication, July 15, 2005). The Great Law of Peace calls for leaders who can serve as mentors to the people by having hearts "full of peace and good will," endless patience, calm deliberation, and skin that is "seven spans thick," as "proof against anger, offensive actions, and criticism" (Akwesasne Notes 1970, p. 13).

The AFS prepares students for leadership roles by teaching Haudenosaunee history, the Great Law of Peace, and the Ohenton Kariwahtekwen, which give a firm foundation in Mohawk identity. The school cultivates self-confidence and nurtures empathy. According to Alfred (1999), Native leaders must promote education "both in the conventional Western sense and in terms of re-rooting young people within their traditional cultures. In time, such education will produce a new generation of healthy and highly skilled leaders who will be able to interact with the changing mainstream society from a position of strength rooted in cultural confidence" (Alfred 1999, p. 133).

Stereotypes often depict Native people as quiet and stoic. The myth of the "silent Indian learner" has been created and perpetuated by colonial education (Lomawaima and McCarty 2006, p. 19). Such stereotypes and myths persist when Native students are seen as rude and disrespectful when looking a teacher directly in the eyes. The preferred stereotypical response is to lower one's gaze in an act of "dignified" respect. The stereotype may also characterize Native students as being impolite if they ask questions or challenge other's viewpoints. While some Native communities may indeed encourage young people to listen more than to question, in Haudenosaunee culture understanding also comes from critical thinking. One parent says, "My children came out far more innocent, very environmentally conscious, [and] opinionated, not in a bad way. They have principles, morals, beliefs. They look at the world differently. They look at themselves differently. They are critical thinkers. That was the goal, to allow children the ability to ask questions and know it's okay to question things. This worked against them at public school, where it can be viewed as disrespectful. They are taught to question, almost resist in some ways. They came out confident" (Interviewee P8: October 8, 2004).

The Great Law of Peace is an expression of Haudenosaunee oral tradition, and becoming a great orator is an important part of Haudenosaunee leadership. Emphasis has been placed on a leader's ability to not only recite the Great Law but also understand it, live by it, and pass it on to future generations. To restore harmony and balance to the world, Alfred writes, "the development of powerful oratorical abilities is imperative" (1999, p. xix). I heard such oral skills when I visited the Native North American Indian Travelling College, located on Cornwall Island at Akwesasne. Students from the AFS had been asked to participate in an art exhibit depicting themes from the Ohenton Kariwahtekwen. The artwork was fascinating, colorful, and imaginative. What really struck me, however, was the small group of AFS students reciting the Ohenton Kariwahtekwen. Confident yet humble, these young people spoke in the language of their heritage as they expressed gratitude to all living things.

It has become quite common for students from the AFS to be invited throughout the community to recite the Ohenton Kariwahtekwen, particularly because there are few speakers of the Mohawk language who are able to do so. A proud parent told me how his child was willing and able to recite the Ohenton Kariwahtekwen while at a meeting in Albany, New York: "She gave the Opening and I did a summary in English of what she said. But the fact that she knew it all in Mohawk was just amazing, and it just amazed the people that I presented to. It just showed the value, for her, and her speaking skills quickly became evident. She's comfortable speaking in front of groups of people, and that's one of her talents" (Interviewee P9: July 15, 2005). She confidently carried out her responsibilities as a Mohawk leader in following the Great Law's instructions to give thanks and gratitude before and after the gathering of minds.

AFS students are able to share their knowledge of the Ohenton Kariwahtekwen and take a leadership role in their community. The AFS has prepared them with a foundation and the self-confidence to speak for themselves. "The Akwesasne Freedom School made them stronger," one parent says. "It made my children more vocal and able to speak for themselves" (Interviewee P12: July 15, 2005). Because these students know who they are and are not afraid of speaking their minds, they exude self-confidence and a quiet calmness. As a teacher says, "They have a stronger identity, confidence. They know it's okay to make mistakes. They can feel good about themselves" (Interviewee T6: July 20, 2005).

By acquiring the values of respect, kinship, responsibility, stewardship, cooperation, and leadership, AFS students are carrying out their duties and becoming "fully Mohawk." These values comprise individual branches of the tree in the Indigenous model of holistic education (see fig. 14). As students live by these values, they move toward the top of the tree.

Becoming Fully Mohawk: A Good Mind

> I don't drink or do anything illegal. . . . I always try and stay calm and treat people how I want to be treated. I always try to keep a good mind.
> —*Interviewee A4: October 18, 2004*

In *To Become a Human Being*, the late Tadodaho (head chief of the Haudenosaunee) Leon Shenandoah reminds us, "We're always to have a Good Mind. If our mind is clouded, how can good decisions be made? Laughter clears our mind and reminds us of the creator" (qtd. in Wall 2001, p. 14). Having a "good mind" means moving through life with respect, dignity, honor, and responsibility. Young people especially must be equipped with a solid sense of right and wrong to make good decisions. One alum whose sister also attended the AFS says,

> I look at my sister and see that she's different. I think it's because of the Akwesasne Freedom School. She has different priorities. She thinks differently. It's hard to explain. When you're tuned into your culture and you know what it takes to be a good human being—the stories, teachings—you live your life that way. I think she does that. It's just how she carries herself. What's important to her is language. She's sixteen, and at sixteen I couldn't care less about language. It's important to be Onkwehonweh. I think [knowing this is] because of the Akwesasne Freedom School. (Interviewee A6: October 13, 2004)

To be Onkwehonwe is to have a good mind, which is necessary for becoming fully Mohawk.

Orenda

A "good mind" is also necessary for accumulating the spiritual power of orenda, or magic power (Hewitt 1902). As mentioned in chapter 1, orenda is a spiritual force that flows in and between all things. A lengthier analysis of the varying interpretations is provided here in attempting to understand the spirituality that propels AFS students toward becoming fully Mohawk. Hewitt compared orenda to *wakan* of the Sioux, *manitou* of the Algonquins, and *pokunt* of the Shoshones. He defined the word "orenda" as a "hypothetic potence or potentiality to do or affect results mystically" (p. 37). This power, he believed, was in all living things and was accompanied by sounds or utterances.[1] Shamans have powerful orenda, hunters have superior orenda, and to win a game of skill or chance one overcomes the orenda of one's opponent. Singing, Hewitt explains, was a method of "putting forth" one's orenda (p. 38). One could also lay down one's orenda by surrendering or submitting:

> A shaman, *rarendiowane,* is one whose orenda is great, powerful; a fine hunter, *rarendiio,* is one whose orenda is fine, superior in quality; when a hunter is successful in the chase, it is said, *watharendogennt,* he baffled,

> thwarted their orenda, . . . should the huntsman return unsuccessful, it is said, wathorendogenni, they (the game) have foiled, outmatched his orenda; . . . when the elements are gathering and a storm is brewing, it is said, *watrendonni,* it (the storm-makers) is making, preparing its orenda; . . . a prophet or soothsayer, *ratren'dats* or *hatrendotha',* is one who habitually puts forth or effuses his orenda, . . . anything whose orenda is reputed or believed to have been instrumental in obtaining some good or in accomplishing some purpose is said "to possess orenda." Singing was interpreted to signify that the singer, chanter whether beast, bird, tree, wind, man or what not, was putting forth his orenda, his mystic potence, to execute his will. (Hewitt 1902, pp. 38–39)

One might conclude that orenda is a demonstration of power, but orenda is not superiority over others or a show of might. Orenda is used for the benefit of others and conveys the general idea of "inherent power of resistance to evil" (Henry 1955, p. 62), which maintains a sense of balance. Ceremonies are an important element in channeling individual orenda for the well-being of others, which "leads to development of a power, an orenda, of the community" (Saraydar 1990, p. 23). Such benevolent personal power is what allowed the Peacemaker to unite the Haudenosaunee community into a confederacy that ended internal warfare (Johansen and Mann 2000). It is this personal power that helps AFS students to feel a sense of connection and responsibility to their community.

Orenda, then, can be considered a power made of dual forces that must be in balance to maintain order in the world. Those dual forces are known as Uki (Ugi) and Otkon (also Otgont or Okton).[2] AFS students are continually trying to negotiate these opposing forces in their world as they struggle to live with a good mind. According to Johansen and Mann (2000) the term "orenda" alone does not adequately represent the idea of the "spirit force." They suggest that Uki and Otkon are two halves that make up the force known as orenda and are represented by the twins, Sapling and Flint, introduced in the Creation Story. It is only when "taken together do *uki* and *okton* form the universe of medicine" (p. 231). It was Uki who created light, trees, and grass, and Otkon who created night, poison, thorns, and earthquakes.[3] Johansen and Mann conclude that the pair should "not separated from each other's influence and certainly not conflated with the Christian Manichean dichotomy" (p. 231).

Johansen and Mann (2000) provide examples demonstrating Uki and Otkon. For one, in the Haudenosaunee creation story, the Sky People "were greatly gifted with *uki-okton* power," they write, especially Sky Woman, who was more gifted than the Fire Dragon, a malevolent Otkon spirit (p. 85).[4] By singing medicine chants, Sky Woman used her Uki power to help the Earth, Turtle Island, increase in size after she fell upon it.

To clarify this idea of orenda further, I consulted Haudenosaunee knowledge holders and Mohawk language speakers. Most had never heard of a contemporary use of the term "orenda" but recognized "karen:na" as song. Fluent Mohawk speaker Karhowane (Cory McComber), from Kahnawà:ke, who has an extraordinary knowledge of Mohawk and Huron linguistics, informed me that the term orenda by itself is not a balance of good and bad. "Orenda" is a noun, and to be "good" or "bad" it must have a suffix: *karenni:io* (good song), *karennakshen* (bad song). "Orenda or Karenna is therefore not good or bad, it just is" (Karhowane, personal communication, August 14, 2014).[5] There are still many questions, then, as to the meaning and usage of the term "orenda" both historically and in contemporary Mohawk lives.

Yet I still found myself grappling with the existential questions posed by John Mohawk (2005): "What is the meaning of all this? Why are we here? How did we get to be here? What is our role in the great measure of things?" This section of the book came about during a difficult time in my personal life while I was grieving the death of my parents. I met with healers and traditional knowledge holders. I read everything I could, from Buddhist philosophy to our own stories of creation, searching for answers. I wanted to know where my parents were. Would I ever see them again? What is our purpose in life? These questions then began to merge back into my writing on what it means to be Mohawk. There had to be some concept in Haudenosaunee culture and language that helped explain the internal force that propels us through life. "Orenda" may not be the proper term, but as I struggled with how to articulate these ideas for the book, I took the advice of Haudenosaunee scholar Brian Rice. Rice said that this discussion of orenda is necessary, as there have been many aspects of our traditions, especially the Creation Story, that have been lost but are slowly making a resurgence.

So orenda or karen:na or some other term for a spiritual life force seems to address at least some of the questions of our existence. In the context of the Creation Story, orenda is a concept that entails accumulating personal power for the benefit of the greater good and living with a "good mind" in order to return to the place of our creation and to the Creator. Mohawk continues, "Why do we do these ceremonials of thanksgiving? Because we recognize our great good fortune as receivers of the gifts of the Giver of Life" (p. v). Our cosmology addresses such issues: "It is to questions about the meaning of existence that grand mythologies, sometimes called meta-narratives, turn their attention. Mythologies construct visions of the past which address the question about how the world became the way it is and, equally important, how we, as cultural beings in a certain culture, came to be the way we are. Such stories also urge upon us the expectation that things have been known to happen in a certain way, and are likely to happen in that way again" (Mohawk 2005, p. vi).

John Mohawk stresses that because of colonization and concomitant assimilation policies, residential schools, Western education systems, and the replacement of traditional governments, the Haudenosaunee have abandoned some of their original belief systems. He describes the result: "It would not be an exaggeration to state the Iroquois creation story has not been recounted in a public ceremony in any longhouse in all of Iroquoia for something over one hundred years. The story of the woman who fell from the sky and landed on Turtle's back, initiating the creation of Turtle Island, is not recounted or read in the Iroquois communities except by a few souls who have access to research libraries and who make a point of studying Iroquois culture" (2005, p. xi). One of those souls was the late Cayuga chief Jacob Thomas who last told the Creation Story over a period of twelve days in 1994 (Rice, 2013). It is also worth stating that the goal of Western education is to gain knowledge and skills in preparation for the work force, not to create good human beings who live a balanced life. There is little opportunity, then, for Haudenosaunee students to accumulate orenda or spiritual power in a Western education system. This could change, with revitalization of Haudenosaunee culture, in an Indigenous holistic education setting such as the Akwesasne Freedom School. The AFS provides for continuation of a Haudenosaunee way of life, realizing personal potential, and gaining the spiritual power of orenda.

Through daily social interaction AFS students are immersed in Kanienke:ha and the Mohawk way of life. The school's pedagogy includes an enculturation process that deeply roots students in Mohawk values, beliefs, and traditional knowledge. Stories of creation, original instructions provided in the Great Law and the Ohenton Kariwahtekwen, traditional songs, and social practices such as Longhouse ceremonies and dances—all convey the values of cooperation, respect, peace, gratitude, and responsibility.[6]

As AFS students follow the original instructions and live a balanced life, they accumulate orenda. And for the Haudenosaunee, this orenda is said to be at its peak when children reach puberty (Rice n.d.). As with the children of the Skyworld, their inner light will be protected from harm. Brian Rice states that "once the oren:ta was acquired, the children could never be harmed and the Sky World would remain lit" (Rice 2013). As our children accumulate orenda they will eventually return to the Skyworld, the place of our creation, via the Milky Way Trail. It is said that this path will lead the Onkwehonwe to the Creator's lodge "on the upper side of the sky" (Rice n.d.).

Free to Be Mohawk

> Most of my poems are about the nature of things. The pollution and how it affects me. I write what I feel and that even though it makes me feel better I know it won't change anything. Sometimes it's hard to imagine that I write these poems with these hands and think of them with this mind. I am very proud of the poems that I write. When I was in other schools I had never written any poems. But since I've been to the Freedom School all my feelings came out. I guess that's why they call it the Freedom School.—*Perkins 1994*

We must ask ourselves if becoming fully human is still important. Western public schooling is geared to producing obedient cogs in the global economy and people who are successful at some level in a capitalistic society where material wealth is valued most, and many Native people have lost the original purposes of education. Tewa educator Gregory Cajete (1994) writes, "What has been called education today was for Native Americans a journey for learning to be fully human" (p. 43). The original purpose of education for the Haudenosaunee, according to Leon Shenandoah (Wall 2001, p. 57) was to "reform you for the benefit of yourself and your people so that you may get back to where the Creator is . . . that's what He wants." In other words, to strive to become fully human, fully Onkwehonwe. To become fully human, Chief Shenandoah said, "the best path is a spiritual one. It's the only one that helps you become a Human Being" (Wall 2001, p. 71). Western education will not take us on this path. "Your schools don't teach you those things," Shenandoah said. "There's coming a day when your education will fail you because they don't teach you the spirituality. You learn how to get a job, make money, and manage business, but you don't know about the Creator's place or about what your path is" (ibid., p. 26).

Shenandoah says: "Giving thanks is to give honor and to honor is to show respect. Doing that means you're becoming a 'Human Being.' The more you become a 'Human Being' the more you remember your ceremonies. All the people on Mother Earth were given their ceremonies. Carrying them on is one of the duties of 'Human Beings'" (Wall 2001, p. 40). The Akwesasne Freedom School provides hope for the future of Mohawk culture, the Mohawk way of life. Its past and current students continue to carry out their responsibility, living as fully Mohawk for future generations. At the AFS, students can fulfill their human potential and find personal meaning. They are learning to be good Onkwehonwe and are given the space to be *free to be Mohawk.*

Conclusion

Final Thoughts on Self-Determination and Educational Freedom

> The Akwesasne Freedom School has to exist. Otherwise *we* will cease to exist.
> —*Interviewee P11: July 20, 2005*

From its early days of kerosene stoves to its present as a full-immersion school, the Akwesasne Freedom School has impacted many lives. "I don't want my kids to feel like that priest made me feel," Theresa "Bear" Fox says as she explains why Kanienke:ha has become a priority for her and her children. She says her oldest daughter doesn't drink or do drugs and is a good role model: "her spirit is really strong" (personal communication, October 11, 2004). She attributes these characteristics in part to the AFS, where her daughter learned about her own culture, which nurtured her self-confidence and self-esteem. Although she still does not consider herself a fluent speaker of Mohawk, Bear has become more proficient in Kanienke:ha and is teaching young Mohawks to find their way through music.

Like Akwesasne, other Indigenous communities can create self-sufficient education programs that support cultural and linguistic survival. Growing out of an extreme internal conflict and in response to the lack of culturally appropriate curriculum in public education systems, the AFS came to provide a space where students are free to be Mohawk and use their own language. It is akin to the Rough Rock Navajo School, which serves as "a place to be Navajo," where Navajo students are "free to be Navajo, in Navajo" (McCarty 2003).

Educational Self-Determination

The Akwesasne Freedom School serves as an exemplary model of educational self-determination and sovereignty. In 2005 it was honored by the Harvard Project on American Indian Economic Development for its work in creating a self-sufficient education program. Other Native communities seeking to gain control over education programs and develop their own language renewal initiatives can look to the grassroots AFS cultural and language immersion program, which serves as a "counter-force to the myriad forces that seek to marginalize and erase Indigenous voices and identities" (McCarty 2003, p. 18). The AFS is a decolonization effort, and there the balance of power between colonizing forces and Indigenous peoples has shifted in favor of the people of Akwesasne. Mohawk youth thrive in an institution once used to subjugate their parents and grandparents.

The AFS has been highly successful in creating future leaders for the community, but creating such education programs from scratch takes considerable motivation, community effort, and perseverance. Reversing decades of assimilation policies and practices and their effects can seem like an insurmountable struggle, especially when greatly limited by financial constraints. Complete control of education may seem impossible for many Native communities, but the empowering aspects of financial independence should be considered. Dependence means adhering to regulations by overarching powers whose main concerns are Western standards and accountability. Such public education creates problems for non-Native students and mass society as well as Native students and communities.

Deloria and Wildcat (2001) find that "the problem with Indian education in America is really the problem of education in America, regardless of whether recipients of the education are, figuratively speaking, red, yellow, black, or white" (p. 9). One response to problems in public education has been the creation of charter schools, and some Indigenous communities have turned to charter schools in an effort to create educational opportunities that are culturally grounded, in hopes of improving student academic performance (Bielenberg 2000; Goodyear-Ka'ōpua 2013). Charter schools however, must still abide by state-mandated guidelines, making "teaching to the test" the norm, while Native culture and language can get squeezed out of the curriculum (Fenimore-Smith 2009).

Cultural Continuity

Regardless of where Indigenous children attend school, cultural continuity between home and school is an important factor in their success. Holistic education programs that are grounded in cultural traditions and emphasize development of the whole child have the potential for great success. Experiential and holistic perspectives on teaching and learning, pedagogy that differs from the Western view of compartmentalized knowledge, means acknowledging how academic disciplines relate to one another and to the surrounding universe (Kawagley and Barnhardt 1998, p. 3). Indigenous communities are creating more comprehensive holistic education systems that integrate Indigenous knowledge and Western pedagogies. The Alaska Rural Systemic Initiative is attempting to bridge the gap between Alaskan Native epistemologies and Western science by documenting Indigenous knowledge systems of Alaskan Native peoples and developing "pedagogical practices and curricula that incorporate Indigenous knowledge and ways of knowing into the formal education system" (Alaska Rural Systemic Initiative 2005, p. 5). The initiative has developed cultural standards for schools and guidelines for teachers and has seen an increase in student achievement scores, a decrease in dropout rates, an increase in post-secondary attendance, and an increase in numbers of Alaska Native college students in the fields of math, science, and engineering. Indeed, Native and non-Native educators and parents share the goal of creating a better future for coming generations.

Raising up Indigenous Languages

An additional goal for many Native educators is the revitalization of their languages. Indigenous communities who wish to see hear their languages spoken by future generations must take action now. When Indigenous communities have more control over their schools, culture and language programs are more likely to be incorporated into the curriculum. However, as I have argued in this book, language instruction must take place in both the home and the school for young people to attain a level of proficiency that ensures continuance of the language. Native nations have become more dependent on schools to provide language instruction, but whether or not students are hearing and using the language in the home is a major factor in their language abilities.

The linguistic ability of AFS students varies from fluency in Kanienke:ha to limited proficiency. Parents, teachers, and other community members at Akwesasne often emphasize the level of Mohawk language ability achieved at the school. Measures of success are stated in terms of the number of fluent speakers produced and the level of fluency attained in any given year, while a relative lack of fluent speakers is seen as a measure of failure. While producing speakers is a worthwhile accomplishment in terms of Mohawk language revitalization, it should be kept in mind that students are achieving other markers of success, like increased self-confidence, self-esteem, and the establishment of strong identities. These are foundational in language revitalization efforts. The fact that these students, while not always fluent, highly value the Mohawk language, speaks volumes to the shaping of positive language ideologies.

Most of the AFS youths I interviewed indicated that they valued the Mohawk language, took pride in it, and viewed it as an integral aspect of their identities. A lesson I learned from these students is that attaining language fluency, while the ultimate goal, should not overshadow the importance of valuing the traditional language. McCarty, Romero-Little, and Zepeda (2006, p. 674) assert: "Youth have much to teach us about the strategies we might employ in creating policies and practices that support heritage-language retention. Our role then is to listen and to act." The young Mohawks of the Akwesasne Freedom School have spoken. They have told us that when language revitalization efforts are meaningful, grounded in specific cultural histories and the contemporary lives of Native communities, they can successfully revive the language as a valuable resource for those communities.

While schools alone cannot save Indigenous languages, ones like the AFS that serve as cultural extensions of the community can play a significant role in language revitalization. Fostering positive beliefs and feelings about Indigenous cultures and languages are essential to language revitalization efforts.

Empowerment through Language and Culture

Indigenous languages are in danger of disappearing, and efforts are desperately needed to maintain and revitalize them. While language is an important factor in the formation of individual and cultural identity, it would behoove us to remember that Indigenous identities are complex, dynamic, and influenced by various factors.

When I asked respondents what it meant to be Mohawk, very few felt that the language was the number one element to their unique identity as Mohawk people. They felt they needed to know traditional songs and stories, their own history, and most importantly, to have a "good mind." Kanienke:ha allows for deeper understanding of what it means to be Mohawk. However, language is only one aspect of one's individual and cultural identities.

Indigenous language loss and revitalization efforts are delicate subjects in Native communities, and we should remember that it is not always the fault of the Native individual, family, or even community if they don't know their ancestors' language. We have to remember the ongoing assaults to Native cultures and languages and the campaigns to destroy them. We likewise have to be cautious when ascribing strict standards to defining who can claim Native identity and who cannot. Communities and individuals who have intact cultural practices, where their languages are strong and vibrant, are few and far between. Not all Native peoples have access to such strong cultural traditions (Garroutte 2003). Those individuals should consider themselves fortunate, and we should all remember that to believe that language equals identity ignores the complexities and nuances—and the history of colonial forces aimed to destroy those languages.

I support the claim that Native students can be successful in school when their culture and language are incorporated into the curriculum. We know that, as Brayboy and Castagno write, "When teachers, curricula, and schools provide a challenging and high-quality education that is intimately connected and relevant to tribal communities, they will be far more likely to graduate youth who are academically prepared, connected to, and active members of their tribal communities, and knowledgeable about the dominant and their home communities" (Brayboy and Castagno 2009).

Deeply entrenched language ideologies informed by colonial forms of education that largely ignored Native cultures have strongly influenced parents' ideas about language immersion. The belief that language immersion will hinder academic success must be dispelled. The future of Indigenous language survival is at stake. Some language immersion students may fall behind temporarily, as was the case with some AFS students, but the majority catch up quickly and excel beyond expectations in their academic and social lives. I hope that this book, in conveying this message, will help some parents become more supportive of language immersion programs.

When students learn their own history and culture they can be empowered. Their self-confidence and self-esteem grow. Indigenous students can become more firmly grounded in their unique individual and cultural identities. Abiding by the unique cultural values of Indigenous communities can help further strengthen those identities, as young people live their lives striving for spiritual fulfillment. Reaching toward this spiritual power—orenda for the Haudenosaunee—is akin to what psychologists and Indigenous scholar Willie Ermine call self-actualization and gives us a higher purpose in life:

> As with many other cultures around the world, the holy people and philosophers among Aboriginal people have explored and analyzed the process of self-actualization. The being in relation to the cosmos possessed intriguing and mysterious qualities that provided insights into existence. In their quest to find meaning in the outer space, Aboriginal people turned to the inner space. This inner space is that universe of being within each person that is synonymous with the soul, the spirit, the self, or the being. (Ermine 1995, p. 103)

Lessons from the Akwesasne Freedom School

As reform is sought in both Native and non-Native education systems, much can be learned from the Akwesasne Freedom School. Community control of education, culturally appropriate curricula, and the adoption of traditional educational principles and practices can have far-reaching influence on young people in a global society that increasingly emphasizes individuality, competition, and material gain. As political and social powers threaten Native languages through marginalization and standardization, education systems can provide a countering force. The AFS empowers its community through the expression of its sovereign rights to educational self-determination while perpetuating Mohawk language and culture.

Teachers and administrators at mainstream schools interested in exploring alternative ways of teaching and learning can benefit from tribally controlled schools that emphasize traditional knowledge and Native ways of knowing (Tippeconnic 2000). By making schooling meaningful, emphasizing parental and community involvement, and engaging students through use of experiential methods and the natural world, schools can better serve the needs of their diverse student bodies. The AFS, like other Native schools "run by parents and communities in accord with their deeply rooted, persistent, but not unchanging cultural values," is "a model for meaningful, challenging, locally controlled education for all Americans" (Lomawaima and McCarty 2006, p. 170). Likewise, inclusion of Indigenous perspectives and ways of knowing in mainstream schooling raises awareness of Indigenous cultures, communities, and contemporary life, enhancing understanding of multiculturalism and diversity.

Reclaiming Research

In response to an expressed need for documenting the history of the Akwesasne Freedom School and determining how the school has affected its alumni, this book allows students, teachers, and parents to tell their own story of a community-wide effort in cultural and linguistic revitalization. AFS administrators, teachers, parents, and other community members were directly involved through reviews of the initial research proposal and reading of individual chapters and the whole manuscript. Their feedback has been invaluable. Given the long history of academic research in Native communities whereby Native people were often not consulted, were rarely involved in the research process, and were sometimes subjected to harm, involving the AFS community was important to me as a Native researcher and as a member of the Akwesasne community.

Linda Tuhiwai Smith (1999, 2012) articulates the importance of Indigenous research methodologies that consider community protocols and cultural values. She advocates for reclaiming research through a deconstruction of Western research paradigms that have historically marginalized Indigenous peoples. She argues for Indigenous peoples to become active participants in healing and decolonizing—and in their own transformation.

Looking Ahead

Protecting Indigenous languages is a priority for the international Indigenous community. The United Nations Declaration on the Rights of Indigenous Peoples (UNDRIP) states that Indigenous peoples have the right to "revitalize, use, develop, and transmit to future generations their histories, languages, oral traditions, philosophies, writing systems and literatures, and to designate and retain their own names for communities, places, and persons" (United Nations 2007, Article 13.1). Further: "Indigenous peoples have the right to establish and control their educational systems and institutions providing education in their language in a manner appropriate to their cultural methods of teaching and learning" (ibid., Article 14.1).

The UNDRIP is a non–legally binding document addressing the collective rights of Indigenous peoples globally. While it is a significant step and indicates potential for a brighter future, there remains an imminent need for protective legislation and significant financial support in both the United States and Canada for Indigenous control of education and language programming. It is imperative for policy makers to support school-based language revitalization efforts that support academic achievement without sacrificing cultural and linguistic identity (Lomawaima and McCarty 2002). The continuance of Indigenous languages depends on consistent funding for language programming in addition to commitment from language educators.

Several themes for further research emerged as I worked on this book. The Akwesasne community has yet to undergo a thorough, formal assessment of the status of the Mohawk language. Language statistics are all rough estimates by various community members. Information regarding fluency rates among various age groups could better inform language revitalization efforts and language planning.

Additionally, further investigation of AFS students might provide documentation regarding the effects of language immersion on academic performance. Several AFS students appear to have had some difficulties in academic and social adjustment in their first year of high school. Additional research might help the AFS community strategize how better to prepare students for the transition to high school and help high school teachers better accommodate students coming from a full Mohawk language immersion program. The idea of a feasibility study to assess the possibility of adding a high school is of interest to AFS parents and teachers. When AFS students go to a public school away from the community, although they can take Mohawk language courses as separate subjects, many have found that they were losing their Kanienke:ha speaking ability because of the heavy influence of English throughout their school day.

Tending the Garden

I end with words from traditional Mohawk leader Tom Porter, whose grandmother told him that he would one day go to the next world. She told him that when his time on earth was completed he would travel to the Skyworld and in doing so face two paths. One path would lead to happiness if the original instructions had been followed while on earth. The other path would lead to eternal visions of destruction. Tom's grandmother instructed him to go toward the ancestors. He remembered these words later when he spoke at a 2004 conference organized by the Ontario-based Sweetgrass First Nations Language Council: "In order to take that route you need to have your language, your Mohawk name, and be dressed in your traditional clothing. Students at the Akwesasne Freedom School will be prepared to take that road and greet their ancestors. The Akwesasne Freedom School gives freedom, dignity, respect, [and] love, and allows students to talk from the heart. The school and its children have to be cared for like a garden. They need water, they need to be weeded, and they need to be talked and sung to each day and need room to grow. In the fall the corn will grow tall and the melons will be ripe for picking" (Porter 2004).

Notes

Introduction

1. "Kanienke:ha" is a Mohawk term referring to the Mohawk language, as noted on p. xvii. The language is also referred to as "Mohawk." Many Akwesasne community members, particularly elders, simply say they are speaking "Indian."
2. Tsi Snaihne is a district within Akwesasne territory that falls within Quebec's borders.
3. See note 12 below regarding methodology of identifying interview subjects and maintaining anonymity.
4. I generally use the terms "Native American," "Native," "Indian," "Indigenous," and "American Indian" interchangeably in this book. "Indigenous," which I prefer, is a more inclusive term used when referring to tribal groups not just in the United States and Canada but also elsewhere. "Indian" has fallen out of use but is used when referring to legislation such as the Indian Act and in other governmental policies and is used as such here. "Aboriginal" is an accepted term in Canada, as is "First Nations." "Aboriginal" is also used when referring to Australian tribal groups. "Alaskan Native" is used when referring to the many tribal groups in Alaska. The preferred choice among most tribal groups, however, is to call them by their original individual names.
5. Officially titled *The Problem of Indian Administration*, the Meriam Report was commissioned by the Institute for Governmental Research to investigate the conditions of US Indian boarding schools and reservations. The report detailed the deplorable overcrowded conditions, lack of medical attention, poor curriculum, and inadequate teacher credentials. It also called for the inclusion of Indian students into public schools (Meriam 1928; Prucha 1995).
6. Throughout this book I refer to "Indian control," "tribal control," and "community control" to mean that Indian people are deciding the fate of their own education programs without outside interference.
7. The National Indian Brotherhood (NIB) was a precursor of today's Assembly of First Nations (AFN). The NIB started in the late 1960s as a lobby group for Aboriginal rights in Canada and as an avenue for First Nations to change Canada's policies. The organi-

zation brought many Aboriginal issues to mainstream awareness, including concerns about housing, education, and poverty. The NIB grew and became the AFN in 1982, reflecting a more cohesive representative organization for all Aboriginal peoples in Canada (see Assembly of First Nations, http://www.afn.ca/index.php/en).

8. "Residential schooling" is a term primarily used in Canada, whereas "boarding school" is used in the United States. Both refer to government-sponsored education programs that were aimed at assimilating Native children into white-European Canadian or US society. I use the Canadian term "residential schooling" when speaking of institutions in both countries to avoid confusion with other types of mainstream boarding schools.
9. In 2004 Senator Sam Brownback (R-Kansas) introduced a Native American apology resolution in partnership with Daniel K. Inouye (D-Hawaii) and Senator Ben Nighthorse Campbell, a Northern Cheyenne. President Obama signed the resolution into law in December 2009 as part of a defense appropriations bill. While it apologizes for "ill-conceived policies and acts of violence against American Indians," it was not meant to authorize or support any claims against the US government and is a symbolic gesture only. While representatives from the Cherokee, Choctaw, Creek, Sisseton Wahpeton Oyate, and Pawnee Nations were present during Senator Brownback's reading of the apology, it was not made public and was largely unnoticed by many Native Americans (see "Brownbeck, Dorgan Applaud Senate Passage of Native American Apology Resolution," www.indian.senate.gov/news/press-release/brownback-dorgan-applaud-senate-passage-native-american-apology-resolution).
10. See Palmater (2011), which discusses Canada's Indian Act and the Canadian government's discriminatory policies against women and offers alternative solutions to determining Indigenous identity.
11. For further discussion on the topic of insider/outsider research and "working from home" in Indigenous communities, see Hill and McCallum 2009).
12. For the purposes of this study, interviewees are identified by the following codes: P—parent, S—student, A—alum, V—volunteer or non-teacher staff member, and T—teacher. Some respondents fit in more than one category. For example, I interviewed several alumni who were also parents of AFS students (AP). Additionally, some alumni are teachers at the AFS (AT).

1. The Haudenosaunee

1. The terms "Haudenosaunee" and "Iroquois" are used interchangeably in this book. The more commonly used descriptor, "Iroquois," is derived from the Algonquian name for "killer people," or some similar negative connotation, and the later French linguistic influence (see Fenton 1978 for an extensive linguistic history; Snow 1994). Most early written accounts use "Iroquois," while "Haudenosaunee" has had a more recent resurgence as the preferred term. "Haudenosaunee" (sometimes spelled Hotinonshonni or Rotinonshonni) translates as "People of the Longhouse."

2. There are dozens of versions of the Haudenosaunee Creation Story; "a single [authoritative] version does not exist" (J. Mohawk 2005, p. iv). This version is compiled from Barnes (1984), Mohawk (2005), and Snow (1994, pp. 2–4). For additional elaboration and analysis, see Bonaparte (2006), Cornplanter (1986), Fenton (1978), Hewitt (1928), Rice (2013), and Tehanetorens (1992). Abler (1987) has conducted research on the forty variants of the Iroquois creation myth. *Traditional Teachings* (Barnes 1984), published by the Native North American Travelling College at Akwesasne, is one of the first sources I read on the Creation Story many years ago. Mohawk's version (2005) is a modern interpretation of Hewitt's publication of the story (1928) as told to him by Onondaga chief John Arthur Gibson at the end of the nineteenth century. Gibson's story is the longest and most detailed, and it is one of the first written recordings of the Creation Story.
3. The concept of a "good mind" (Kanikonri:io) was introduced to the Haudenosaunee by the Peacemaker and refers to a code of conduct by which one should live. "Having a good mind" means that one has positive thoughts and lives in peace.
4. "Orenda" is an anglicized version of the Huron term "*iarenda*." Huron is an Iroquoian language and the Huron or Wendat people, although not a part of the Haudenosaunee Confederacy, share a similar culture with the Haudenosaunee. Orenda or "hypothetic potence" is called "*orenna*" or "*karenna*" in the Mohawk language (Hewitt 1902, p. 37). There is a lack of recent detailed literature on orenda, with its varied spelling and meanings. "Orenda" is typically incorporated into a verb within the Mohawk language, such as "*renn*" in the verb "*enionterennoten*," meaning "to sing for power" or to "stand up my karenna" (Karhowane Cory McComber, personal communication, August 15, 2014). See J. Bruyas, *Radical Words of the Mohawk Iroquois with their Derivatives* (New York: Cramoisy Press, 1862), for examples of seventeenth-century Mohawk and Huron languages. See J. Steckly, *Words of the Huron* (Waterloo, Ontario: Wilfred Laurier Press, 2007), for a discussion of the Huron form of "orenda" and its noun root and usage relating to ceremonies. While "*karenna*" may be the Mohawk spelling noted by Hewitt, "*orenda*" or "*orenta*" appears to be a more contemporary spelling by the Haudenosaunee as evidenced in Mohawk scholar Brian Rice's *The Rotinonshonni* (2013), Oneida singer Joanne Shenandoah's music CD titled *Orenda*, and Anishanabe author Joseph Boyden's novel *The Orenda* (New York: Alfred A. Knopf, 2013). Thus, for consistency, I have used "orenda."
5. The idea of "good" versus "evil," the Good-Minded Twin (Sapling or Uki) and versus the Evil-Minded Twin (Flint or Otkon), suggests a concept of completely opposite forces. But Johansen and Mann (2000) note: "The Twins, Sapling and Flint, were not, in fact, displaying good versus evil. They illustrate the cosmic balance of spirit elements. . . . Flint was what Western anthropologists like to call a 'trickster figure,' a powerful spirit with a sense of humor and an immature lack of patience. . . . The Twins embodied the certainty-uncertainty principle, but each was necessary to balance out the excesses of the other" (p. 84). Johansen and Mann also observed that the concepts of "good" versus "evil" were perpetuated by the agenda of Christian missionaries who

cast Flint as Satan and Sapling as God. Subsequently many versions of the Creation Story "contained blatantly Euro-Christian interpolations" (p. 84) and are still widely accepted.

6. As with the Creation Story, there are many versions of the Great Law of Peace and stories regarding the founding of the Haudenosaunee Confederacy. Gibson and others (1992) provide the most extensive written account of the Great Law. Other original translations can be found in Hewitt (1892), Parker (1916), and Tooker (1978). For anthropological descriptions of the confederacy and discussions of the Great Law, see Fenton (1968), Morgan and Lloyd (1901), Snow (1994), and Tooker (1978). Alfred (1999) and Mohawk (2005) provide contemporary perspectives as Haudenosaunee scholars. Grinde and Johansen (1991) counter early anthropological narratives and offer an alternative view of the Haudenosaunee's and the Great Law's historical influences on the founding of the US Constitution. This is a highly controversial topic that scholars debate (Snow 1994; Tooker 1988). A more recent account of the Great Law is given by Mohawk elder Tom Porter (2008), who served as translator for a ten-day recitation. See also Trigger (1978) and Johansen and Mann (2000). Most versions of the Great Law are similar in their core elements. I choose here to defer mainly to written accounts based on oral tradition printed in *Traditional Teachings* (Barnes 1984). The rich descriptions presented therein are generally accepted by the Haudenosaunee.
7. The formation of the confederacy is often a matter of dispute between scholars and traditional Haudenosaunee. Mann and Fields (1997) consider documented history, oral accounts, and solar eclipse data to determine the date of August 31, 1142. Other scholars (Snow 1994; Tooker 1978) do not take oral history or solar eclipse data into their estimates of the founding of the confederacy and date it as late as 1451.
8. Wampum is made from quahog or whelk shells cut into cylindrical shapes of purple and white. The beads were woven into belts as records of historical events, treaties, and stories (Fadden 1987; Fenton 1971; R. Hill 1990; Tehanetorens 1999).
9. The name "Mohawk," given by enemy tribes, has a negative connotation, meaning "man-eaters." "Kanienkeha:ka," although not frequently used, is widely thought to mean "People of the Flint," referring to the flint or chert found in the region (Fenton and Tooker 1978). However, an alternative translation replaces "flint" with "crystal" or "ice," referring to the abundance of quartz found in the Mohawk Valley (Hewitt 1903; Rice 2013; Snow 1994). Also see Hamell (1983) for a discussion of flint as "ice-stone" or "crystal." Although their usage is rare among Mohawks today, these crystals, now called Herkimer Diamonds, are popular for their beauty and alleged healing properties.
10. The use of the term "Akwesasne" has only come into popular use since the 1970s as a part of reclamation of Mohawk language and connection to the traditional land.
11. See also Brad Bonaparte's website Wampum Chronicles for references to the oral and written history of Akwesasne and the first families who settled there: www.wampumchronicles.com/.
12. It was not until after federal recognition in 1972 that the St. Regis Tribal Council began to administer health, welfare, and social service programs (George-Kanentiio 2006).

13. For more regarding the Code of Handsome Lake, see Fenton (1968), Morgan (1962), Parker (1913), and Wallace and Steen (1972, 1978). Thomas (1994) provides a contemporary interpretation of Handsome Lake.

2. Drums along the St. Regis

1. The Jay Treaty of 1794 between the United States and Britain increased trade and averted war. Article III declared Aboriginal rights to trade and travel between the United States and Canada, then a British territory (Hauptman 1986).
2. Now known as the Native North American Travelling College, this organization continues to produce small publications, offer crafting classes, host an art gallery, and put on summer festivals. The focus is a troupe of traveling singers, dancers, and storytellers who provide historical and cultural presentations to the public (www.natc.org).
3. The conflict has also been commonly referred to as "the barricades," and "the Raquette Point standoff." For more regarding the details of the incident, see Ciborski 1990; Garte 1981; George-Kanentiio 2006; Lemelin 1997; and Matthiessen 1984.
4. As stated in the US Constitution, Congress has the power to regulate trade with Indians, and the executive branch has the power to enter into treaties with Indians. In *Worcester v. Georgia* in 1832, Chief Justice John Marshall ruled that the states have no jurisdiction in Indian affairs (Canby 1998; Cohen 1982; Deloria and Lytle 1983; Getches 2005). French Jesuits established Akwesasne as a mission site in 1755 (Frisch 1970). In 1796 the Seven Nations of Canada, a French organization of Christian allies, allegedly including the St. Regis Mohawks, entered into an unauthorized treaty with New York State, setting limits to Mohawk land and relinquishing future land claims by the Seven Nations (Frisch 1970; George-Kanentiio 2006). New York State ignored federal jurisdiction in dealing with the Iroquois and "obtained land sales and cessions in defiance of the 1790 Trade and Intercourse Act" (Jemison 2000, p. xiv), which "promised that the federal government would guarantee that Indians would not be cheated by the states in dealings over land" (p. xii). Unauthorized individuals who did not represent the Seven Nations of Canada or the St. Regis Mohawks signed the treaties that were negotiated with New York State. The War of 1812 created political divisions between Mohawks at St. Regis, and while the international boundary was at first ignored by the Mohawks, the United States, and Canada, the war made the international boundary a permanent imposition in the community. Akwesasne's land was further diminished through a series of New York State treaties between 1816 and 1845. Not held in trust by the US government, it is still subject to control by Congress (Frisch 1970; George-Kanentiio 2006).
5. George-Kanentiio is referring to crackdown by state police and national guard troops during the infamous Attica prison uprising of 1971 at the Attica Correctional Facility in New York State, during which prisoners rioted and seized control of the prison. Dozens of people were killed including prisoners, correctional officers, and other civilians (Jackson 1999).

6. This is not the first time Mohawks of Akwesasne have protested the imposition of outside authorities. In 1899, not long after the Canadian government instituted an elected band council, a Mohawk known as "Jake Ice" was shot and killed by Canadian authorities. He was part of a group opposed to the Indian Act and its "alien system of elections" and was shot inside the Indian Agent office during a fight with authorities who were determined to make sure band council elections proceeded as planned (Bonaparte n.d.).
7. Title VII is a federally funded grant program that began at the Salmon River High School in 1973, was authorized by the Bilingual Education Act of 1968, and is also known as Title VII of the Elementary and Secondary Education Act. See Evans and Hornberger (2005) for a review of federal language education policies in the United States.
8. "Ahkwesahsne" is an alternative spelling of "Akwesasne."
9. The SRMS used to be under the auspices of the Catholic Church and was referred to at one time as "the convent," as it was operated by nuns. But by the time Tom Porter attended, the school had been made public. In 1955–56 the school became a part of the Salmon River Central School District. However, the nuns would still visit the school in the years when Porter attended to provide religious instruction (John Kahionhes Fadden, personal communication, January 17, 2015).
10. Tom Porter, whose first language is Mohawk, is describing the nun's habits. They were fully covered except for their faces.

3. The Akwesasne Freedom School

1. There is no one clear definition of holistic education theory or practice, which is attributed to its interdisciplinary nature: "The holistic education movement does not have a single source, a predominant proponent, or a major form of expression. Consequently it is difficult to define holistic education" (Forbes 1996). Holistic education draws from philosophy, psychology, pedagogy, and theology. The progressive education movement (Dewey 1938; Tanner 1997) and Waldorf and Montessori school models (Pope-Edwards 2002; Montessori 1964) have also influenced holistic educators. Indigenous communities in Hawaii (Schonleber 2006), and in the southwestern United States (Oberly 2002) find the Montessori approach in particular to be congruent with their own educational goals and values.

4. Kanienke:ha and the Akwesasne Freedom School

1. For early missionary writing and documentation of Mohawk and other Iroquois languages—and for a survey of antiquarian materials in the British Library—see Edwards (2008).
2. See Mithun (1999, p. 425) for a comprehensive list of research on Iroquoian languages including grammar, dictionaries, phonology, lexicon, and literacy.

3. See also Peters and Peters (2013).
4. Examples from Mohawk (Stairs, Peters, and Perkins 1999); Navajo (Holm and Holm 1995); Hualapai (McCarty and Watahomigie 1998), and Native Hawaiian communities (Kamanā and Wilson 1996) attest to the ability of schools to help reverse language shift.
5. See Hinton (2013) for autobiographical accounts of language revitalization efforts at home.
6. The "20x20" rule is that a learner must hear or use a word twenty times in twenty different situations before it is mastered. Whereas just saying a word four hundred times will not result in mastery (Hinton and Hale 2001, p. 184)
7. Waldorf education was started in Germany by Austrian scientist Rudolf Steiner in 1919. His vision was independently administered education for a just and peaceful society. Waldorf addresses the needs of the whole child—"the heart and the hands, as well as the head" (Why Waldorf Works, www.whywaldorfworks.org/).

5. Language and Identity

1. "The Department, under its legal name the Department of Indian Affairs and Northern Development, was established by the Government Organization Act, 1966 and continued by the Department of Indian Affairs and Northern Development Act (R.S., 1985, c. I-6). It is named in Schedule I of the Financial Administration Act. However, the Department is more commonly known by its applied title under the Federal Identity Program (FIP) as Aboriginal Affairs and Northern Development Canada (AANDC)" (https://www.aadnc-aandc.gc.ca/eng/1330446017663/1330446256610).
2. This event took place with a southwestern tribe; the speaker was not Mohawk. The example however, illustrates the difficulties many Native language speakers face when they attempt translating ceremonies from their language to English.

6. Becoming "Fully Mohawk"

1. Hewitt found orenda to be distinctly related to singing: "The speech and utterance of birds and beasts, the soughing of the wind, the voices of the night, the moaning of the tempest, the rumble and crash of thunder, the startling roar of the tornado, the wild creaking and crackling of wind-rocked and frost-river trees, lakes, and rivers, and the multiple other sounds and noises in nature, were conceived to be the chanting—the dirges and the songs—of the various bodies thus giving forth voice and words of beastlike or birdlike speech in the use and exercise of their mystic potence" (1902, p. 36). Based on Seneca linguistic studies, Pratt (1998) concludes that "orenda" means "its song" or "its voice." Isaacs's dissertation (1973) on the Seneca concept of orenda focuses on orenda as power and manifestations of that power in Seneca medicine practices.
2. The Code of Handsome Lake, which was influenced by Christianity, associated Otkon with evil or witchcraft and outlawed its use, replacing the concept with the singular

Sapling as sole Creator. Johansen and Mann also attribute errors in the interpretation of Uki and Otkon to Hewitt (1902), who singled out Uki "for elevation as orenda and then presented it as the totality of spirit access, ignoring otkon" (Johansen and Mann 2000, p. 231). Hewitt (1902) notes that Otkon represents the "malign, deadly, lethal, or destructive half of orenda" (p. 37). While Herrick (1995) also notes that Otkon stems from Sawiskera, the so-called Evil-Minded Twin, and is represented by undesirable creatures like mice and rats, he acknowledges that when Otkon is out of control, the balance between good and evil is disrupted.

3. Grim and John (2005) write: "The Huron concept of oki referred both to a superabundance of power or ability and to spirit-forces of the cosmos, or guardian spirits. An oki could be either benevolent or malevolent. The supreme oki, louskeha, dwelt in the sky, watched over the seasons and the affairs of humans, witnessed to vows, made crops grow, and owned the animals. He had an evil brother, Tawiskaron. The Iroquois orenda, a magico-religious force, was exercised by spirit-forces called Okton and Oyaron (p. 6680)."
4. I am inclined to concur with Johansen and Mann's consideration of both forces, Uki and Otkon, constituting orenda and Hewitt's (1902) interpretation: "*Orenda* is of easy utterance and of simple orthography, and so is readily enunciated. So, until a better name for the mystic potence under discussion is found, let *orenda* be used for it" (p. 38).
5. Karhowane reminded me of the Jesuit influence on early Mohawk writing, coupled with the influence of Huron linguistics and linguistics of other closely related cultures. He feels that Hewitt may have been wrong in his interpretation of orenda, as it can also be applied to Otkon. "Uki," he informed me, is the same as Mohawk "otkon." He indicated that some of the language and its meaning has been lost in modern Mohawk dialects. For example, "atohnhets" is a modern Mohawk term meaning soul or spirit. The root word—"ohnhe"—means "to be alive." A seventeenth-century Mohawk term, "tionhehkwen," which is the same word used to describe the Three Sisters (corn, beans, squash), means something akin to the spirit as a life force. Another similar term meaning spirit or life force of the mind is "o'nihkonra." This is still used in the context of describing one's state of being: "i:iah te sa'nihkonra(t)," which Karhowane translated to mean "you have no mind." When words are thus broken down, one can see the importance of understanding every aspect of the language for the deeply embedded cultural knowledge it contains: "sa" (you), "nihkonr" (mind/spirit), and "a(t)" (to be contained in).
6. The Creation Story became a more central aspect of the AFS curriculum in recent years with the help of a faithkeeper. A faithkeeper, an expert on Haudenosaunee culture and Longhouse ceremonial practices, has helped reinvigorate the ceremonial and cultural aspects of the AFS curriculum.

References

Abate, W. 1985. "Iroquois Control of Iroquois Education: A Case Study of the Iroquois of the Grand River Valley in Ontario, Canada." PhD diss., University of Toronto.

Abler, T. S. 1987. "Dendogram and Celestrial Tree: Numerical Taxonomy and Variants of the Iroquois Creation Myth." *Canadian Journal of Native Studies* 2, no. 2, 195–221.

Adams, D. 1988. "Fundamental Considerations: The Deep Meaning of Native American Schooling, 1880–1900." *Harvard Educational Review* 58, no. 1: 1–28.

———. 1995. *Education for Extinction: American Indians and the Boarding School Experience, 1875–1928*. Lawrence: University Press of Kansas.

Agbo, S. 2001. "Enhancing Success in American Indian Students: Participatory Research at Akwesasne as Part of the Development of a Culturally Relevant Curriculum." *Journal of American Indian Education* 40, no. 1: 31–56.

Akwesasne Freedom School. 1999. *Mid-Term Report*. Akwesasne: Akwesasne Freedom School.

———. 2002–2004. *School Report*. Akwesasne: Akwesasne Freedom School.

———. n.d. *Akwesasne Freedom School* [Brochure]. Akwesasne: Akwesasne Freedom School.

Akwesasne Notes. 1970. *Kaianerekowa Hotinonsionne: The Great Law of Peace of the Longhouse People*. Akwesasne: White Roots of Peace.

———. 1972. "Are White People Ready to Handle Their Own Affairs?" *Akwesasne Notes* 4, no. 3: 43–44.

Akwesasne Task Force on the Environment. 1997. "Superfund Clean-up at Akwesasne: A Case Study in Environmental Justice." *International Journal of Contemporary Sociology* 34, no. 2: 267–90.

———. 2001. *Cultural Resources Study*. Akwesasne: Akwesasne Task Force on the Environment.

———. n.d.(a) "Environmental Contamination." Akwesasne Task Force on the Environment, https://sites.google.com/site/atfeonline/environmental-contamination.

———. n.d.(b) "Update on Superfund Cleanup." Akwesasne Task Force on the Environment, https://sites.google.com/site/atfeonline/update-on-superfund-clean-up.

Alaska Rural Systemic Initiative. 2005. "Final Report: Phase II." Alaska Native Knowledge Network, http://www.ankn.uaf.edu/curriculum/articles.html.

Alfred, T. 1999. *Peace, Power, and Righteousness: An Indigenous Manifesto.* Don Mills, Ontario: Oxford University Press.

———. 2005. *Wasase: Indigenous Pathways of Action and Freedom.* Peterborough, Ontario: Broadview Press.

Arbuthnot, B. R. 1984. *Kahnawake Survival School: A Community Based Case Study in Bicultural Education.* Master's thesis, Department of Education, Concordia University, Montreal.

Archuleta, M. C., B. Child, and K. T. Lomawaima. 2000. *Away from Home: American Indian Boarding School Experiences, 1879–2000.* Phoenix: Heard Museum.

Arviso, M., and W. Holm. 2001. "Tse'hootsoo'di Olta'gi Dine' Bizaadbihoo'aah: A Navajo Immersion Program at Fort Defiance, Arizona." In Hinton and Hale 2001, 203–15.

Baker, C. 1992. *Attitudes and Language.* Cleveland, UK: Multilingual Matters.

Baker, M. C. 1996. *The Polysynthesis Parameter.* New York: Oxford University Press.

Barik, H., and M. Swain. 1976. "A Longitudinal Study of Bilingual and Cognitive Development." *International Journal of Psychology* 11, no. 4: 251–63.

Barnes, B., ed. 1984. *Traditional Teachings.* Akwesasne: North American Indian Travelling College.

Barnhardt, R. 1981. *Culture, Community and the Curriculum.* Fairbanks: Center for Cross Cultural Studies, University of Alaska, Fairbanks.

Barnhardt, R., and O. Kawagley. 1999. "Education Indigenous to Place: Western Science Meets Indigenous Reality." In *Ecological Education in Action,* edited by G. Smith and D. Williams, 117–40. New York: State University of New York Press.

———. 2005. "Indigenous Knowledge Systems and Alaska Native Ways of Knowing." *Anthropology and Education Quarterly* 36, no. 1: 8–23.

Barth, J. 1989. "Toxic Lesson Taught at Freedom School." *Syracuse Herald American,* September 10.

Bates, R. 2001. "Developing Haudenosaunee Heritage Based Literacy Curriculum at the St. Regis Mohawk School." PhD diss., State University of New York at Albany.

Beauchamp, W. 1905. *A History of the New York Iroquois, Now Commonly Called the Six Nations.* Bulletin of the New York State Museum, Archaeology 9. Albany: New York State Education Department.

Bell, G. 1998. "Telling Tales Out of School: Remembering the Carlisle Indian Industrial School, 1879–1918." PhD diss., Stanford University.

Bielenberg, B. 2000. "Charter Schools for American Indians." In *Learn in Beauty: Indigenous Education for a New Century,* edited by J. Reyhner, J. Martin, L. Lockard, and W. Sakiestewa Gilbert, 132–50. Flagstaff: Northern Arizona University.

Bonaparte, D. 2006. *Creation and Confederation: The Living History of the Iroquois.* Akwesasne: Wampum Chronicles.

———. n.d. "Saiowisakeron: The Jake Ice Story." Wampum Chronicles, http://www.wampumchronicles.com/saiowisakeron.

Boyer, G. 1979. “May Incident Triggered Trouble on Reservation.” *Malone (N.Y.) Herald*, December 31.
Brady, P. 1995. “Two Policy Approaches to Native Education: Can Reform Be Legislated?” *Canadian Journal of Education* 20, no. 3: 349–66.
Brayboy, B., and A. Castagno. 2009. “Self-Determination through Self-Education: Culturally Responsive Schooling for Indigenous Students in the U.S.A.” *Teaching Education* 20, no. 1: 31–53.
Brothers, C., and E. Emery. 1980. “Weapons Turned over to State Police: Tatlock's Burns.” *Massena (N.Y.) Observer*, December 30.
Brown, F. L. 2004. “Making the Classroom a Healthy Place: The Development of Affective Competency in Aboriginal Pedagogy.” PhD diss., University of British Columbia, 2004.
Cajete, G. 1994. *Look to the Mountain: An Ecology of Indigenous Education*. Skyland, N.C.: Kivaki Press.
Canby, W. C. 1998. *American Indian Law in a Nutshell*. 3rd ed. St. Paul: West Group.
Cantoni, G., ed. 1996. *Stabilizing Indigenous Languages*. Flagstaff: Northern Arizona University Center for Excellence in Education.
Castile, G. P. 1998. *To Show Heart: Native American Self-Determination and Federal Indian Policy, 1960–1975*. Tucson: University of Arizona Press.
Chavira, V., and J. Phinney. 1991. “Adolescents' Ethnic Identity, Self-Esteems and Strategies for Dealing with Ethnicity and Minority Status.” *Hispanic Journal of Behavioral Sciences* 13, 226–27.
Child, B. 1998. *Boarding School Seasons: American Indian Families, 1900–1940*. Lincoln: University of Nebraska Press.
Ciborski, S. 1990. “Culture and Power: The Emergence of Politics in Akwesasne Mohawk Traditionalism.” PhD diss., State University of New York at Albany, 1990.
Cohen, F. 1982. *Handbook of Federal Indian Law*. Charlottesville, Va.: Bobbs-Merrill. First published 1942.
Collister, R. 2001. “Revitalizing Marginalized Communities by Increasing Social Capital through Holistic Education and Lifelong Learning Strategies of Indigenous Peoples.” Paper presented at the National Biennial Conference of the Australian Curriculum Studies Association, Canberra, Australia, September 29–October 1.
Cook-Peters, K. 2003. *Report on the Ahkwesahsne Mohawk Board of Education Kanien'keha Program*. Akwesasne: Ahkwesahsne Mohawk Board of Education.
Cornplanter, J. J. 1986. *Legends of the Longhouse*. Ohsweken, Ontario: Iroqrafts.
Crawford, J. 1996. “Seven Hypotheses on Language Loss Causes and Cures.” In Cantoni 1996, 51–68.
Cross, M. 1991. *Shades of Black: Diversity in African American Identity*. Philadelphia: Temple University Press.
Cummins, J. 1992. “The Empowerment of Indian Students.” In *Teaching American Indian Students*, edited by J. Reyhner, 3–12. Norman: University of Oklahoma Press.
———. 1998. “Immersion Education for the New Millenium: What We Have Learned

from 30 Years of Research on Second Language Immersion." In *Learning through Two Languages: Research and Practice,* edited by M. R. Childs and R. M. Bostwick, 34–47. Japan: Katoh Gakuen.

Dauenhauer, N., and R. Dauenhauer. 1998. "Technical, Emotional, and Ideological Issues in Reversing Language Shift: Examples from Southeast Alaska. In *Endangered Languages: Current Issues and Future Prospects,* edited by L. A. Grenoble and L. J. Whaley, 57–98. Cambridge, UK: Cambridge University Press.

Dejong, D. 1998. "Is Immersion the Key to Language Renewal?" *Journal of American Indian Education* 37, no. 3: 1–11.

Deloria, V., and C. Lytle. 1983. *American Indians, American Justice.* Austin: University of Texas Press.

Deloria, V., and D. Wildcat. 2001. *Power and Place: Indian Education in America.* Golden, Co.: Fulcrum.

Dewey, J. 1938. *Experience and Education.* New York: Macmillan.

Dick, G., and T. McCarty. 1996. "Reclaiming Navajo: Language Renewal in an American Indian Community School. In *Indigenous Literacies in the Americas: Language Planning from the Bottom Up,* edited by N. Hornberger, 69–94. New York: Mouton de Gruyter.

Dorais, L. J. 1995. "Language, Culture, and Identity: Some Inuit Examples." *Canadian Journal of Native Studies* 15, no. 2: 293–308.

Eastman, C. 1971. *Indian Boyhood.* New York: Dover Publications. First published 1902.

Edwards, J. 1997. "Language Minorities and Language Maintenance." *Annual Review of Applied Linguistics* 17: 30–42.

Elder, J. 1979. "Indian Faction Wants Akwesasne Police to Resign." *Watertown (N.Y.) Times,* May 29, 7–8.

Emery, E. 1979. "Mohawk Language Taught as a Cultural Enrichment." *Massena (N.Y.) Observer,* July 12.

———. 1981. "Freedom School Celebrates First Year." *Massena (N.Y.) Observer,* July 20.

Ermine, W. 1995. "Aboriginal Epistemology." In *First Nations Education in Canada: The Circle Unfolds,* edited by M. Battiste and M. Barman, 101–12. Vancouver, B.C.: University of British Columbia Press.

Evans, S. 2001. "The Potential Contribution of Comparative and International Education to Education Reform: An Examination of Traditional, Non-Western Education." *ERIC Digests,* March, ED4511979, 1–7.

Evans, B. A., and N. H. Hornberger. 2005. "No Child Left Behind: Repealing and Unpeeling Federal Language Education Policy in the United States." *Language and Policy* 4, no. 1: 87–106.

Fadden, R. n.d. "The Record, Laws and History of the Akwesasne Mohawk Counselor Organization." Unpublished manuscript, John Kahionhes Fadden personal collection.

Fadden, S. 1987. "Beaded History." *Northeast Indian Quarterly* 4, no. 3: 17–20.

Faries, E. 2009. "Closing the Gap for Aboriginal Students." Paper presented at the Education Research Symposium, Toronto, February. http://www.edu.gov.on.ca/eng/research/efaries.pdf.

Fear-Segal, J. 2006. "The Man on the Bandstand at Carlisle Indian Industrial School." In *Boarding School Blues: Revisiting American Indian Educational Experiences*, edited by C. Trafzer, J. Keller, and L. Sisquoc, 99–122. Lincoln: University of Nebraska Press.

Fenimore-Smith, J. K. 2009. "The Power of Place: Creating an Indigenous Charter School." *Journal of American Indian Education* 48, no. 2: 1–17.

Fenton, W. 1968. *Parker on the Iroquois*. Syracuse: Syracuse University Press.

———. 1971. *The New York State Wampum Collection: The Case for the Integrity of Cultural Treasures*. Proceedings of the American Philosophical Society 6. Philadelphia: American Philosophical Society.

———. 1978. "Northern Iroquois Culture Patterns." In Trigger 1978, 296–321.

Fenton, W. N., and E. Tooker. 1978. "Mohawk." In Trigger 1978, 466–80.

Fishman, J. A. 1991. *Reversing Language Shift: Theoretical and Empirical Foundations of Assistance to Threatened Languages*. Clevedon, UK: Multilingual Matters.

———. 1996. "What Do You Lose When You Lose Your Language?" In Cantoni 1996, 80–91.

Fiske, J. 1995. "Political Status of Native Indian Women: Contradictory Implications of Canadian State Policy." *American Indian Culture and Research Journal* 19, no. 2: 1–30.

Forbes, S. H. 1996. "Values in Holistic Education." Paper presented at the Third Annual Conference on Education, Spirituality, and the Whole Child, Roehampton Institute, London, June 28.

———. 2003. *Holistic Education: An Analysis of its Ideas and Nature*. Brandon, Vt.: Solomon Press/Foundation for Educational Renewal.

Fortune, T., and D. Tedick. 2003. "What Parents Want to Know about Foreign Language Immersion Programs." *ERIC Digests*, August. EDO-FL-03-04.

Foster, B. 1995. "Keeping Language Alive: Mohawk Students Write, Illustrate Story-Books." *Standard-Freeholder* (Cornwall, Ontario), December 4.

Foster, M. W. 1998. *Being Comanche: A Social History of an American Indian Community*. Tucson: University of Arizona Press.

Foster, T. 1981. "At Site of Confrontations: 'Freedom' Is an Indian School." *Watertown (N.Y.) Times*, September 18.

Four Arrows (D. T. Jacobs). 2013. *Teaching Truly: A Curriculum to Indigenize Mainstream Education*. New York: Peter Lang.

Fox, S. J. 2001. American Indian/Alaska Native Education and Standards Based Reform. *ERIC Digests*, ED 459039.

Francis, N., and J. Reyhner. 2002. *Language and Literacy Teaching for Indigenous Education: A Bilingual Approach*. Clevedon, UK: Multilingual Matters.

Freeman, K., A. Stairs, E. Corbiere, and D. Lazore. 1995. "Ojibway, Mohawk, and Inuktitut: Alive and Well? Issues of Identity, Ownership, and Change." *Bilingual Research Journal* 19, no. 1: 39–69.

Freire, P. 1993. *Pedagogy of the Oppressed.* New York: Continuum. First published 1970.
Friedman, T. 1980. "Drums along the St. Regis: Indians Fighting for Their Heritage." *Massena (N.Y.) Observer,* January 12.
Frisch, J. A. 1970. "Revitalization, Nativism, and Tribalism among the St. Regis Mohawks." PhD diss., Indiana University, 1970.
Gardner, H. 1983. *Frames of Mind: The Theory of Multiple Intelligences.* New York: Basic Books.
Garroutte, E. M. 2003. *Real Indians: Identity and the Survival of Native America.* Berkeley: University of California Press.
Garte, E. 1981. "Where the Partridge Drums." *Journal of American Indian Education* 2, no. 1: 24–30.
Genessee, F. 1994. *Integrating Language and Content: Lessons from Immersion.* Educational Practice Report 11. Santa Cruz, Calif.: National Center for Research on Cultural Diversity and Second Language Learning.
———. 2008. "Dual Language in the Global Village." In *Pathways to Multilingualism: Evolving Perspectives on Immersion Education,* edited by T. W. Fortune and D. J. Tedick, 22–45. Clevedon, UK: Multilingual Matters.
George-Kanentiio, D. 1993. "Iroquois History Rooted in Ganondagan." *Syracuse Herald American,* July 5.
———. 2000. *Iroquois Culture and Commentary.* Santa Fe, N.M.: Clear Light.
———. 2006. *Iroquois on Fire: A Voice from the Mohawk Nation.* Lincoln: University of Nebraska Press.
Getches, D., C. Wilkinson, and R. Williams. 2005. *Cases and Materials on Federal Indian Law.* 5th ed. St. Paul: Thompson West.
Gibson, D. n.d. *Cycle of Ceremonies.* Akwesasne: Ranathahon:ni Cultural Center.
Gibson, J. A., W. Woodbury, R. Henry, H. Webster, and A. Goldenweiser. 1992. *Concerning the League: The Iroquois League Tradition as Dictated in Onondaga by John Arthur Gibson.* Winnipeg: Algonquian and Iroquoian Linguistics.
Giles, H., and P. Johnson. 1987. "Ethnolinguistic Theory: A Social Psychological Approach to Language Maintenance." *International Journal of Sociology of Language* 68: 69–99.
Gilliland, H. 1999. *Teaching the Native American.* Dubuque, Iowa: Kendall/Hunt.
Giroux, H. 2001. *Theory and Resistance in Education: Towards a Pedagogy for the Opposition.* Westport, Conn.: Bergin & Garvey.
Goodyear-Ka'ōpua, N. 2013. *The Seeds We Planted: Portraits of a Native Hawaiian Charter School.* Minneapolis: University of Minnesota Press.
Grande, S. 2004. *Red Pedagogy: Native American Social and Political Thought.* Lanham, Md.: Rowman and Littlefield.
Grant, J. 1984. *Moon of Wintertime: Missionaries and the Indians of Canada in Encounter since 1534.* Toronto: University of Toronto Press.
Greene, A. (Gah-wohn-nos-doh). 1972. *Forbidden Voice: Reflections of a Mohawk Indian.* London, England: Hamlyn House.

Greymorning, S. 1999. "Running the Gauntlet of an Indigenous Language Program." In *Revitalizing Indigenous Languages*, edited by J. Reyhner, G. Cantoni, R. N. Clair, and E. P. Yazzie, 6–16. Flagstaff: Northern Arizona University.

Grim, J., and D. John. 2005. "North American Indians: Indians of the Northeast Woodlands." In *Encyclopedia of Religion*, 2nd ed., edited by L. Jones, 6679–88. Detroit: Macmillan.

Grinde, D. A., and B. E. Johansen. 1991. *Exemplar of Liberty: Native America and the Evolution of Democracy.* Los Angeles: American Indian Studies Center, University of California, Los Angeles.

———. 1995. *Ecocide of Native America: Environmental Destruction of Indian Lands and Peoples.* Santa Fe, N.M.: Clear Light.

Hamell, G. R. 1983. "Trading in Metaphors: The Magic of Beads: Another Perspective upon Indian-European Contact in Northeastern North America." In *Proceedings of the 1982 Glass Trade Bead Conference*, edited by C. F. Hayes III, 5–28. New York: Rochester Museum and Science Center.

Hanzeli, V. 1969. *Missionary Linguists in New France.* The Hague: Mouton.

Harper, Stephen. 2008. "Prime Minister Harper Offers Full Apology on Behalf of Canadians for the Indian Residential Schools System." Prime Minister of Canada, June 11, www.pm.gc.ca/eng/.

Harris, M. 1990. "Emics and Etics Revisited." In *Emics and Etics: The Insider/Outsider Debate*, edited by T. Headland, K. Pike, and M. Harris, 48–60. Newbury Park, Calif.: Sage Publications.

Harrison, B. 1998. "Te Wharekura'oRakaumangamanga: The Development of an Indigenous Language Immersion School." *Bilingual Research Journal* 22, no. 2–4: 297–316.

Haudenosaunee Environmental Task Force (HETF). 1998. *Words That Come before All Else.* Akwesasne: Native North American Travelling College.

Hauptman, L. 1986. *The Iroquois Struggle for Survival: World War II to Red Power.* Syracuse: Syracuse University Press.

Henry, T. R. 1955. *Wilderness Messiah: The Story of Hiawatha and the Iroquois.* New York: Bonanza Books.

Hermes, M. 2008. "Ma'iingan is Just a Misspelling of the Word Wolf:" A Case for Teaching Culture through Language." *Anthropology and Education Quarterly* 36, no. 1: 43–56.

Herrick J. W. 1995. *Iroquois Medical Botany.* Syracuse: Syracuse University Press.

Hewitt, J. N. B. 1902. "Orenda and a Definition of Religion," *American Anthropologist*, New Series 4, 33–46.

———. 1903. "Iroquoian Cosmology: First Part." In *Report of the Bureau of American Ethnology to the Secretary of the Smithsonian Institution*, vol. 21, 127–360. Washington, D.C.: Smithsonian Institution, Bureau of American Ethnology.

———. 1928. "Iroquoian Cosmology: Second Part." In *Forty-Third Annual Report of the Bureau of American Ethnology*, 449–828. Washington, D.C.: Smithsonian Institution, Bureau of American Ethnology.

Hill, R. 1990. "Oral Memory of the Haudenosaunee." *Northeast Indian Quarterly*, Spring, 21–30.

Hill, S., and M. J. L. McCallum. 2009. "Working from Home in American Indian History." Special issue, *American Indian Quarterly* 33, no. 4.

Hinton, L. 2013. *Bringing Our Languages Home: Language Revitalization for Families.* Berkeley: Heyday.

Hinton, L., and K. Hale. 2001. *The Green Book of Language Revitalization in Practice.* San Diego: Academic Press.

Hoffman, K. 2001. "Their Native Tongue: Children of the Mohawk Nation Work to Save Their Ancient Language and Culture." *Time for Kids*, January 26, 6.

Holm, A., and W. Holm. 1995. "Navajo Language Education: Retrospect and Prospects." *Bilingual Research Journal* 19, no. 1, 141–67.

Hoover, M. L., and Kanienkeha:ka Raotitiohkwa Cultural Center. 1992. "The Revival of the Mohawk Language in Kahnawa:ke." *Canadian Journal of Native Studies* 12, no. 2: 269–87.

Horn, G. 2011. "Karihwanoron Mohawk Immersion Needs Donations." *Iori:wase Kahnawake News*, January 6. http://kahnawakenews.com/karihwanoron-mohawk-immersion-needs-donations-p1115-1.htm.

Hornberger, N. 1996. "Language Planning from the Bottom Up." In *Indigenous Literacies in the Americas: Language Planning from the Bottom Up*, 357–66. New York: Mouton de Gruyter.

———. 2008. *Can Schools Save Indigenous languages? Policy and Practice on Four Continents.* New York: Palgrave Macmillan.

Howe, L. 1999. "Tribalography: The Power of Native Stories." *Journal of Dramatic Theory and Criticism*, Fall, 117–25.

———. 2002. "The Story of America: A Tribalography." In *Clearing a Path: Theorizing the Past in Native Studies*, edited by N. Shoemaker, 29–48. New York: Routledge.

Hoxie, F. 1984. *A Final Promise: The Campaign to Assimilate the Indians, 1880–1920.* Cambridge: University of Cambridge Press.

Indian Tribes of Manitoba. 1971. *Wahbung: Our Tomorrows.* Winnipeg: Manitoba Indian Brotherhood.

"Indian Way School." 1972. *Akwesasne Notes* 4, no. 2: 19.

Innes, R. 2007. "The Importance of Family Ties to Members of Cowessess First Nation." PhD diss., University of Arizona, 2007.

Isaacs, H. 1973. "*Orenda*: An Ethnographic Cognitive Study of Seneca Medicine and Politics." PhD diss., State University of New York at Buffalo, 1973.

Itin, C. 1999. "Reasserting the Philosophy of Experiential Education as a Vehicle for Change in the 21st Century," *Journal of Experiential Education* 22, no. 2: 91–98.

Jackson, B. 1999. "Attica: An Anniversary of Death," Bruce Jackson website, University at Buffalo, http://www.acsu.buffalo.edu/~bjackson/attica.htm. First published in *Artvoice* (Buffalo, N.Y.), September 9, 1999.

Jemison, P. G., and A. M. Schein. 2000. *Treaty of Canandaigua 1794: 200 Years of Treaty*

Relations between the Iroquois Confederacy and the United States. Santa Fe, N.M.: Clear Light.

Jennings, N. 1998. "In the Spirit of the Kaswentha: Cultural Literacy in Akwesasne Mohawk Culture." PhD diss., University of Pennsylvania, 1998.

Jennings, N., and B. Montour. 1992. "Akwesasne Freedom School and the New Paradigm: In the Year of Columbus, 1992: Is the New World Rediscovering Native America?" Unpublished manuscript, Barry Montour personal archives.

Jocks, C. 1998. "Living Words and Cartoon Translations: Longhouse 'Texts' and the Limitations of English." In *Endangered Languages: Current Issues and Future Prospects,* edited by L. A. Grenoble and L. J. Whaley, 217–33. Cambridge, UK: Cambridge University Press.

Johansen, B. E., and B. A. Mann. 2000. *Encyclopedia of the Haudenosaunee (Iroquois Confederacy).* Westport, Conn.: Greenwood Press.

Johnston, B. 1989. *Indian School Days.* Norman: University of Oklahoma Press.

Kamanā, K., and W. Wilson. 1996. "Hawaiian Language Programs." In *Stabilizing Indigenous Languages,* edited by G. Cantoni-Harvey, 153–56. Flagstaff: Northern Arizona University Center for Excellence in Education.

Kana'iaupuni, S. M., and K. Ishibashi. 2005. *Hawai'i Charter Schools: Initial Trends and Select Outcomes for Native Hawaiian Students.* Honolulu: Kamehameha Schools-PASE.

Kaplan, J., and A. Bernays. 1997. *The Language of Names: What We Call Ourselves and Why it Matters.* New York: Simon and Schuster.

Kasten, W. 1992. "Bridging the Horizon: American Indian Beliefs and Whole Language Learning." *Anthropology and Education Quarterly* 23, no. 2: 108–19.

Kawagley, A. O., D. Norris-Tull, and R. A. Norris-Tull. 1998. "The Indigenous Worldview of Yupiaq Culture: Its Scientific Nature and Relevance to the Practice of Teaching in Science." *Journal of Research in Science Teaching* 35: 133–44.

Kennedy, B. 1981. "Mohawk School Decries Public Culture, Defies State Law." *Syracuse Post-Standard,* September 26.

Kipp, D. R. 2000. *Encouragement, Guidance, Insights, and Lessons Learned for Native Language Activists Developing Their Own Tribal Language Programs.* Browning, Mont.: Piegan Institute.

Kirkness, V. 1999. "Aboriginal Education in Canada: A Retrospective and a Prospective." *Journal of American Indian Education* 39, no. 1: 14–30.

Krashen, S., and T. Terrell. 1983. *The Natural Approach: Language Acquisition in the Classroom.* New York: Pergamon Press.

Krauss, M. 1998. "The Condition of Native North American Languages: The Need for Realistic Assessment and Action." *International Journal of Social Language* 132, 9–21.

Kroskrity, P. V., and M. C. Field. 2009. *Native American Language Ideologies: Beliefs, Practices and Struggles in Indian Country.* Tucson: University of Arizona Press.

LaFlesche, F. 1978. *The Middle Five: Indian School Boys of the Omaha Tribe.* Lincoln: University of Nebraska.

LaFrance, B. 1994. "Empowering Ourselves: Making Education and Schooling One." "Negotiating the Culture of Indigenous Schools," special issue, *Peabody Journal of Education* 69, no. 2: 19–25.

LaFrance, R. 1982. "Akwesasne Freedom School Newsletter." Unpublished manuscript, AFS Archives.

LaFrance, R. 1985. "Indian Education or Education of Indians: The Saint Regis Mohawk Experience." PhD diss., Cornell University.

Lambert, W., and G. R. Tucker. 1972. *Bilingual Education of Children: The St. Lambert Experiment*. Rowley, Mass.: Newbury House.

Landis, B. 2006. "Putting Lucy Pretty Eagle to Rest." In *Boarding School Blues: Revisiting American Indian Educational Experiences*, edited by C. Trafzer, J. Keller, and L. Sisquoc, 123–30. Lincoln: University of Nebraska Press.

Lazore, C. 2006. "Homeland Insecurity." *Cultural Survival Quarterly* 30, no. 3: 3.

Lazore, D. 1993. "The Mohawk Language Standardization Project." Conference report, Mohawk Language Standardization Conference, Tyendinaga Mohawk Territory.

Lee, T. 2006. "I Came Here to Learn How to Be a Leader: An Intersection of Critical Pedagogy and Indigenous Education." *Interactions: UCLA Journal of Education and Information Studies* 2, no. 1: 1–24.

Lemelin, R. H. 1997. "The Great Law of Peace and Social Movement in the Mohawk Territory of Akwesasne." Master's thesis, University of Ottawa.

Liebkind, K. 1999. "Social psychology." In *Handbook of Language and Ethnic Identity Development*, edited by J. Fishman, 18–31. Oxford, UK: Oxford University Press.

Loether, C. 2009. "Language Revitalization and the Manipulation of Language Ideologies: A Shoshoni Case Study." In *Native American Language Ideologies: Beliefs, Practices and Struggles in Indian Country*, edited by P. V. Kroskrity and M. C. Field, 238–54. Tucson: University of Arizona Press.

Loftlin, C., et al. 2002. "Teaching Anthropological Ethics at the University of South Carolina: An Example of Critical Ethical Dialogue Across Communities." In *Ethics and the Profession of Anthropology: Dialogue for Ethically Conscious Practice*, edited by C. Fluehr-Lobban, 197–224. Walnut Creek, Calif.: AltaMira Press.

Lomawaima, K. T. 1993. "Domesticity in the Federal Indian Schools: The Power and Authority over Mind and Body." *American Ethnologist* 20, no. 2: 1–14.

———. 1994. *They Called It Prairie Light: The Story of Chilocco Indian School*. Lincoln: University of Nebraska Press.

———. 1995. "Educating Native Americans." In *Handbook of Research on Multicultural Education*, edited by J. Banks, 331–47. New York: Macmillan.

———. 1999. "The Un-natural History of American Indian Education." In Swisher and Tippeconnic 1999, 1–33.

———. 2000. "Tribal Sovereigns: Reframing Research in American Indian Education." *Harvard Educational Review* 70, no. 1: 1–21.

Lomawaima, K. T., and T. McCarty. 2002. "When Tribal Sovereignty Challenges Democracy: American Indian Education and the Democratic Ideal." *American Educational Research Journal* 39, no. 2: 279–305.

———. 2006. *To Remain an Indian: Lessons in Democracy from a Century of Native American Education.* New York: Teachers College Press.

Lyons, O., and J. Mohawk. 1992. *Exiled in the Land of the Free: Democracy, the Indian Nations, and the U.S. Constitution.* Santa Fe, N.M.: Clear Light.

Lyons, S. 2010. *XMarks: Native Signatures of Assent.* Minneapolis: University of Minnesota Press.

Lysne, M., and G. Levy. 1997. "Differences in Ethnic Identity in Native American Adolescents as a Function of School Context." *Journal of Adolescent Research* 12372–89.

MacLean, M., and L. Wason-Ellam. 2006. "When Aboriginal and Métis Teachers Use Storytelling as an Instructional Practice." Grant report to the Aboriginal Education Research Network, Saskatchewan Learning. Saskatchewan Ministry of Education, http://www.education.gov.sk.ca/storytelling.

Mann, B. A. 2010. "Where Are Your Women? Missing in Action." In *Unlearning the Language of Conquest: Scholars Expose Anti-Indianism in America,* edited by Four Arrows (Don Trent Jacobs), 120–33. Austin: University of Texas Press.

Mann, B., and J. L. Fields. 1997. "A Sign in the Sky: Dating the League of the Haudenosaunee." *American Indian Culture and Research Journal* 21, no. 2: 105–63.

Mar-Molinero, C. 2000. *The Politics of Language in the Spanish-Speaking World: From Colonisation to Globalization.* London: Routledge.

Matthiessen, P. 1984. *Indian Country.* New York: Penguin.

May, S., and R. Hill. 2008. "Māori-Medium Education: Current Issues and Challenges." In Hornberger 2008, 66–98.

McBeth, S. 1983. *Ethnic Identity and the Boarding School Experience of West-Central Oklahama American Indians.* Washington, D.C.: University Press of America.

McCarty, T. L. 1998. "Schooling, Resistance, and American Indian Languages." *International Journal of the Sociology of Language* 132: 27–41.

———. 2002. *A Place to Be Navajo: Rough Rock and the Struggle for Self-Determination in Indigenous Schooling.* Mahwah, N.J.: Lawrence Erlbaum.

———. 2003. "Revitalising Indigenous Languages in Homogenising Times." *Comparative Education 39,* no. 2: 147–63.

———. 2008. "Schools as Strategic Tools for Indigenous Language Revitalization: Lessons from Native America." In Hornberger 2008, 161–79.

———. 2013. *Language Planning and Policy in Native America: History, Theory, and Praxis.* Bristol, UK: Multilingual Matters.

McCarty, T. L., M. E. Romero-Little, and O. Zepeda. 2006. "Native American Youth Discourses on Language Shift and Retention: Ideological Cross-Currents and Their Implications for Language Planning. *International Journal of Bilingual Education and Bilingualism* 9, no. 5: 659–77.

McCarty, T. L., and L. J. Watahomigie. 1998. "Language and Literacy in American Indian

and Alaskan Native Communities." In *Sociocultural Contexts of Language and Literacy,* edited by B. Perez, 69–98. Mahwah, N.J.: Lawrence Erlbaum.
McCarty, T. L., and O. Zepeda. 1995. "Indigenous Language Education and Literacy. Special issue, *Bilingual Research Journal 19,* no. 1.
McCaskill, D. 1987. "Revitalization of Indian Culture: Indian Cultural Survival Schools." In *Indian Education in Canada,* vol. 2, *The Challenge,* edited by J. Barman, Y. Hébert, and D. McCaskill, 153–79. Vancouver: University of British Columbia Press.
Merrell, J. H. 2008. *The Lancaster Treaty of 1744 with Related Documents.* Boston: Bedford/St. Martin's.
Meriam, Lewis. 1928. *The Problem of Indian Administration: Report of a Survey Made at the Request of Honorable Hubert Work, Secretary of the Interior.* Baltimore: Johns Hopkins University Press.
Merriam, S. 1998. *Qualitative Research and Case Study Applications in Education.* San Francisco: Jossey-Bass.
Miller, H. 1931. *Treaties and Other International Acts of the United States of America,* vol. 2, *Documents 1–40: 1776–1818.* Washington, D.C.: Government Printing Office.
Miller, J. R. 1996. *Shingwauk's Vision: A History of Native Residential Schools.* Toronto: University of Toronto.
Miller, R. 1990. *What Are Schools For? Holistic Education in America.* Brandon, Vt.: Holistic Education Press.
Milloy, J. 1999. *A National Crime: The Canadian Government and the Residential School System—1879 to 1986.* Winnipeg: University of Manitoba Press.
Mithun, M. 1999. *The Languages of North America.* Cambridge, UK: Cambridge University Press.
Mohawk, J. 2005. *Iroquois Creation Story: John Arthur Gibson and J. N. B. Hewitt's Myth of the Earth Grasper.* Buffalo, N.Y.: Mohawk Publications.
Momaday, N. S. 1969. *The Way to Rainy Mountain.* Albuquerque: University of New Mexico Press.
Montessori, M. 1964. *The Montessori Method.* New York: Schocken Books.
Montour, B. 1992. "Akwesasne Freedom School and the New Paradigm: In the Year of Columbus, 1992, Is the New World Rediscovering Native America?" Unpublished manuscript, Barry Montour personal archives.
———. 2000. "First Nations Jurisdiction over Education at Ahkwesahsne: A Case Study." Master's thesis, McGill University, Department of Educational Studies.
Morgan, L. H. 1962. *League of the Iroquois.* Secaucus, N. J.: Citadel Press.
Morgan, L. H., and H. M. Lloyd. 1901. *League of the Ho-dé-no-sau-nee or Iroquois.* New York: Dodd, Mead.
Moshman, D. 1999. *Adolescent Psychological Development: Rationality, Morality, and Identity.* Mahwah, N.J.: Lawrence Erlbaum.
Nagel, J., and M. Snipp. 1993. "Ethnic Reorganization: American Indian Social, Economic, Political, and Cultural Strategies for Survival." *Ethnic and Racial Studies* 16, no. 2: 203–35.

National Indian Brotherhood/Assembly of First Nations. 1972. "Indian Control of Indian Education." Policy paper presented to the Minister of Indian Affairs and Northern Development, Ottawa.

Newman, D. 2005. "Ego Development and Ethnic Identity Formation in Rural Native American Adolescents." *Child Development* 76, no. 3: 734–46.

Nicholas, S. 2008. "Becoming 'Fully' Hopi: The Role of the Hopi Language in the Contemporary Lives of Hopi Youth—A Hopi Case Study of Language Shift and Vitality." PhD diss., University of Arizona.

———. 2009. "'I Live Hopi, I Just Don't Speak It': The Critical Intersection of Language, Culture, and Identity in the Lives of Contemporary Hopi Youth." *Journal of Language, Identity, and Education* 8, no. 5: 321–34.

———. 2010. "How Are You Hopi If You Can't Speak It? An Ethnographic Study of Language as Cultural Practice among Contemporary Hopi Youth." In *Ethnography and Language Policy*, edited by T. L. McCarty, 53–76. New York: Routledge.

Nieto, S. 1992. *Affirming Diversity: The Sociopolitical Context of Multicultural Education*. New York: Longman.

Niezen, R. 2013. *Truth and Indignation: Canada's Truth and Reconciliation Commission on Indian Residential Schools*. Toronto: University of Toronto Press.

Oberly, S. 2002. "Pinunuuchi Po'og'ani: Southern Ute Indian Academy." *Montessori Life* 14, no. 4: 30.

Ortiz, S. 2006. Untitled paper presented at the National Association for Bilingual Education conference, Phoenix, Arizona.

Palmater, P. 2011. *Beyond Blood: Rethinking Indigenous Identity*. Saskatoon, Saskatchewan: Purich.

Parker, A. C. 1913. *The Code of Handsome Lake, the Seneca Prophet*. Ohsweken, Ontario: Iroqrafts, 1983. First published 1913.

———. 1916. *The Constitution of the Five Nations of the Iroquois, or The Iroquois Book of the Great Law*. Ohsweken, Ontario: Iroqrafts, 1991. First published 1916.

Parker, A. C., and W. N. Fenton. 1968. *Parker on the Iroquois*. Syracuse: Syracuse University Press.

Parman, D. L., and L. Meriam. 1982. "Lewis Meriam's Letters during the Survey of Indian Affairs 1926–1927 (Part I)." *Arizona and the West* 24, no. 3: 253–80.

Patton, M. 2002. *Qualitative Research and Evaluation Methods*. Thousand Oaks, Calif.: Sage Publications.

Peacock, T., and D. Day. 1999. "Teaching American Indian and Alaska Native Languages in the Schools: What Has Been Learned." *ERIC Digests*. ED438155. http://files.eric.ed.gov/fulltext/ED438155.pdf.

Peacock, T., and M. Wisuri. 2002. *Ojibwe Waasa Inaabidaa—We Look in All Directions*. Afton, Minn.: Afton Historical Society Press.

Perkins, N. 1994. "Poem Dedicated to the Akwesasne Freedom School." Unpublished manuscript, AFS Archives.

Peters, M., and T. Peters. 2013. "Mohawk: Our Kanienkeha Language." In *Bringing Our*

Languages Home: Language Revitalization for Families, edited by L. Hinton, 61–79. Berkeley: Heyday.

Philpott, D. 2010. "Approaching Educational Empowerment: Guidelines from a Collaborative Study with the Innu of Labrador." *International Indigenous Policy Journal* 1, no. 1, http://ir.lib.uwo.ca/iipj/vol1/iss1/6.

Phinney, J. 1989. "Stages of Ethnic Identity Development in Minority Group Adolescents." *Journal of Early Adolescence* 9, nos. 1–2: 34–49.

———. 1993. "A Three-Stage Model of Ethnic Identity Development in Adolescence." In *Ethnic Identity Formation: Transmission among Hispanics and Other Minorities,* edited by M. Bernal and G. P. Knight, 61–78. Albany: SUNY Press.

———. 1996. "Understanding Ethnic Diversity: The Role of Ethnic Identity." *American Behavioral Scientist* 40, no. 2: 143.

Phinney, J., and L. Alipuria. 1996. "At the Interface of Culture: Multiethnic/Multiracial High School and College Students." *Journal of Social Psychology* 136, no. 2: 139–58.

Phinney, J., and D. Rosenthal. 1992. "Ethnic Identity in Adolescence: Process, Context, and Outcome." In *Adolescent Identity Formation,* edited by G. Adams, T. Gulotta and R. Montemayor, 145–72. Newbury Park, Calif.: Sage Publications.

Piaget, J. 1954. *The Construction of Reality in the Child.* New York: Basic Books.

Pike, K. 1954. *Language in Relation to a Unified Theory of the Structure of Human Behavior.* Glendale, Calif.: Summer Institute of Linguistics.

———. 1990. "On the Emics and Etics of Pike and Harris." In *Emics and Etics: The Insider/Outsider Debate,* edited by T. Headland, K. Pike, and M. Harris, 29–47. Newbury Park, Calif.: Sage Publications.

Pope-Edwards, C. 2002. "Three Approaches From Europe: Waldorf, Montessori, and Reggio Emilio." *Early Childhood Research and Practice* 4, no. 1, http://ecrp.uiuc.edu/v4n1/edwards.html.

Porter, T. 2004. Keynote address, Sweetgrass First Nations Language Council conference, Brantford, Ontario, October 21.

———. 2008. *And Grandma Said: Iroquois Teachings as Passed Down through the Oral Tradition.* Bloomington, Ind.: Xlibris.

Pratt, S. 1998. "Ceremony and Rationality in the Haudenosaunee Tradition." In *Theorizing Multiculturalism: A Guide to the Current Debate,* edited by C. Willett, 401–21. Malden, Mass.: Blackwell.

Prucha, F. P. 1995. *The Great Father: The United States Government and the American Indians.* 2 vols. Nebraska: University of Nebraska Press.

Pyles, T., and J. Algeo. 1993. *The Origins and Development of the English Language.* 4th ed. Fort Worth: Harcourt Brace Jovanovich.

Reyhner, J. 1994. "American Indians Out of School: A Review of School-Based Causes and Solutions." In *Taking Sides: Clashing Views on Controversial Issues in Race and Ethnicity,* edited by R. Monk, 104–12. Guilford, Conn.: Dushkin.

———. 1999. "Introduction: Some Basics of Indigenous Language Revitalization." In

Revitalizing Indigenous Languages, edited by J. Reyhner, G. Cantons, R. St. Clair, and E. Yazzie, v–xx. Flagstaff: Northern Arizona University.

———. 2006. *Contemporary Native American Issues: Education and Language Restoration*. Philadelphia: Chelsea House.

———. 2010. "Indigenous Language Immersion Schools for Strong Indigenous Identities." *Heritage Language Journal* 7, no. 2: 137–51.

Reyhner, J., and J. Eder. 1988. *Teaching American Indian Students*. Norman: University of Oklahoma Press.

———. 2004. *American Indian Education: A History*. Norman: University of Oklahoma Press.

Rice, B. n.d. "The Sky World and the First Cosmological Beings." Wampum Chronicles, http://www.wampumchronicles.com/creationstory1.html.

———. 2013. *The Rotinonshonni: A Traditional Iroquoian History through the Eyes of Teharonhia:wako and Sawiskera*. Syracuse: Syracuse University Press.

Richter, D. 1983. "War and Culture: The Iroquois Experience." *William and Mary Quarterly* 40, no. 4: 528–59.

Romero-Little, M. E., and T. L. McCarty. 2006. *Language Planning Challenges and Prospects in Native American Communities and Schools*. Tempe: Arizona State University Education Policy Studies Laboratory. http://epsl.asu.edu/epru/documents/EPSL-0602-105-LPRU.pdf.

Ryle, J. 2002. "Ganondagan: Town of Peace." *National Museum of the American Indian* 3, no. 1: 10–13.

Saraydar, S. C. 1990. "No Longer Shall You Kill: Peace, Power and the Iroquois Great Law." *Anthropology and Humanism Quarterly* 15, no. 1: 21–28.

Schneider, P. 1997. *The Adirondacks: A History of America's First Wilderness*. New York: Henry Holt.

Schonleber, N. S. 2006. "Culturally Congruent Education and the Montessori Model: Perspectives from Hawaiian Culture Based Education." PhD diss., University of Hawaii.

Seidman, I. 1998. *Interviewing as Qualitative Research: A Guide for Researchers in Education and the Social Sciences*. New York: Teachers College Press.

———. 2006. *Interviewing as Qualitative Research: A Guide for Researchers in Education and the Social Sciences*. 3rd ed. New York: Teachers College Press.

Senese, G. 1986. "Self-Determination and American Indian Education: An Illusion of Control," *Educational Theory* 36: 153–64.

Skinner, L. 1999. "Teaching through Traditions: Incorporating Languages and Culture into Curricula." In Swisher and Tippeconnic 1999, 107–34.

Skutnabb-Kangas, T. 1984. *Bilingualism or Not: The Education of Minorities*. Cambridge, UK: Cambridge University Press.

———. 1990. *Language, Literacy, and Minorities*. London: Minority Rights Group.

———. 2000. *Linguistic Genocide in Education—or Worldwide Diversity and Human Rights?* Mahwah, N.J.: Lawrence Erlbaum.

Slaughter, H. B. 1997. "Indigenous Language Immersion in Hawai'i." In *Immersion Education: International Perspectives*, edited by R. K. Johnson and M. Swain, 105–29. Cambridge, UK: Cambridge Press.

Smith, L. T. 1999. *Decolonizing Methodologies: Research and Indigenous Peoples*. London: Zed Books.

———. 2012. *Decolonizing Methodologies: Research and Indigenous Peoples*. 2nd ed. London: Zed Books.

Snipp, M. C. 1989. *American Indians: The First of this Land*. New York: Russell Sage Foundation.

Snow, D. R. 1994. *The Iroquois*. Oxford, UK: Blackwell.

Sorensen, M. 2014. "STAR (Service to All Relations." In *Place-Based Education in the Global Age: Local Diversity*, edited by D. A. Gruenewald and G. A. Smith, 49–64. New York: Routledge.

Spack, R. 2002. *America's Second Tongue: American Indian Education and the Ownership of English, 1860–1900*. Lincoln: University of Nebraska Press.

Stairs, A., M. Peters, and E. Perkins. 1999. "Beyond Language in Indigenous Language Immersion Schooling." *Practicing Anthropology* 20, no. 2: 44–47.

Standing Bear, L. 1988. *My Indian Boyhood*. Lincoln: University of Nebraska Press.

Stanton, K. 2011. "Canada's TRC: Settling the Past?" *International Indigenous Policy Journal* 2, no. 3: 1–18.

Stiles, D. B. 1997. "Four Successful Indigenous Language Programs." In *Teaching Indigenous Languages*, edited by J. Reyhner, 248–62. Flagstaff: Northern Arizona University.

Swain, M., and S. Lapkin. 1986. "Immersion French in Secondary Schools: The 'Goods' and the 'Bads.'" *Contact* 5, no. 3: 2–9.

Swisher, K., and M. Hoisch. 1992. "Dropping Out among American Indians and Alaska Natives: A Review of Studies." *Journal of American Indian Education* 31, no. 2: 3–23.

Swisher, K., and J. Tippeconnic. 1999. *Next Steps: Research and Practice to Advance Indian Education*. Charleston, W.Va.: ERIC Clearinghouse on Rural Education and Small Schools.

Szasz, M. 1999. *Education and the American Indian: The Road to Self-determination since 1928*. Albuquerque: University of New Mexico Press.

Tanner, L. N. 1997. *Dewey's Laboratory School: Lessons for Today*. New York: Teachers College Press.

Tehanetorens (R. Fadden). 1992. *Tales of the Iroquois*. Ohsweken, Ontario: Iroqrafts.

———. 1999. *Wampum Belts of the Iroquois*. Summertown, Tenn.: Book Publishing Company.

Thomas, J. 1984. "Articles of the Kariwiio." In *Traditional Teachings*, edited by B. Barnes, 73–101. Cornwall Island, Ontario: North American Indian Travelling College.

———. 1992. "Words That Come Before All Else." In *Indian Roots of American Democracy*, edited by J. Barreiro, 10–11. Ithaca, N.Y.: Akwe:kon Press.

Thomas, J., and T. Boyle. 1994. *Teachings from the Longhouse*. Toronto: Stoddart.

Thompson, N. 1979a. "Unrest at Indian Reservation Discussed at Closed Meeting." *Massena (N.Y.) Observer,* August 28.

———. 1979b. "Incident Ends Friendships, Splits up Families." *Massena (N.Y.) Observer,* September 13.

———. 1980. "Tensions Subside, but Problems Far from Over." *Massena (N.Y.) Observer,* December 30.

Tippeconnic, J. 2000. "Towards Educational Self-Determination: The Challenge for Indian Control of Indian Schools." *Native Americas.* Winter, 42–49.

Toohey, K. 2000. *Learning English at School: Identity, Social Relations and Classroom Practice.* Clevedon, UK: Multilingual Matters.

Tooker, E. 1970. *The Iroquois Ceremonial of Midwinter.* Syracuse: Syracuse University Press.

———. 1978. "The League of the Iroquois: Its History, Politics, and Ritual." In Trigger 1978, 418–41.

———. 1988. "The United States Constitution and the Iroquois League." *Ethnohistory* 35, no. 4: 305–36.

"Traditionalists under Siege." 1980. *Syracuse Post-Standard,* December 30.

Trigger, B. G., ed. 1978. *The Handbook of North American Indians,* vol. 15, *Northeast.* Washington, D.C.: Smithsonian Institution.

Tse, L. 2001. *"Why Don't They Learn English?" Separating Fact from Fallacy in the U.S. Language Debate.* New York: Teachers College Press.

Tulloch, S. 1999. "Language and Identity: An Inuit Perspective." In *Papers from the 23rd Annual Meeting of the Atlantic Provinces Linguistic Association,* edited by W. Burnett, and R. Adams, 106–16. Sackville, New Brunswick: Atlantic Provinces Linguistic Association.

United Nations. 2007. United Nations Declaration on the Rights of Indigenous Peoples. United Nations. http://www.un.org/esa/socdev/unpfii/documents/DRIPS_en.pdf.

Venne, S. H. 1981. *Indian Acts and Amendments: 1868–1975: An Indexed Collection.* Saskatoon: University of Saskatchewan Native Law Center.

Vygotsky, L. S. 1978. *Mind in Society: The Development of Higher Psychological Processes.* Cambridge, Mass.: Harvard University Press.

———. 1986. *Thought and Language.* Edited and translated by A. Kozulin. Cambridge, Mass.: MIT Press.

Wall, S. 2001. *To Become a Human Being: The Message of Tadodaho Chief Leon Shenandoah.* Charlottesville, Va.: Hampton Roads.

Wallace, A. F. C., and S. C. Steen. 1972. *The Death and Rebirth of the Seneca.* New York: Vintage Books. First published 1970 (copyright 1969).

———. 1978. "Origins of the Longhouse Religion." In Trigger 1978, 442–48.

Wallace, P. 1994. *White Roots of Peace: The Iroquois Book of Life.* Santa Fe, N.M.: Clear Light.

Wan, C., et al. 2007. "Perceived Cultural Importance and Actual Self-Importance of

Values in Cultural Identification." *Journal of Personality and Social Psychology* 92, no. 2: 337–54.

Warloski, P. 1991. "Mohawk Freedom School Follows Native Traditions." *Malone (N.Y.) Herald*, May 9.

Warner, S. 1990. "The Delay of the Formal Introduction of English in the Hawaiian Language Immersion Program until Grade Five." Paper submitted at the request of the Hawaiian Language Advisory Council to the Committee on Hawaiian Affairs, State of Hawaii Board of Education.

———. 1999. "Kuleana: The Right, Responsibility, and Authority of Indigenous Peoples to Speak and Make Decisions for Themselves in Language and Cultural Revitalization." *Anthropology and Education Quarterly* 30, no. 1: 68–93.

———. 2001. "The Movement to Revitalize Hawaiian Language and Culture." In Hinton and Hale 2001, 134–44.

Wertsch, J. V. 1991. *Voice of the Mind: A Sociocultural Approach to Mediated Action.* Cambridge, Mass.: Harvard University Press.

White, L. 2003. "Athabascan Region: Old Minto Cultural Orientation Program." *Sharing Our Pathways* (newsletter of Alaska Native Knowledge Network, Fairbanks, Alaska).

Wilkins, D. E., and K. T. Lomawaima. 2001. *Uneven Ground: American Indian Sovereignty and Federal Law.* Norman: University of Oklahoma Press.

Wilson, W., and K. Kamanā. 2001. "'Mai Loko Mai O Ka 'I'ini: Proceeding from a dream': The 'Aha Pūnana Leo Connection in Hawaiian Language Revitalization." In Hinton and Hale 2001, 147–76.

Woolard, K. A. 1998. "Introduction: Language Ideology as a Field of Inquiry." In *Language Ideologies: Practice and Theory*, edited by B. B. Schieffelin, K. A. Woolard, and P. V. Kroskrity, 3–47. New York: Oxford University Press.

Yamauchi, L. 2003. "Making School Relevant for At-Risk Students: The Wai'anae High School Hawaiian Studies Program." *Journal of Education for Students Placed at Risk* 8, no. 4: 379–90.

Zavala, M. 2000. "Puerto Rican Identity: What's Language Got to Do with It?" In *Puerto Rican Students in U.S. Schools*, edited by S. Nieto, 115–36. Philadelphia: Lawrence Erlbaum.

Zaytoun, K. 2005. "Identity and Learning: The Inextricable Link." *About Campus* 9, no. 6: 8–15.

Index

Page numbers in italic type indicate illustrations.